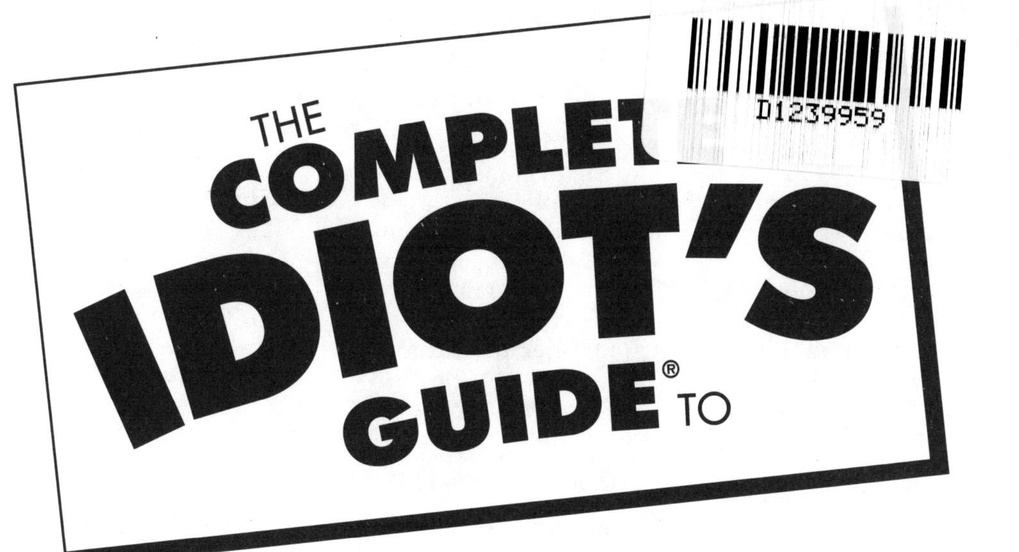

Running Your Small Office with Microsoft® Office

Laurie Ulrich
John San Filippo

que®

A Division of Macmillan Computer Publishing
201 W. 103rd Street, Indianapolis, IN 46290

The Complete Idiot's Guide to Running Your Small Office with Microsoft Office

International Standard Book Number: 0-7897-1748-4

Library of Congress Catalog Card Number: 98-85916

Printed in the United States of America

First Printing: *January 1999*

01 00 99 4 3 2 1

Trademarks

Executive Editor
Jim Minatel

Acquisitions Editor
Jill Byus

Development Editor
Angelique Brittingham

Managing Editor
Thomas F. Hayes

Project Editor
Tom Stevens

Copy Editor
Julie McNamee

Indexer
Greg Pearson

Proofreader
Tricia Sterling

Technical Editor
Don Roche

Illustrator
Judd Winick

Production Team
Cynthia Davis-Hubler

Contents at a Glance

Contents

Dedication

I dedicate this book with love to my parents, Ann Talbot and Karl Ulrich. I owe all that I have to the talents you gave me, the values you taught me, and the love you showed me. —Laurie Ulrich

Acknowledgments

I must thank so many people for their help with this Complete Idiot's Guide! Many friends, vendors, and clients provided information and suggestions, helping me to make this book as accurate and relevant as possible. I also took a lot of notes as I fielded daily support calls, enabling me to provide some real-life cautionary tales for the readers. I must thank all the people whose problems made me smack my forehead and think, "This one goes in the book!"

Some people I must thank individually for their help:

- *Richard Maurone, computer salesman extraordinaire, provided pricing on computers, printers, and memory, and sent me a lot of dirty jokes.*
- *Dave Van Wert, owner (with his wife, Susan) of a Kwik Kopy in Langhorne, PA, provided (with his typical wit) pricing and information on reproducing marketing materials.*
- *Rick Shuster knows everything there is to know about computer service and support contracts and makes me laugh hysterically whenever I call him.*
- *Linda and John Kline, friends, clients, and owners of two home-based businesses, were in my mind and heart through many of this book's pages. I've been cajoling, teasing, and finally begging them to buy a computer, and my efforts paid off. Please pray for me as I teach them to use it!*
- *Adrienne Patrick is raising three kids and runs a business with her husband from their home. She's a great friend and a source of many of the do's and don'ts found throughout this book.*
- *Mike Reilly (my accountant) helped me out by providing the latest and greatest tax advice and information pertaining to the purchase of a computer. He's the best.*

At Macmillan, I must thank Jim Minatel for seeing the potential in the proposal I submitted for this book, and for placing the project in the capable hands of Jill Byus, my acquisitions editor. The editorial staff, especially Tom Stevens, deserves a big thank you for wading through a lot of loose ends. Thanks also to John San Filippo, my contributing author, for his experience, knowledge, and the ability to share it with our readers.

Finally, special thanks must go to Angelique Brittingham, my development editor. Brought into the project late in the game, Angelique whipped things into shape and was a great ally for me in defending my vision for this book and getting things done on time. I don't know what I'd have done without her!

Tell Us What You Think!

As the reader of this book, *you* are our most important critic and commentator. We value your opinion and want to know what we're doing right, what we could do better, what areas you'd like to see us publish in, and any other words of wisdom you're willing to pass our way.

As the Executive Editor for the General Desktop Applications team at Macmillan Computer Publishing, I welcome your comments. You can fax, email, or write me directly to let me know what you did or didn't like about this book—as well as what we can do to make our books stronger.

Please note that I cannot help you with technical problems related to the topic of this book, and that due to the high volume of mail I receive, I might not be able to reply to every message.

When you write, please be sure to include this book's title and author as well as your name and phone or fax number. I will carefully review your comments and share them with the author and editors who worked on the book.

Fax: 312-581-4663

Email: office@mcp.com

Mail: Executive Editor
General Desktop Applications
Macmillan Computer Publishing
201 West 103rd Street
Indianapolis, IN 46290 USA

Introduction

Okay, let's be honest. You don't have to be a rocket scientist to use Microsoft Office. Sure, Office provides an extremely sophisticated suite of business applications, but anyone with even the slightest bit of computer experience probably wouldn't have too much trouble, say, creating a new document in Word. As for learning the features that may not be quite as intuitive as we'd like them to be, there are computer books like *The Complete Idiot's Guide to Microsoft Office,* or serious references like the *Special Edition Using Microsoft Office*.

Although these books might be very thorough in their coverage of Microsoft Office, they lack something important. They focus purely on teaching you how to perform various tasks within a given application or suite of programs. This makes sense from the publisher's marketing perspective, because it enables the book to appeal to the widest possible audience. However, it also means that the author can only include information that's going to be relevant to that wide audience. A typical computer book might teach you *how* to use various Office features, but it won't necessarily teach you *when* or *why* to use those features or how those features fit into the much bigger picture of running a small business.

This book is different. I try to show you where and when to use Office tools to get things done, and once I've done that, I give you the basic information on how to use the software. The primary focus is your small business, the secondary focus is using Microsoft Office to perform business tasks such as writing letters, marketing your business, or maintaining your schedule. How have I managed to write about Office without writing about Office? You don't find step-by-step instructions for every single Office feature (although you do find procedures for some more complex operations). What you do find are practical ideas and real-world suggestions on how to run your small business using Microsoft Office.

And another thing! Because this isn't a typical computer book, I don't always stick to computer topics. I've injected insight from my years of experience running a small business and consulting to other small businesses to give you a better sense of the "big picture". What that means is that in addition to useful information about using Microsoft Office, you also find tips and advice that are applicable to any small business—even if you decide to scrap Microsoft Office tomorrow.

How to Use this Book

To make this book idiot-proof, I've organized it into four major sections, described as follows:

- **Part 1: Should My Office Be a Microsoft Office?** starts with the basics of computerizing your business. Flip through the pages of any computer magazine, or simply browse the aisles at your favorite computer store, and you quickly realize that the number of options can be overwhelming. Just as important as what you do need is what you don't need. Running a small business means getting the most bang for your buck with everything you do, and this section helps you do just that with your computer investment.

- The amount of mediocre business correspondence floating around the business world is staggering. In **Part 2: Mastering Business Communication**, you discover tips, tricks and important advice that helps you to avoid being labeled a communications novice (or a complete idiot). From letters, reports, and proposals to email and faxing, this section covers it all.
- Every year, hundreds of otherwise viable businesses fold because they fail to effectively communicate their message to the buying public. "If you build it, they will come," may work for Kevin Costner in the movies, but it doesn't work for businesses that expect to turn a profit in the real world. If you want to draw in customers, you need to take advantage of every possible opportunity to let the world know you're there. And that's exactly what you learn in **Part 3: Marketing: Cheaper and Safer Than Skywriting**.
- Finally, there's **Part 4: You're Late! Scheduling Your Time and Resources**. One of the biggest problems small and home business owners have is making productive use of their time. Whether a tendency to be late or forget appointments is your problem, or you go the other way and try to be in three places at one time, this section helps you to keep your schedule and projects organized, and keep track of your own comings and goings.

Extras

Throughout this book, you find the following elements—bits of advice, warnings, definitions, and scenarios designed to give you the benefit of my personal experience and what I've learned working with other small businesses:

Faster, Better, More

Like having me right there, whispering advice in your ear, these boxes contain tips and tricks to make your office-related efforts more productive and efficient. Notice the small "o" in office—we're not just talking about software tips here.

Whaddya Mean by That?

If I use a term I'm not sure you know, I define it in one of these boxes. Although we also have a glossary in this book, a quick explanation, right were you read the term, is something I thought you'd like. No need to thank me...

Watch Out!

You know those big orange cones in the road that warn you to steer clear of the huge pothole? These Watch Out! boxes serve the same purpose by pointing out potential pitfalls and things to avoid in business and in your use of Microsoft Office. In addition to warnings, you also find advice to get you out of the hole!

Office Confidential

The names have been changed to protect the innocent, but the stories are true. My years of working with small businesses have netted me hundreds of stories, and you find some of them in these boxes. Plans that didn't work, shortcuts that wasted time, and oversights that cost money—Office Confidential enables you to learn from others' mistakes!

Part 1

Should My Office Be a Microsoft Office?

It's easy to say you should use a computer to accomplish tasks in your small office, but where do you start? Even if you already have a computer and are making strides toward effective automation, you probably need some direction. Chapters 1 through 6 give you the lowdown on choosing the tasks to automate, selecting a new computer or upgrading the one you have, and making sense of your software options.

Chapter 1

If I Had a Hammer: Choosing the Right Tool for the Job

In This Chapter

- Learn to identify tasks you should do on your computer from those that you're better off doing with a paper and pencil
- Choose which tasks you should tackle with your computer
- What size hammer do you really need? Learn to tell want from need
- Will you need a fax machine or a fax modem? Choose the other types of computer-related equipment your office requires

Even if you already have a computer, you may not be sure whether you're getting everything out of it that you can. The computer's not going to tell you that it can do much more than you're asking of it. It isn't trying to get a raise, and it doesn't care if you fire it. From your perspective, it's hard to tell if you're getting your money's worth. If your brother-in-law gave you the computer, chances are you're getting your money's worth even if you're using it as a doorstop. If you paid for it, you probably want to actually type stuff in and have useful stuff come out from time to time. The more you paid, the more it should do. At least that's the goal, right?

Deciding which office tasks are worth computerizing is a big first step, followed by choosing from that list the tasks you're willing or able to tackle. After you've decided that, look at your current computer (or the computer you're going to buy) and decide whether it can handle these tasks.

Identifying Tasks to Be Done with Your Computer

Let's look at my office. No, we're not going to comment on the neatness (or lack thereof). I'm sitting here in a cluttered office. Everything's in neat piles, but there are a lot of piles. Some of these piles could be smaller or disappear completely if I used my computer to do more things. I don't catalogue my magazines or newspaper articles that I save, I just throw them in a bin. I have to rifle through them to find something when I need it. I don't keep up-to-date records of my contacts, so I have a couple of address books, in varying stages of completeness, lying around. I tell you this for two reasons: So you don't think I'm some freak who does everything right, and so you start to think about your own desk and the stuff on it you could handle with your computer.

Maybe you need some help thinking of your desk as a pile (excuse me, I meant to say neat stack) of tasks. The following is a list of daily office tasks. Some are done with a computer, others are not. We may disagree, however, about which category each item falls into:

- **Make phone calls** Do you work from a written list that you check off with a pen throughout the day? Or do you put your calls in a to-do list in the computer?
- **Answer phone calls** Do you log business calls, write down what was discussed, and list any actions you're supposed to take? Please say that you don't, or I'm going to start worrying about you. No, actually, it's a good idea, depending on your line of work. And, it's something you can do on your computer.
- **Write letters** Tell me you're not using a typewriter. Okay, tell me the truth. It's okay to use a typewriter, really it is. I hope you're using carbon paper or making photocopies, however, so that you have a record of what you wrote and to whom you wrote it. Obviously, I think this falls into the "Should Be Done On The Computer" category.
- **Open your mail** No, there isn't a computerized gadget to rip open the envelopes. But if you aren't making use of the Internet for electronic mail (email), you're missing some real time-saving and convenient benefits.
- **Answer your mail** See previous item.
- **Go to the bank** I still go to the bank in person, even if I only go to the cash machine to make a deposit or get some money. But I know I can use the computer to move money around between my accounts and verify my balances. I can also check my stock portfolio. I would do all these things, I swear I would—if I had money to transfer, if I had balanced my checkbook in this decade, or if I had any stocks.
- **Buy office supplies** You can go to the store, call for a delivery, or buy them online and have them shipped. I like to browse in the store and buy cool pens (that end up in my drawer, never used). When I need to order paper or labels, and if I'm too busy to go to the store and am willing to wait a day or two to get them, I order them online.

Banking by Computer

Ask your bank about computerized banking. Find out about fees, and what sort of transactions you can perform online. Get everything in writing, so you can compare your bank statement to the costs and services that were described. Some banks offer free services until you hit a calls-per-month limit or your balance dips below a certain level. Also, make sure adequate technical support from a live person is available should you have questions or problems with the online system.

- **Bill your customers** You can write or type on preprinted invoice forms that come in pads at the office supply store, or you can use an accounting package that has an invoicing module. You can also create an invoice template in Excel or Word and create an invoice. If you take this route, you'll have to enter the billed amount into another system. If not, you'll end up with an audit trail no better than if you had handwritten the invoice.
- **Create marketing materials** You can go to a graphic designer and ask him or her to design your business card and deliver a box of 500 next week. Or, you can design the cards yourself, store the designs on your computer so you can make minor changes (addresses, phone numbers, new product or service), and then create the *camera-ready* copy and take it to a printer yourself.

Camera-Ready Copy

Camera-ready copy is printed material that's clean, detailed, and crisp enough to be used as the original for a large printing job. You can create camera-ready copy for business cards, brochures, newsletters, flyers, or any other printed document on your computer, if you have a laser printer that prints at least 600 dots per inch.

You may do other things in addition to these, or you may not do all the things on the list. I can't possibly know what every person in every business does, but I've tried to cover the most common daily or weekly office tasks. Every item on the list can be computerized. If they can be computerized, should every aspect of the task be computerized?

To help you think about that, use this example. You have a bank deposit to make. A check is in your hand, endorsed and ready for deposit. You can't slip it into your floppy disk drive and have it end up in the credit column on your bank statement. You have to walk or drive up to the bank teller (or cash machine) and deposit it. What you can do on the computer, however, is enter the deposit into some accounting package or a checkbook spreadsheet that you've created in Microsoft Excel. You'll have a record of the transaction, and you'll be assured that the deposit of $546.75 isn't added to the balance as $456.75, unless that's what you type in. The computer can only mess up the math if you give it the wrong numbers.

What if you keep scrupulous manual records of your bank transactions? Why computerize them? Computerizing those transactions gives you easy ways to see patterns and trends. How simple is it to use your manual system to see if you made as many deposits from customer A last year as you did this year? Can you tell quickly if you've made more cash withdrawals this year than last? Can you see which season or month is your busiest in terms of bank activity? Can you get a quick tally of your bank fees so you can compare them to what the new bank down the street is offering to new business accounts?

If you had it all in your computer, you could.

Choosing Which Tasks to Automate

So you've decided that you can use your computer to do many, if not all, of your daily office tasks. If the entire task can't be computerized, major portions of it can be, resulting in more and better information, available quickly.

Now snap out of it. Who do you think you are? Unless you're wearing a cape and a leotard and have super powers, you can't computerize every task in your office. Not unless the following things happen:

- **You add to or hire a staff** If you have some employees to answer the phone, log calls, enter your invoices, and update your accounting system, you can probably computerize nearly everything on your list of tasks.
- **You stop doing anything else** Unless you can add more hours to the day (please don't, I'm happy when bedtime rolls around, and I don't want to wait longer for it), you're going to need to offload all your personal tasks—errands and appointments that have nothing to do with "business"—to someone else, delay them until the weekend, or not do them at all.

Hiring or adding to your staff may not be feasible right now. Doing nothing but business, all day, every day, isn't possible, nor is it a healthy decision to make. You need time to take care of you, to do things that have nothing to do with the office. If you don't, sooner or later (and sooner than you expect), you'll begin to hate the office. You need to like the office and look forward to going there, whether it's across town or right off the kitchen.

You're faced with automating only the tasks that you can reasonably expect to do and do well. Don't take on more than you can handle, and don't lie to yourself when you think about it. You know in your heart how much time you have to enter and maintain a daily to-do list, log incoming and outgoing calls, enter banking and billing information, and handle all your correspondence. We haven't even mentioned the time you need to actually do what it is you do! If you're a salesperson, a plumber, a dentist, a lawyer, a landscaper, or whatever, you need time to be that. Don't overload your office hours with more tasks than you can really do. If you don't leave time for doing your billable work, you won't need that office for long.

No Backup? No Calendar!

A certain computer consultant I know switched to a computerized scheduling program. She spent hours putting her past, current, and future appointments into the computer, created to-do lists, and started setting up a contacts list. After using the computerized version, she was so happy, she let her manual appointment book/calendar lapse, no longer keeping it up-to-date. Then one day her hard drive died. There was no saving it. "Did you do a backup?" they asked. "No," she said. "I forgot, and I never have time." Her schedule was lost, and her manual system was no longer a substitute. She had to call her clients and ask if they were expecting her, and when. She looked silly, missed a couple of appointments, and was stressed out. I admit it, I'm talking about myself here. The moral of my story? Run parallel scheduling systems (manual and computer) for several months before giving up the manual system. If you're on the road a lot, consider maintaining the manual system so you can take your current schedule with you (or buy a laptop). Last but not least, always, I repeat, ALWAYS do a backup of your computerized schedule, at least every other day.

How Much Machine Do You Need?

You need a computer that can run the software you need. That begs the question, "What software do I need?" and the following is a general idea, based on the list of tasks that can be done on a computer:

➤ **Word processing** Use a word processing program, such as Word (part of Microsoft Office), to create letters, reports, invoices, brochures, newsletters, and business cards. (To find out more about choosing software for your office, see Chapter 4, "Smart Businesspeople, Foolish Choices: Selecting the Right Software.")

- **Data storage and analysis** Use a spreadsheet program, such as Excel, to keep track of your checkbook balance or maintain a list of contacts, including the date of your last phone call to or from them. A more powerful database program, such as Access, can be used to store large and complex databases, like your customers and their purchase history. Create customized reports to assist you in making your own purchasing decisions.
- **Sales and marketing** Use a presentation program, such as PowerPoint, to create presentations, flyers, signs, or a Web page. The things you create in PowerPoint can be used in Word and Excel documents, and vice versa.
- **Scheduling** Maintain your schedule (appointments, events, to-do lists) with a program such as Outlook, which is part of Microsoft Office. You can create and maintain your schedule on a daily, weekly, monthly, or yearly basis, as well as keep a journal and an address book.
- **Electronic mail** Stay in touch with customers, vendors, friends, and family via the Internet. Establish an Internet account and check your email daily through a program such as Outlook. Use Outlook to send, receive, and respond to your email. Store your email so you can refer to past messages. This can be handy when you need to blame someone else or keep people from blaming you for some office mishap. (For more information on using email, see Chapter 10, "Email: Getting Connected and Staying in Touch.")

Does it sound as if I'm endorsing Microsoft Office? Well, check the front of the book! That's what we're here for. The goal is to show you how to use Microsoft Office to run your small office. That means using it to do your daily office tasks, and keeping those neat piles on your desk from getting out of hand. Virtually any task in your office can be computerized with Microsoft Office. Yes, you still have to water the plants yourself, but Office can do just about everything else.

How much machine do you need to run Microsoft Office? Computers become obsolete every five minutes, or so it seems. The specifications I give you today will be out of date tomorrow, so I'm not going to commit to anything terribly specific. You should look for the following in a computer for your small office:

- At least 32MB (megabytes) of memory, preferably more
- A big hard drive, at least 4GB (gigabytes)
- A fast processor, at least 333MHz (megahertz)
- An internal modem that transfers data at 56.6bps (bits per second)
- An internal CD-ROM drive (standard on new computers)
- A Zip or Jaz drive, either internal or external, for doing fast backups

Of course you need a monitor, a keyboard, and a mouse, and you should be able to find package deals (some even include an inkjet printer) at your local computer store or from large-scale mail order vendors.

Does this sound like a lot of machine? Am I suggesting you need to spend thousands? No. At this writing, the specifications above are average. The point is, Microsoft Office, like most Windows applications, takes a lot of drive space just to live in your computer, as much as 500MB, maybe a little less, maybe a little more, depending on what you install. That's not counting all the files it installs all over your computer to help it work properly. Consider 1GB of your drive for just Microsoft Office. That's not including the space you'll need to store the files you create and any other programs you buy.

WYSIWYG

WYSISYG stands for What You See Is What You Get. It means that documents (letters, spreadsheets, reports, and graphic designs) look onscreen just as they will look when printed. It promotes creativity and saves paper.

Microsoft Office also uses a lot of memory. Not more than other software, but a lot. Windows-based software is graphical, meaning a lot of pictures. Toolbar buttons, *WYSIWYG* text, graphs, charts, and clip art takes a lot of memory to store, display, and manipulate.

All Windows-based software works best with a fast processor, and Microsoft Office is no exception. Just like it's important to have a lot of memory to handle all concurrent jobs happening on your computer, it's also important that those jobs happen as quickly and efficiently as possible. (To find out more about upgrading your existing PC, read Chapter 3, "Already Got a PC? Consider Upgrading.")

You don't need a major computer to run your office. But you don't want to skimp, either. You don't want to have system failures, crashes, or a slow-running system. All these things make using the computer a major pain, by limiting your productivity and creativity, and making you avoid the computer, slipping back to your manual systems. It's worth the investment to buy a machine with enough "juice" to do the job, or to upgrade the machine you have (as needed) to handle the tasks you want to accomplish. (For more information about buying a computer, see Chapter 2, "Buying a Reliable, Reasonably Priced Computer for Your Business.")

Fax Machine or Fax Modem?

The way you share documents with the outside world can create another set of decisions for you. When it comes to your fax machine needs, your new computer most likely will come with a fax modem (a modem capable of sending a fax to a fax machine as well as transferring data to and from other computers). You'll have no choice, and that's fine. Even if you don't use it for faxing, it will work fine for other modem needs, such as Internet access.

If you fax things that are created with your computer, this fax modem may be all you ever need in terms of faxing. If, however, you find yourself faxing magazine and newspaper clippings, photocopied checks, pictures, brochures, and other things that didn't come from your computer, you'll need an actual fax machine, separate from your computer. You can run the fax machine through a phone line and set it up so it only activates if it hears another fax machine on the other end of the line.

Some other devices you'll want to buy to complement your office include

- **A shredder** Many shredders (under $50) sit on top of your trash can, so no special setup is required, and they take up little space. You'll need one to shred rough drafts, financial information you print out but don't need to save, and any name and address reports you don't want to keep. Don't throw people's addresses and phone numbers in the trash where anyone can find them. Keep your financial information private by shredding it before throwing it out.

Beg, Borrow, or Buy?

The Magic Carpet didn't have a fax machine. They borrowed a friend's fax, or went to the drug store down the street and paid 25 cents per fax to use theirs. This was a nuisance when they needed the fax early in the morning or late at night. Their friend started to feel guilty if she went out and they needed her fax while she was out. She even gave them her key so they could come in and fax whenever they needed to. At long last, they bought a fax machine. $250 later, they not only sent faxes, they made photocopies. Hey! I think they still have the key to my house!

- **A copier** Although your fax machine (if you decided you needed one) can make copies, the quality isn't great on many of the fax machines under $500. If you need to make crisp, clear copies and you make them often enough to make going to a commercial copy store prohibitive, make the investment.

- **A reliable answering machine** Better yet, get the answering service through your phone company. No tapes to get tied up, no need to remember to turn the machine on. And best of all, the system works even if your power is out. Each call is logged with the time of the call, and can be stored for up to 30 days. You can even set up a system with more than one voicemail box, so if you have a staff, each person can have voicemail and accumulate his or her own messages. Now that you're logging all business calls into your computer, you really can't afford to miss a call.
- **Communication devices** Get a beeper and a cell phone. Safety and convenience aside, giving your clients another way to find you (or you another way to call them when you're on the road) can be the difference between closing the sale and losing the client.

The Least You Need to Know

- You should carefully analyze the work on your desk to see what tasks you're performing on a daily basis, and which ones can be computerized.
- Don't commit to computerizing something that you don't have time to build and maintain, such as a contact list or a banking transaction database. Sometimes a manual system is best, if you'll be able to keep it up-to-date.
- Choose a computer that can do what you need. Don't skimp on the basics.
- Remember to invest in the other types of office equipment that make it easier to move data and the paper it's printed on from place to place.

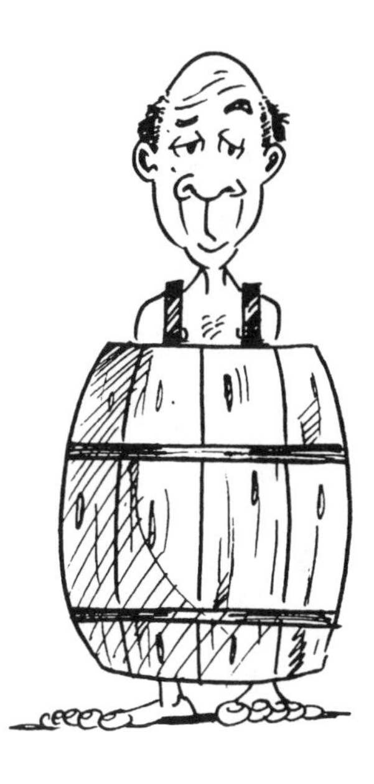

Chapter 2

Buying a Reliable, Reasonably Priced Computer for Your Business

In This Chapter

- Figure out how much computer you can afford
- Make the rounds before plunking down a check
- Should you buy the package deal or go a la carte?
- Sleep better at night with the right warranty coverage
- Consider whether to install a network in your office

Buying a computer isn't as big a financial decision as buying a car, but because you rely on it for so many things—correspondence, financial information, your calendar—you're under pressure to find one that's perfect, that does everything short of picking out your clothes in the morning and driving you to work. You also want to pay as little as possible for all that power.

So many computers are available, from so many different manufacturers, at so many stores, the prospects can be dizzying. Before you spiral and collapse on the linoleum at your local Big Computer Warehouse, you should do your homework. Much of the preparation and research can be done on your current computer if you have Internet access. If you don't have a computer, borrow time on a friend's. You can also make the rounds of computer stores, and buy a newspaper once or twice a week. Don't go crazy and spend months on the decision, however. You can go too far in terms of preparation. Give yourself a target "I Will Have a Computer By This Date," and stick to it.

Determining Your Computer Purchase Budget

It's easy for me to say that you'll spend somewhere in the $1,500–$3,000 range for your computer. My saying that doesn't make it so. Perhaps you can't afford to spend that kind of money right now. Maybe you need to spend more for tax reasons. Let's take the approach that you're trying to spend as little as possible. You have some options for reducing and deferring your costs:

- **Buy a used computer** Some stores only sell used equipment, and many so-called superstores have some used equipment to sell. You can also check the newspaper classifieds, or look online. "Used" doesn't have to mean useless. Someone may have needed a more powerful computer and traded up, leaving you a perfectly appropriate computer for your needs. You can expect to pay approximately two-thirds to one-half the price of a new computer if you buy a used computer that's less than a year old. When buying a used computer, make sure you have access to someone who does computer repair—used computers, even recent models, are rarely under warranty. Some stores may offer a 30-day or similar guarantee, but be prepared to foot the bill for any required service on the computer.
- **Lease a computer** You can spread your purchase over a long period, from 12 to 36 months. Most computer stores have leases available, and if you're a real business with a business bank account and have been in business for six months or more, you should have little or no trouble getting a lease. At the end of the lease period, you can usually buy the computer for about 10% of its original price, or start a new lease on a bigger and better computer. Your lease can include the computer, software, and even training, if the store offers it. Make sure you clarify the terms of the lease as they apply to service for the computer—if it needs repairs during the lease period, it may be the store's responsibility. This is important if the length of the lease exceeds the warranty on your computer, so it pays to have a real understanding of the fine print.
- **Scale back** If your wish list resulted in the need to purchase a $3,000 computer, cut a few things from the list. Remember that memory and hard drive space are the key items on which you don't want to compromise. Giving up the DVD CD drive, or the 21-inch monitor may cut the price back to $2,000, making your purchase do-able.

How can you tell what you can afford? With leasing in the list of possible solutions, determine what monthly payment you can afford. "Afford" means that you don't have to give up any essentials to do it. Food, clothes, utilities, and other business expenses (paying vendors, your cell phone, business credit cards, legitimate travel expenses) are things you shouldn't sacrifice, or your life and business may suffer.

What if you don't want or can't qualify for a lease? Look at your savings or business checking account. Can you live with taking $1,500 to $3,000 out of it in one chunk? If your savings are tied up in CDs or an IRA, the penalty might be higher than if you put the purchase on a credit card instead. Only you know those particulars. If you don't have a credit card or one with enough credit on it to make such a purchase (and still leave yourself some available credit for emergencies or other purchases), you may have to delay the purchase until you've saved the money to buy the computer outright.

Death and Taxes...and Computers?

It's a good idea to contact your accountant before making your purchase. In tax year 1998, for example, you can write off up to $18,500 in computer-fixed assets. You can also depreciate that amount over five years, at varying percentages of the total each year. Your accountant will know which one is best for you. You can get up-to-date tax information at **http://www.el.com/elinks/taxes/**. This site contains links to various tax information resources, including the IRS.

If you can't wait until you've saved the full purchase price, check into personal or business financing through the store where you buy the computer—many computer stores offer a variety of financing options. Depending on the length of the financing, your monthly payment on a $3,000 computer can be as low as $85. If financing doesn't work (maybe your credit report isn't great or you don't want to incur any debt right now), you can wait until the financial climate is better. If you've been computerless or living with your current computer this long, another few months won't kill you. Unlike equipment required to actually perform your service or manufacture your product, you can live without a new computer for a short time!

You Better Shop Around

Assuming that you've decided you can afford to buy or lease the computer, what next? Run into the first computer store and buy something? Shop for months until you find the absolute best deal possible? No, and no.

First, set up a two-column list as shown in Table 2.1. In the first column, your dream computer, in the second, the computer you'll settle for. You can look in the newspapers to start your wish list, and then add the computers you find when you start shopping the stores. List the specifications of each computer, and as you go through the newspaper, shop in the stores, and use online resources, you can note the places that are offering computers like those on your list, and mark down who's selling them and for what price. This will give you a one- or two-page organized place to compare your findings.

Table 2.1 Computer Comparison Shopping List

Dream Computer	Acceptable Alternative	
Processor		
RAM		
Hard drive		
Monitor size		
Modem specs		
Sound specs		
CD equipment		
Extras		
Graphics card		
Printer		

At the bottom of your Computer Comparison shopping list, be sure to list the prices and shopping information for the computers you find that match your dream and acceptable alternative computer specifications.

When you're shopping the stores, bear in mind that although most of them sell the same computers, they sell at different prices and offer different companion services. Basically you'll find two types of computer stores:

- **Superstores** The big computer department stores, such as CompUSA and MicroCenter—different chains exist throughout the country. These stores buy in bulk, so their prices are fairly low. They usually have a service department, where you can bring your computer back for repairs or to install upgrades (memory, hard drives, and so on). You can use their service department whether you bought your computer from them or not. After your computer is out of warranty, however, beware the charges for diagnosing and then fixing the problem.
- **Boutiques** The small storefronts in the mall or shopping center. Boutiques offer more personalized service than the superstores, and their staff is usually more well-informed. The downside? Their prices tend to be somewhat higher because they don't buy in the quantities that a larger store does, so their costs from the manufacturer or aggregator (the middleman between manufacturer and reseller) are higher.

Desktop or Laptop?

A few years ago, this was a no-brainer. Laptops (a.k.a. notebook computers) were too expensive, had notoriously small hard drives, and had lousy monitors. Not so anymore. Because their prices have become more reasonable (generally just $500 to $1,000 more than their desktop equivalents) and they now have decent-sized hard drives and fairly nice monitors, the decision to buy a laptop can be a difficult one.

Laptops generally come with all the same devices as a desktop computer, except some have one external disk slot. You can insert a CD-ROM drive or a floppy drive (both drives come with the laptop), but you're restricted to using them one at a time. Sound is another feature you may lose, great speakers rarely come built-in to a laptop.

With these pros and cons in mind, should you go with a laptop? Consider this checklist of questions—your answers should make the answer clear.

- ❑ Do you travel a lot?
- ❑ When you travel, do you need access to email and the capability to create documents?
- ❑ Do you have a large office with lots of desk space?
- ❑ Do you do presentations and sales calls at customer sites?
- ❑ Do you want to do your computer work outside or on the couch in front of the TV?

If you answered Yes to all but the third question, you should seriously consider the purchase of a laptop. If you already have a desktop computer, consider buying a laptop as your "spare," the one you take on trips and sales calls or use at home on the weekends—you can enter your expenses while your kids play in the yard.

Buyer Beware

Small computer stores often build their own systems, and offer them at low prices. Beware! You may run into repair problems, compatibility problems (when trying to upgrade or add a peripheral device), and these smaller stores tend to go out of business more frequently than the larger ones. You don't want to hear that their number's been disconnected when you call for tech support.

Laptop to Desktop to Laptop

If you decide to buy a laptop, remember you can attach your desktop computer's monitor and mouse to it if you feel the need to have a bigger or better viewing area, or if you're tired of the laptop's "mouse" (usually a pointer embedded in the keyboard or a pad/buttons gadget). You might also consider a docking station that you can plug the laptop into at the office.

If this laptop will be a second computer, you can take it easy on the bells and whistles. A fall-back computer doesn't have to have the huge hard drive you have on your primary (desktop) computer, and it doesn't need the best or biggest laptop monitor available because you won't be staring at it all day, every day.

To laptop or not to laptop is a decision based on needs, wants, and budgets. All the rules for picking one out (after you've decided you want one) are the same as those I've outlined for selecting a desktop computer—shop around, get your best deal, and make sure you get a great warranty.

Mail Order or Off the Shelf?

While you're researching your options, consider mail order. Buying a computer by mail (from a catalog or Web site) is usually cheaper (no store or salesperson to finance), and you'll usually get a greater variety of system combinations. Match computer A with monitor B and printer C, with the bigger hard drive and a memory upgrade, and you've got your system. If this sounds too impersonal or risky because you could make a mistake by checking off the wrong product on some catalog or online order form, don't worry. Most mail-order companies have patient and well-informed customer service reps who will discuss your purchase with you on the phone, via a toll-free number. Their job is to make sure the system you buy is viable and will run what you need it to run. Nobody wants you to send it back.

Even with customer service reps on the phone, if you don't think you could tell a RAM chip from a tortilla chip, you probably won't feel comfortable with mail order, be it ordering from a catalog or a Web site. You're probably underestimating yourself, but if you're feeling unsure of your technical savvy, don't do anything you're not 100% comfortable with.

For some people, mail order isn't worth the savings. Some people like to see and touch the computer before they buy it, or at least an identical model. They want to look the sales rep in the eye when they ask a question. One computer manufacturer has resolved the mail order discomfort issue. Although I'm not endorsing their products (nor am I saying they're not great), Gateway has stores throughout the country where you can see their computers in person, talk to a live sales rep, and then make your purchase. Rather than leaving the store with a big box, however, you go home and await a shipment (which could take up to two weeks) from their warehouse in South Dakota.

Whether you're shopping by mail, online, or just nosing around for pricing and product information, it pays to look at the major computer manufacturer's Web sites. They list their products, describe their capabilities, and in some cases, list current retail prices.

http://www.gateway.com/

http://www.dell.com/

http://www.compaq.com/showroom/index.html

http://www.nec.com/products/products.html

http://www.ibm.com/Products/

http://www.toshiba.com

For more online shopping alternatives, try **www.yahoo.com** or **www.excite.com** (or any Web-search page), and click the **Shopping** link you'll find on the home page. You can scan a list of items from Apparel to Wine & Spirits. Don't get distracted, here! Click **Computer Hardware** and **Computer Software** to access online computer shopping using your credit card. You can also order most items to be shipped after the manufacturer has received your check, if you're not comfortable using your credit card on the Internet.

If you'd rather have a catalog to leaf through, you can grab a copy of the Computer Shopper catalog at most computer stores. It will set you back about $4. You can also go to their Web site, at **www.computershopper.com**, and view their pages online for free. If you receive computer catalogs in the mail, use them carefully. They often advertise great prices, but may not be as competitive as they lead you to believe. Hundreds of catalogs are out there, and as soon as you make any inquiries for computer information (at stores, online, through the mail), you're likely to end up on their mailing lists.

Sold! Check Out Online Computer Auctions

If you already have access to a computer that's connected to the Internet (yours or a friend's), check out online auctions. Whole computer systems and peripheral devices (monitors, printers, scanners, modems) are auctioned off via the World Wide Web. You enter your bid and your email address (you'll have to register with the auctioneer beforehand to get a password and ID number), and submit your bid. Although each auction site operates a little differently, auctions generally take place over the course of a day or two. You can check back with the site periodically to see how the bidding is going (some sites update you via email throughout the day to let you know how your bid stacks up against the other participants). You can submit newer, higher bids if someone tops your last bid. If your bid wins, the auctioneer will contact you to let you know, and you can send a check or pay by credit card. Prices range from 25% to 75% of the original retail price.

Check the following auction Web sites:

http://www.3dauction.com/

http://www.onsale.com/

http://www.ebay.com/—This site is more like a swap meet—individuals use the site to run their own mini-auctions. You deal with the seller directly, not with the company that hosts the site.

Buyer Beware, Again

Beware of the Big Computer Show and Sale at your local convention center. These shows are tempting because they offer big savings on computers and software. Although many of the companies that you'll see there are reputable, many fly-by-night outfits will sell you a computer and then skip town, leaving a disconnected phone number and a lot of disillusioned customers. No iron-clad way exists to tell the good guys from the bad. If no warranty is offered in writing, walk away. At least if you have a warranty, you have legal recourse if they disappear.

Many sites have new and used equipment, and older equipment that the manufacturers get rid of to free up warehouse space for new stuff. Auctions offer great savings and a wide variety of products to choose from, although you may have to shop around to find the auction that's selling what you want. Go to the following site to search for a particular computer or piece of computer equipment—you'll be given a list of the auctions currently offering the product.

http://www.pricefinder.com

Is a Package Deal Your Best Deal?

You can't open the paper or turn on the TV without seeing a package deal on a computer. Buy it this week and you get a printer (usually a low-end color inkjet) or free software. Some deals include training or a free year's service. Whatever the offer, the seller's goal is to move product.

By purchasing a package, you normally get a good deal, but you may give up some flexibility. In many cases, the deal price is an "as is" price. If you want to increase memory or get a bigger hard drive, you'll end up paying the a la carte prices for each piece of the package. Some package deals do offer options, however, and these are the deals to go for.

When isn't a package deal your best deal? When you can't add or delete options without increasing the price, or when the products in the package are obsolete technology. Because you listened to me and made your handy-dandy computer wish list, you can compare what they're selling to what you want. Don't let a "free" printer or software package make you give up on important computer features such as a big hard drive or extra memory. Don't buy an old processor just to get a larger monitor.

Remember, people who sell computers are in the game to make money—nothing is really free. Your package deal is opening up his warehouse space or getting him in good with a manufacturer. These are not wrong motives—as a business person, you can certainly empathize. You can also benefit from the seller's predicament.

Warranties and Service Plans

Most computers come with at least a one-year warranty. Unless you violate the warranty by letting your 12-year-old computer-wiz nephew take your new computer apart, you're safe for the warranty period. If anything stops working, it will be replaced, free of charge. You may have to take it to a service center or ship it to the manufacturer for the repair/replacement to be made, but the shipping will be free. If you're leasing your computer, you may find that the cost of repairs and maintenance are the responsibility of the seller, because the seller actually owns the product until, and unless, you buy the product outright at the end of your lease.

Technical Turnaround

If you need your computer back immediately, you have to pay for the express shipping, and probably a small fee for quick turnaround. Make sure you find out what kind of timeframe your warranty or service plan offers for fixing the computer and getting it back to you. Of course if your computer comes with *on-site maintenance* (the best option, which means the company will send a repair person to your location), you've got it made in the shade.

Some computers are covered by more than one warranty. For example, your computer package—computer, monitor, and printer—may be under one warranty, but your hard drive may be on another one. Using my own computer as an example, I was upset when I had owned my computer for two years (and the computer warranty was over), and my hard drive died. I figured I would have to buy a new one, out of my pocket. Wrong! I had a three-year warranty from the hard drive manufacturer, and I was given a free replacement. Be sure to ask about all the warranties on your system.

You can, however, purchase additional coverage (called a *service agreement*) from the store or mail-order company from whom you buy the computer. This can supplement the year that the manufacturer gives you, extending your service for up to five years. The cost of these plans is usually less than the cost of parts and labor for replacing one major part in your computer, such as the hard drive or motherboard.

Warranty Warning

If the manufacturer doesn't offer at least a one-year warranty, you should reconsider buying that computer. Even if you can buy coverage from the seller, the manufacturer's unwillingness to guarantee its own product sends a clear message—buy something else.

If you only intend to keep your new computer for a year or two (no longer than the warranty that comes with it), you may not want to go to the extra expense of the service plan. Bear in mind, however, that if your plans to replace the PC don't become a reality, it may be more expensive to buy the service plan later. Ask the sales rep to clearly explain all of your service plan purchase options.

What do service agreements include? Typically, they come in one of several flavors:

- **Hardware Support agreements** Include an agreed-upon response time and on-site repair of your hardware. Some plans require you to pay a retainer up front—your costs are deducted from that payment—which is held in escrow for the duration of the agreement. Others require monthly, quarterly, or yearly payments that cover you no matter how much service you require. For a small office (two computers), costs for such an agreement shouldn't exceed $500.
- **Time and Materials agreements** Cover the labor costs in repairing your system. You pay only for the parts that need replacing. This sort of coverage isn't advisable for older equipment, which is more likely to break down and have no other warranties to cover the cost of parts.

What About Networks?

Do you need a network? If you do, what considerations does it require? To determine whether you need a network for your small business, you should first determine what a network is and what it does.

A network is a group of computers tied together through networking software and physically connected via cables or phone lines. A network can be a LAN (Local Area Network) where all the computers in the network are in one small, centralized area, such as an office or group of offices in one building. A network can also be a WAN (Wide Area Network), with computers spread across the street, the city, or the globe. For small businesses, however, networks tend to be small and simple, enabling a handful of users to share software, files, and printers. You may also hear small networks referred to as workgroups.

To determine whether you need a network, review the following list. If you see yourself in this list, you may benefit from a network:

- ➤ More than one person is working in the office most of the time. If so, you can share printers and other peripheral devices like a fax modem if you're networked.
- ➤ You frequently share files with your coworkers. If you have found that giving files to each other on disk is too time-consuming or that many of your files are too big to fit on a disk, it's time for a network.
- ➤ You have more than one computer and you want to use one for a specific task (such as graphic design or industrial drawings) and use the other(s) for general office use? A network will enable both computers to use the same printer.

If you're a one-person office with one computer, you obviously don't need a network. If you have a small staff and you want to share devices or files, you might need one. A traditional network, which is the best option if your business is growing, consists of the following parts:

- ➤ **A server** This computer contains the network software, and is usually the home of shared files.
- ➤ **Connection devices** External wiring and internal connection cards that connect your computers to each other or the server.
- ➤ **Network software** This can take the form of an operating system (Windows NT) or a software package that runs with your operating system, such as Novell NetWare.
- ➤ **A networking consultant** You need an expert who knows networks, and can make an informed, unbiased suggestion about which type of network you need, and can set it up for you. This consultant should also be available to support you when you have questions or problems with your network.
- ➤ **A network service agreement** The consultant who can fix your network software or help you with administering the network may not be the same person who does physical repairs—replacing broken parts, repairing the server. A service contract that assures you a fast response and lowers your repair costs after the hardware is out of warranty is not just a good idea, it's essential.

If you don't imagine that your office will grow beyond two or three computers in the next few years (and that doesn't mean your business won't grow, just that you won't need more computers to manage it all), you might consider using a less hardware-intensive solution. Assuming you're using Windows 95 or Windows 98, you can take advantage of Microsoft's simpler "peer-to-peer" networking capabilities. This technology allows each computer on the network to function as both a user (also known as a "client") and a server (see definition in the previous list of network components). You'll need cabling and adapter cards for each computer (peer) in the group, and I strongly suggest you pull in some technical expertise for the project. Make sure this person is available to set you up, train you, and offer technical support. Although this solution is less expensive and less complex than a traditional network, it's not like setting up your VCR, either. Don't be ashamed to seek out a consultant to help you.

What if neither of these networking solutions seems right for you? Try some inexpensive alternatives for a small office—they may not be wise long-term solutions, but they're working for many of my clients right now:

Zip It Up

To make a large file smaller (for storage or transmission over the Internet), you may choose to *compress* or "zip" the file. This process reduces the file size by up to 75%, depending on the file's content. After a file has been compressed, it must be expanded (returned to its normal size) before it can be used.

- If your primary reason for having a network is to share files, consider emailing them to each other. Although some email systems can't handle large file attachments, you can compress the files before sending them to make sure they're 3MB or less. Each user must have a connection to the Internet, and each user must have an email address.
- Add an external Zip or Jaz drive. These devices work similarly to the internal floppy drive on your computer now, but they use larger-capacity disks, ranging from 100MB to 1GB. When installed, the drives appear in your Windows Explorer and My Computer windows, and can be used as the target for backups and copied files. Copy files from your computer to the Zip or Jaz disk, and then give it to your coworker who needs to use the file. At around $100 each, you can probably afford to get one for every PC in the office, although you can move a single external drive from computer to computer as needed.
- Again, if file sharing is your primary goal and you find that swapping floppy disks doesn't do it (they don't hold enough and they're vulnerable to damage and corruption of data), try adding a CD drive that writes to blank CDs. Each write-able CD can hold up to 650MB. You can write (copy) needed files to the CD, and share it with coworkers, who can access the data through their normal CD-ROM drive. You can get one for under $500, most in the $200 to $300 dollar range, from companies like Panasonic and Mitsumi. Check the Computer Shopper (**www.computershopper.com**) for specific information.
- If you need to share a printer, consider a switch box. It's a junction box that forms a Y-connection between two computers and a printer. You have to take turns using the printer, but it's much cheaper than a network. Switch box

pricing depends on how the device works—mechanical switch boxes (where you manually flip a switch) are at the low end of the price range ($20). Automatic switch boxes are software driven (the software comes with the box, and you install it on your computer). You can choose your printer/computer via the software, and for this convenience, you will pay a higher price, in the neighborhood of $100.

A network is not something to leap into, because it adds to your starting and maintenance costs. It's also a good idea that you become well-informed about your network software or operating system so you can do a lot of your own troubleshooting. That requires training (few people can just pick up a book and become a network expert), and training for Novell Netware or Windows NT is pricey, sometimes up to $1,000 for a two- or three-day basics class.

The Least You Need to Know

- Figure out what you can afford—a lump expense or monthly payments—and shop carefully for your new computer.
- Use stores, newspapers, even the Web to find computer deals on the technology you need to get the job done.
- You may give up some warm fuzzy feelings when you buy a mail-order computer, but what you save may be worth the lack of personal attention.
- Don't buy a computer that doesn't have at least a one-year warranty. After that runs out, pick up a service contract that limits down-time and saves you real money.
- Although a network can facilitate file and device sharing in your office, some common sense alternatives can save you money and the expense of a consultant.

Chapter 3

Already Got a PC? Consider Upgrading

In This Chapter

- Give your computer a kick in the RAM
- Buy a larger hard drive to store more software and files
- Find instant gratification with cool peripherals

So you already have a computer. Maybe you've had it for a long time, maybe you bought it just last year. In either case, chances are you wish it had...more. More speed? More room? More stuff? Speed is good. Room is good. And stuff? Well stuff is always good, especially when it gives you pretty pictures and sound.

Your current PC probably does what you need it to do. It probably runs your word processing software, and you can run a couple of other programs at the same time, hopping over to a game of solitaire when the mood strikes. But does it do these things quickly? Do programs crash frequently? Do your storage limitations cause you to think twice before you download a new game or some clip art from the Web? Adding memory and hard drive space to your computer will make it more productive and turn it into a more powerful tool for everything you do. Adding peripherals that bring color, sound, and Internet access to your office isn't essential to some offices, but it is a great deal of fun. Making work fun can be as important as the work itself.

Don't Forget to Add Memory

Your computer's memory, measured in megabytes of RAM (Random Access Memory), is where the various tasks that your computer is performing are stored while they're happening. Like thoughts in your head that you hang on to until a job is finished and then you replace them with a new thought, your computer's memory maintains "thoughts" about programs, documents, print jobs, and the files that support them. As each job is completed, a new job takes its place. The word random (the R in RAM) refers to the way memory is used—your computer grabs a random open spot in the memory area for a process, and when that spot is emptied (by the task's completion), a new task takes its place—or it might grab another open spot altogether. These open areas are not doled out serially or in any particular order, but in a completely random way.

A Reminder About Memory

Memory is not storage. Let's get that common misconception out of the way right off the bat. Although your computer may use portions of the hard drive (a storage device) for memory-related tasks, the size of your hard drive in terms of how much software you can install and how many files you can store has nothing to do with your computer's memory.

Because your computer's memory handles ongoing tasks, the more memory you have, the more tasks you can juggle at once. Adding memory to your computer is one of the simplest and cheapest ways to give your computer more oomph. If you're running Windows 95 or 98, you've probably been told that 32MB is all you need. Ha! Try 40MB or better. Running with 32MB allows you to get by, but if you run any programs that have a lot going on visually or that create and use large files, things slow down. If you've ever found yourself drumming your fingers on your desk waiting for a program to start or a screen to refresh, you know what I mean.

Adding memory isn't something most people should do by themselves. Most computer technicians charge about $50 for the labor involved, and buying 16–32MB of RAM costs under $200 for most desktop computers. It's worth paying for someone to install the memory for you—you avoid having to research the size and type of memory chips your computer uses, and although problems with most service technicians are rare, you'll have someone to blame if things go wrong. If you do it and mess up, you're stuck, and then you'll have to take the PC in for service, anyway. If you insist on installing your own memory, or if you just want to understand what's going on, ponder these points:

- **How much memory do you already have?** You may be able to use the existing memory and add to it. If you have 32MB, is it in four 8MB chips or in a combination of four 4MB and two 8MB chips? Does your computer require that pairs of like chips be used? Some PCs are finicky about that, although others allow more mixing and matching. Do you have enough sockets to add more or will you have to replace your existing chips with larger chips to achieve your desired RAM? Sometimes you have to replace all the existing chips so you can have all the same kind, although some computers allow different size chips to coexist.
- **What type of memory does your system have?** In addition to different size chips, there are several varieties, such as SIMM, DIMM, and SDRAM. Don't let these acronyms worry you. You don't have to know what they mean, but you might have to write them down when someone tells you what your system requires so you can buy the right kind. Look in your system documentation or call the store or manufacturer from whom you bought the PC.
- **Where is your memory?** If you've never opened your computer case before, you might want to find your system documentation. If there isn't a diagram for you to follow and you're not familiar with the internal parts of your computer, stop right now and give up the idea of doing this yourself.

Elbow Room: Increasing Storage Space

Whether with an increase in memory in a total system improvement process or as the sole upgrade you're doing, adding hard drive space can make a world of difference in the way you work.

If you currently have to worry about whether you have room to add a program or download a file, you need to add space. If you have less than 500MB left on your hard drive, you need to get more space, and get it fast.

You can add hard drive space in a variety of ways, all but one of which (the last) should be done by a qualified technician:

- **Swap your existing hard drive for a newer, larger one** You can copy your data from one to the other before or after installation (a second computer is required for the copying process).
- **Add another internal hard drive to your computer** Depending on your system's configuration and capabilities, you may be able to add an entire extra drive. Your original drive (and all that's on it) will remain intact, and you'll have a brand spanking new drive right next to it, adding space for more software and files. The new drive will probably become drive D: or E:.

Gimme Room

Why is having at least 500MB of free space important? Because your computer uses that extra space for processing while you work. From making use of hard drive space for transient memory-related functions to storing temporary files, you will see major system slow-downs if your computer doesn't have enough elbow room.

- **Add an external hard drive or removable drive like a Zip, Jaz, or SyJet drive** Typically plugged into a parallel port (depending on the type of drive), this extra drive gives you more space without requiring a complete reconfiguring of your computer, and doesn't affect your existing drive at all. You can perform this installation yourself, running an installation program from a disk or CD that comes with the drive. For some types of removable drives, you also can buy a model that installs within your computer, like a floppy disk drive, rather than connecting to the parallel port. This type of drive should be installed by a professional.

External storage drives work a lot like the floppy drive already on your computer—they use disks (or cartridges) for storing data. These disks/cartridges hold from 100MB to 2GB (gigabytes) of data. That's where the similarity to a floppy drive ends—you go from 2MB of capacity to 2GB—a considerable leap in portable data storage.

External storage drives can be used in many ways—like an extra closet to store files you use often or like your attic, where you store stuff you need once or twice a year. The files can be stored in their full open status, or as zipped files. If you choose to zip the files, you can store many more files on the disk. The downside (but it's a small one) of storing zipped files is that you'll have to expand them before using them on your computer.

How about costs? Internal hard drives can cost anywhere from $150 to $350 (plus installation), depending on their size. Obviously, larger drives cost more money. Prices on hard drives are in a perpetual reduction mode, however. The prices in your area may be half of what I'm stating here by the time you read this book. Check online sources, computer stores, and the newspaper for the latest pricing.

Zip and Unzip

A *zipped file* is a file that has been compressed to take up less room, becoming up to 75% smaller after compression. While zipped, a file cannot be used. Zipped files are unzipped before use, restoring them to their full size and functionality. WinZip and PKZip are popular compression programs available as shareware online (see Chapter 4, "Smart Businesspeople, Foolish Choices: Selecting the Right Software" for more).

External drives cost nearly the same as internal drives, starting at $150 for an external Zip drive, and going up to $450 for an internal Jaz drive. Because they come in fancy packages with installation programs and require a warm and fuzzy customer support number for you to call, they may cost more. You'll spend from $10 to $75 on cartridges for Zip and Jaz drives, depending on the capacity of the cartridge.

Want to know more about external drives? Check out the FAQ (Frequently Asked Question) pages for the popular Zip and Jaz drives:

http://www.iomega.com/support/techs/zip/2002/html

http://www.iomega.com/support/techs/zip/4001.html

Major Renovations: Upgrading Your CPU or Motherboard

Your motherboard is a large circuit board on which sits your processor, a.k.a. your CPU. Your CPU (Central Processing Unit) is your computer's brain. Just like a person with a high IQ can process information more effectively, a computer with a high-level processor can process data faster and more efficiently.

So your CPU sits on the motherboard. Why? Because all of your computer's devices—drives, monitor, keyboard, mouse, and so on—must talk to the CPU. Due to the CPU's size (about the size of a postage stamp), you can't physically plug everything into it. You can, however, plug everything into the motherboard—enabling all the devices to talk to the CPU.

Although you shouldn't contemplate performing this upgrade yourself, you can certainly look into the possibilities. Replacing your motherboard/CPU is a big job, and one that you should give to a qualified technician. Unlike plugging in some extra memory chips or adding an external storage drive, installing a new motherboard and CPU can require some changes to your computer's basic configuration—the technician will have to set your PC up to recognize its new brain and use it properly.

The costs of a processor upgrade are higher than adding memory or a hard drive, because it takes longer to do it—it's not a simple plug-it-in process. You'll be charged approximately $100 for installation, plus the cost of the parts you're adding. There's a wide range of prices for different computers and processors. Check with your local computer store for the latest pricing, or go to **www.computershopper.com** to look it up yourself.

Adding the Extras: Printers, Scanners, Modems, and Sound

Adding these devices does two things—adds to your enjoyment of your computer, and increases the types of programs and files you can use. I'm sure the enjoyment part of that statement is obvious—if your computer can print in color, make noises, connect to the Internet, and be used to create graphic files from photographs and drawings, you'll have a lot of fun with it.

If you can print in color, play sounds, connect to the Internet, and turn a printed document into a document you can save and edit, you'll get more done. Good deal, no?

Adding peripheral devices is fairly simple, and not too expensive. You can install most if not all of them yourself. If you shop carefully, you can spend less than $1,000 to add a printer, scanner, modem, and sound equipment to your computer.

Adding a Color Printer

Adding a printer involves plugging it into your computer and using the Control Panel to add a driver for the new printer. Double-click the **Printers** icon in the Control Panel window, and then double-click the **Add Printer** icon. Find your printer manufacturer and model, and be ready to insert the Windows CD-ROM. Follow the onscreen instructions, and Windows copies the required files to the hard drive. If you find your printer model in the list of printers that Windows offers, you're probably safe to use the Windows driver. If, however, you don't find your late model printer in the list, use the floppy disk that came with your printer. The printer disk may come with an actual installation program on it to install the driver, or it may merely require you to insert that disk when Windows prompts you for the disk or CD when you're performing the Add Printer function.

A color inkjet printer can be inexpensive (many are less than $250), and although it doesn't create crisp, photographic-quality printouts (despite recent manufacturer

Call My Driver!

A *driver* is a file that tells your computer how to talk to a particular device. In the case of a printer driver, it tells Windows and the other applications on your computer what the printer is capable of doing, how fast it prints, how much data it can digest at a time, and what fonts it can support. If the right driver isn't available, check the manufacturer's Web site. You can probably download the latest and greatest driver along with instructions for installing it.

claims), it does create cool output. You can create color transparencies for a presentation, create your own color brochures and flyers, or generate greeting cards and announcements. If you already have a black-and-white printer, consider adding a color printer as your second printer.

Color laser printers are more expensive, running you a few thousand dollars, depending on speed. A color laser's printed output is crisp, clear, and nearly photographic. You can use color laser copy as the original for clean photocopies, in color or black-and-white.

Many offices use a black-and-white laser printer (many under $500, some as high as $1,500) and have a color inkjet as a spare printer for jobs that require color. Why have both? Because the laser prints quickly, and creates crisp black-and-white documents—perfect for most business correspondence. Laser printers create output that can be photocopied or faxed cleanly, as opposed to inkjets, which can create nice originals, but the color stripes (formed by the inkjets firing ink at the paper on many horizontal passes) can show when the original is copied or faxed. Inkjets also print slowly, making them frustrating to use for multi-page documents or as a printer used by more than one person in the office.

Maintenance of lasers is also cheaper in the long run. A laser printer's toner cartridge can be used to create thousands of pages, and one cartridge costs less than $100. Inkjet cartridges cost from $10 to $20 dollars each (the color ink cartridges can be more expensive than black), and you may go through 20 or more in a year if you use the inkjet printer for all of your output. That's why inkjets are great for home use—your kid's book reports or your Christmas newsletter—the output rates are low. In the office, however, using an inkjet as your sole printer can be expensive.

Capture Text and Graphics with a Scanner

A scanner works by taking an image—a photograph, a drawing, a document—and capturing the image content. It does this with technology similar to a photocopier: A laser passes by the image (placed face-down on a glass plate), enabling the scanner to read the colors, the lights and darks, and convert them to an image on your computer. The image can then be saved as a file for inserting into documents, spreadsheets, and presentations. You can add photos, maps, drawings—any graphic image—to any Word, Excel, or PowerPoint document. Graphic content makes your documents more interesting, and can convey a message easily where words might fail.

If you're considering adding a scanner to your computer system, it's easy to do, and relatively inexpensive. A decent color scanner costs less than $500, many models less than $200. Depending on the type of scanner, you'll plug it into your parallel or serial port. Many people prefer to use a serial port, because it doesn't tie up their printer's parallel port. You can purchase a device that allows you to share the parallel port, but many printers aren't compatible with it.

Scanners come with a disk or CD that includes an installation program. This program sets up the scanner for recognition by Windows, and gives you a program for scanning images. Most scanning software also includes tools for fine-tuning the image—adjusting sharpness and contrast—as well as cleaning up any stray marks from smudges or wrinkles on the original. To scan an image, you do a preview scan of the entire scanner plate (the glass) and then you choose the area on which to do a final scan. After your final scan, you can save the image as a file, preferably in a graphic file format that Office can use. (For more information on using graphic files in Office documents, check out Chapter 13, "Printed Matter: Do-It-Yourself Marketing.")

If you'll be using your scanner for text documents, you may want to purchase software that converts the text from an image to actual editable text. This type of software is generally referred to as OCR (Optical Character Recognition) software.

Graphic File Formats

Choose a file format for your scanned images that will make it compatible with the greatest number of programs. If you'll be inserting your scanned image in an Office document but want to use it with other programs as well, stick with the three most common file formats: .bmp, .tif, and .jpg. Don't let the initials frighten you—they're file extensions that tell your computer how the image content is stored.

Depending on the program's sophistication, you can pay anywhere from $100 to $500. After scanning your document and using the OCR software to convert the image to text, you can save your image as a document file (.doc for use in Word, for example), and then open it in Word for editing and formatting as needed.

Do you need a scanner? If you find yourself taking photographs, drawings, or graphics to a store and having them scanned (at about $5–$10 per scan) more than once or twice a month, you need a scanner. If you create a lot of marketing materials (newsletters, brochures, flyers), you will definitely benefit from having a scanner—scan a picture of yourself and save it for adding to your brochure, newsletter, or to post on the Internet to find a date.

Just Scan It!

Using OCR software is great for organizations that deal with legal documents such as leases or contracts. By scanning the document, you save the time of retyping it, and you avoid omissions that can change the content and legal spirit of the document.

Reach Out with a Modem

If you bought your computer in the last three years, you probably already have an internal modem. Unless you bought your computer in the last year, however, that modem is probably too slow. If your computer is older or for some reason doesn't have an internal modem, you can add one, or plug an external modem into your computer. Current modems transfer data at a rate of 56.6Kbps (kilobytes per second).

What does a modem do? It allows you to connect to other computers. You can connect to the Internet, putting email and the World Wide Web at your disposal. Newer modems can also handle voice, allowing you to use your computer to make phone calls (you'll need a microphone attached to your PC to pick up the sound of your voice, and sound capability to play the other person's voice over your computer).

Modems also control the flow of data to and from your computer, running at speeds up to 56.6Kbps. Circumstances can lower this transfer rate, however, such as the quality of your phone line, the speed of the modem on the computer you dial into, and traffic at popular Internet sites.

Most new modems are called fax modems, meaning they can transfer data to fax machines and other fax modems as well as perform standard data transmissions between computers. Chapter 1, "If I Had a Hammer: Choosing the Right Tool for the Job," discusses the use of a fax modem, and you'll find more information about the process of sending faxes (via modem or fax machine) in Chapter 11, "Just the Fax, Ma'am."

Modems come in two flavors—internal or external. Internal modems are easy to install, but they require you to remove the computer's cover, plug a modem device into your computer's processing board, and set up the phone jack that will emerge from the back of your computer. In addition, you must run an installation program (it comes with the modem on CD or disk) that sets up the modem so your computer recognizes it as a functioning internal component. You must do separate setups for your Internet software and any local email systems you may use so that these programs know which modem you're using.

An external modem requires the same installation program and software setups, but you need only plug it into one of your serial ports to connect it to your computer. Then plug your phone into the modem, and you're ready to go.

More About Modem

The word *modem* comes from two words—*mod*ulator and *dem*odulator. The modem's original role was to convert analog (voice grade) phone waves to digital input for your computer. Outgoing data is converted from digital back to analog. The modem's second job is to control the flow of data to and from your computer. The computer's *transfer rate* (Kbps or bps) tells you how fast that data is being sent.

Making Noise with Your Computer

With more and more software designed to take advantage of sound, you're missing a lot if your computer isn't equipped to play and record sound.

To play sound, your computer needs a sound card. The sound card is installed inside your computer, plugging into your motherboard and creating a connection on the back of your computer for external speakers. Speakers can sit on the desk or attach to the side of your monitor. The whole setup will set you back from $150 to $300, depending on the quality of the speakers.

Zapped!

A consultant I know (Okay, it's me again) installed her own sound card. Due to a buildup of static electricity (it was winter, I was wearing a wool sweater), I zapped my hard drive when I plugged in my sound card. The drive was irreparably damaged, and I lost all my data (I hadn't done a backup, but that's another story). The technician to whom I took my poor injured PC said that my mishap was a common one, and said I should have had him install the card for me. NOW he tells me!

Installing the card is easy, but as I've said with regard to other installations that require taking the cover off the computer, please know your way around before taking this on yourself. It's much cheaper to let someone else do it for you (take the computer and your sound equipment to your service technician) than to risk messing it up if you're not sure what you're doing.

After the sound card is installed, you can plug your speakers in and install the sound device software. Although Windows 95 and 98 come with sound programs, you may want to use the sound program that comes with your sound card—these programs normally offer more "bells and whistles" for playing and manipulating sound files.

Music Soothes the Savage Worker

You can also play audio CDs on your computer, listening to them through your speakers or with headphones that plug into your CD-ROM drive. This can make a long session working at your computer much more enjoyable.

Recording sound requires that a microphone be plugged into your sound card, through the back of your PC. With recording capability, you can record your voice, music, and extraneous sound, and save these recordings as sound files. You can insert these sound files into your PowerPoint presentations, or even your Word and Excel documents. Recording devices should cost you no more than $150.

The Least You Need to Know

- Adding memory is easy, but if you're not a techie, you might consider hiring one to do it. Increasing your computer's memory will increase it's efficiency and responsiveness.
- Increasing hard drive space allows you to install more software and create more files. It also gives your computer more processing room for handling temporary files and tasks while you work.
- Plugging cool extras like color printers, scanners, sound devices, and modems into your computer will increase your creativity, productivity, and make using the computer more fun.

Chapter 4

Smart Businesspeople, Foolish Choices: Selecting the Right Software

In This Chapter

- Is the free software that comes with your new PC worth the price?
- Research your off-the-shelf software choices
- Should you hire a programmer to design a program just for you?

Your computer hardware can have all the power in the world, leaping tall documents in a single bound, more powerful than a speeding spreadsheet. But if you load software (or use the programs that came with your PC) and it doesn't do what you need, your computer may be as effective as a particular superhero after exposure to kryptonite.

It's not that bad or inappropriate software saps your computer's strength per se—rather, it saps your productivity, turning hours of time entering and processing data into wasted time or time that might have been better spent with better software.

Throughout your computing life, you'll be faced with free software, reduced rates on software upgrades, and seductive offers that promise performance and ease of use. Many of these offers will be legitimate, many will mean well but not deliver. It's up to you to use your innate consumer ability to sniff out a bargain and make intelligent software choices.

Freebies: Software that Comes with Your PC

So you've gone out and shopped for a new computer. Noticed that in addition to package deals that give you a printer with your basic system, many of them also come with free software? This software is in addition to the operating system (Windows), of course, which the computer can't run without. Even a computer that isn't sold as a package deal often comes with a variety of software programs, all supposedly free.

Why is software given away? To encourage you to buy, to forge alliances between the hardware and the software vendors, and to give away software no one would buy. The freebies on your new PC could fall into one or more of those categories.

How do you tell if your free software is worth the price? The first clue is recognition. Have you heard of any of the programs? If you have had any exposure at all to computer magazines, ads in the paper, or just browsed in a computer store, you'll recognize any well-known programs by name. That's not to say that only well-known software is any good, but it's a first clue.

A Computer with the Works, Please!

Many new computers come with Microsoft Works. This is a program that combines some of the basic functions of the Microsoft Office suite—word processing, spreadsheets, database, and communications software—into one integrated software application. Significant differences exist, however, as Works contains scaled-back, simplistic versions of the full-running applications in Office. It's a good place to get started, however. Many new users get their feet wet with Works, and then move up to Office later.

Second, check the local computer store. Is the free software that's on this PC available on the shelves? Look it up in a software catalog. See it? No? If you can't find any information about it, it's probably a throw-away that either didn't sell or was created expressly to be given away with new computers. That means it's not well tested by consumers, and the manufacturer has no vested interest in supporting or upgrading it in the future. Unless it's a game or a simple utility of some sort (a file compression program, for example), you can safely consider it a waste of your time.

Hey, you're saying, it's free! Why not use it? I'm not saying you should remove it the minute you get the PC home. I'm saying you shouldn't assume that you won't need another program that does the same thing—say, word processing or spreadsheets—

because you've got this free software on your PC. The freebie may not do what you need, or it may do it badly, therefore wasting your time. Give it a limited try and see how you like it. Try to do some of the things you may have heard other similar software does. If you like it, that's great. Occasionally, diamonds are hidden amongst the cubic zirconium.

Parental Guidance Suggested

Many of the new programs on your new computer will be games. Some of these games are going to take up a lot of memory to use, and some require video capabilities that a basic computer system doesn't have. Also, many of the games are not for kids. Play it once yourself to find out if the violence level is in keeping with your parental standards.

Read this software checklist and keep it in mind if you're considering using any of your new PC's free software instead of buying a package off the shelf:

Free software viability checklist:

- Have you heard of it?
- Is it available anywhere for purchase?
- After trying it, does it do what you need it to do?
- Do manuals for the software come with the PC? If not, does the manufacturer offer online help at its Web site?
- Can you get the CD for the software for free? This is useful if you decide you like the software and then later need to reinstall for any reason.
- Does the manufacturer offer any technical support?
- Does the manufacturer have any intention of upgrading it as time goes by?

Only you know how many items on the checklist are deal-breakers. Although it's not as important a decision as selecting a doctor or buying a safe car for your family, the software on your PC determines your return on your hardware investment. A computer is just a large doorstop without useful software.

Ready to Wear: Sifting Through Off-the-Shelf Software

Purchasing software is riskier than trying the free software that came with your computer. You paid for it, so money and ego are involved—nobody wants to think they made a mistake, and nobody likes to have paid to make it! Doing your homework is one way to make sure your off-the-shelf program is what you need.

First, do some research:

- **Ask around** Does anyone you know use the software you're considering? If you're not considering anything in particular, does anyone have a specific program to recommend? Ask your friends—they know you and you can trust their opinions to be honest, if not technically expert.

- **Let your fingers do the walking** Look in software catalogs and computer magazines. Your local library will have magazines on file, and many of them do monthly software comparisons. This month they'll do contact management software, last month they did accounting packages. Look for the issue that compared packages in the category you need, and read up.
- **Seek professional help** No, not therapy. I mean ask someone in the field. Taking a training class? Ask the instructor if he or she recommends a particular program. Ask the consultant who comes into your office if the program you're considering is all it's cracked up to be.

Another way to check out a program is to buy it. Check out your store's return policy first, however. Some stores allow you to return software if the packaging is returned with it—the box in one piece, all the manuals, and the envelope the CD was in—so they can return it to their vendor. Others won't take it back unless it's defective, and I wouldn't suggest you lie about that. No, not me!

Many libraries rent software, although it doesn't tend to be the cutting edge, latest releases. Check it out, however. If you can borrow it (you'll have to agree to uninstall it before returning it), you can check it out, risk (ego and money) free!

When you're evaluating the software, use the form in the following figure to assist you:

Software evaluation form.

Feature / Function	Yes	No
Does the software install easily?		
Is the interface (toolbars, menus) visually appealing?		
Check out the Help. Is it helpful?		
Is it easy to start working with the program?		
Are you able to do all that you wanted?		
Are the menus and commands easy to understand?		
Do the dialog boxes contain clear instructions?		
Does the software run smoothly (no crashes, no unresolved error messages)?		
Do you understand the manuals?		
Does the software manufacturer offer technical support?		
Use the technical support if it's free. Did they solve your problem?		

If your check marks fall mostly in the Yes column, it's probably a good program. You can also use the list to evaluate software that someone else is recommending—ask them the questions on the list, and see whether, when pressed for specifics, the software really is worth a recommendation.

Do You Need a Custom Program Created?

Sometimes we find that the tools we have just don't do the job. Like the time my father took an axe to the lawnmower. It wouldn't start, and he didn't have the tool he needed to fix it. Out of frustration (hey, it was hot out) he grabbed the first weapon he could find. After chopping it into pieces, guess what? It still didn't run.

If you're having a similar problem with your software—perhaps a report you really can't live without that your software won't provide, or you need to store data that it doesn't have a place to keep—you may need a program, written just for you.

When a program is written for you, it is either a custom program or a customized program. A custom program is software written for you, from the ground up. A programmer designs and writes a program expressly to meet your needs. He or she may use parts of other programs written for previous customers, but the way these parts are pulled together and the interface you get is just for you.

Customized software starts with an existing program and through a tweaking process is changed so it meets your needs. This is usually done with off-the-shelf software that is programmable. Microsoft Office, for example, comes with VBA (Visual Basic for Applications) that allows a VBA-savvy programmer to create special applications within the Office programs, usually for Excel and Access users with special needs.

How do you know which type of program you need? Two things guide you:

- **Money** Custom programs usually cost thousands, although customized programs can cost just hundreds. Some customized programs may cost thousands, but that's usually a case of Access being used as an application-development tool, not as a program you'll use on its own with some minor modifications.
- **Degree of need** If your only complaint is that you need a report that the software doesn't give you, that's not reason enough to have an entire program written for you, from scratch. If your complaint is that nothing off-the-shelf comes close to what you're looking for, a custom program may be your only answer.

Many a desperate user, horribly unhappy with their off-the-shelf program, has become happy with it upon reading the programmer's proposal. Having a custom program written can take months, and is very expensive. Suddenly, your $159.99 program looks really powerful, and that report isn't so essential to your life. Or maybe upgrading to a software program that's more tweak-able is worth the price.

Pretweaked Software?

Before hiring a programmer (to write something from scratch or to tweak your current program), investigate all possible software programs that could solve your problem. Check software catalogs for industry-specific programs. Many little-known applications are written by people in your field *for* people in your field. They aren't cheap, but they're cheaper than a custom program. Check with professional organizations and look online.

What if you're in a business that requires very specific data be kept and reports written, and no existing software does what you need? You may have no choice, regardless of the cost, than to have the custom program written.

How do you go about it?

1. Write down your needs, clearly. Give examples. Sketch the reports you need on paper.
2. Ask people you trust to recommend a programmer. Get two or three names, and ask each one to give you a proposal.
3. Compare the proposals, but not just on price. That should really be last on your list. Compare time needed to write the program, what guarantees they give you, and other extras, as shown in the following figure.
4. Select the proposal that allows you to put as many checks in the Yes column as possible.

	Yes	No
Will you get to se the program in various stages of completion?		
Will you be given a prototype to test before paying for the final program?		
Can you pay in stages as the software and prototypes are developed?		
Does the program come with a guarantee?		
Does the programmer promise not to market this tool to your local competitors?		
Will you be given training on the program?		
Will the programmer provide free support?		
Will he promise fast response times when/if the software requires repair or changes?		
Will documentation be provided?		

Custom program proposal checklist.

The Least You Need to Know

- Free software that comes with your computer requires some evaluation before you use it, instead of software you have to pay for. Free software is often worth every penny.
- Research and evaluate off-the-shelf software (hands-on, if possible) to make sure it does what you need it to do.
- If you need a custom program written, make sure you're getting what you need and what you pay for. Don't jump into a completely custom program before you check all other alternatives.

Chapter 5

Working the Web: Using the Internet to Find Software

In This Chapter

- Find cool programs and useful files on the World Wide Web
- Can useful online support be found?

Most people only use the Internet to access the World Wide Web. It's no wonder that the Web is so popular—sites of all descriptions bearing products and information are available with a few clicks of your mouse.

Because you can get to the Web with your computer, can you use it *for* your computer? Can you find programs—utilities, tools, applications—and download them easily? Can you find someone who knows what they're doing to help you? Are the help files stored on the Web of any use?

The answers are yes, yes, maybe, and sometimes. A lot of programs are available on the Web, most for a fee, some at no charge. Finding a living, breathing, typing individual to help you online is difficult, but not impossible. Help files stored at various software and hardware manufacturers' sites are easy to come by, and fairly easy to use.

Searching for and Downloading Files

Searching for programs and files is simple, and requires two basic things—a Web browser and knowledge of how to phrase your search criteria for the most appropriate results.

First, the browser. If you're on the Internet, you must have a Web browser program, either Netscape or Internet Explorer, or maybe you're using AOL's browser. The browser gives you the tools to use the Web, including search engines. You can go to the Web site of any number of search engines and begin your treasure hunt with a few simple steps. The following is a list of the most popular search engines:

- **www.yahoo.com** This easy-to-use and popular site searches not only sites but categories, so you can refine your search by starting in a focused area. Most sites make it a point to be listed with Yahoo!. Yahoo! also does full-text searches for your search words, so even sites that are not intentionally listed come up on the list of results.
- **www.altavista.digital.com** Also popular, this site allows you to choose a language for your search, so if, for example, you don't speak anything but French, your list won't include sites in any other language.
- **www.lycos.com** This site enables you to choose where your search will focus—the Web, ftp sites, newsgroups, message boards, or combinations thereof. Like Yahoo!, this site also breaks down sites into categories, so you can start your search from what they call a Web Guide, narrowing the search from the start.
- **www.hotbot.com** This site makes phrasing your search words easier by enabling you to choose from qualifiers such as all the words, some of the words, or the exact phrase. In other ways, it is similar to the other search sites, including the use of categories to refine your search.

After choosing and going to the engine site, type your search word or words into the appropriate box, and click the **Search** button. A list of sites that contain the words you searched for will appear, in order of appropriateness, with the best matches at the top of your list. Don't be surprised if you are informed that thousands of sites met your criteria. If the first five or six sites don't have what you need, you can try rephrasing your search, or try another engine. The following figure shows the Yahoo! search window, with a phrase typed into the search box.

Try the techniques in Table 5.1 to improve the effectiveness of your search.

Table 5.1 Useful Search Techniques

To Find...	Type...
An exact phrase, such as Cable TV Networks	**"Cable TV Networks"** If you don't use the quotes, you'll get sites that pertain to cable wiring, cable TV, cable cars, and networks—the computer kind and the TV kind. By placing it in quotes, you tell the engine you're interested in Cable TV Networks.

To Find...	Type...
A topic, with a specific twist, such as San Francisco Restaurants	**San Francisco + Restaurants**. You'll get sites pertaining to the city, plus sites for restaurants in that city.
A topic, such as pythons, excluding something, such as Monty Python	**Python –Monty**. This will give you information on big snakes, but nothing about British comedy troupes.
Two or more topics together, such as heartburn and the medicines that combat it	**Heartburn + medicine**. You'll get sites that pertain to each word, plus sites that refer to all of them, and these will be at the beginning of the list.

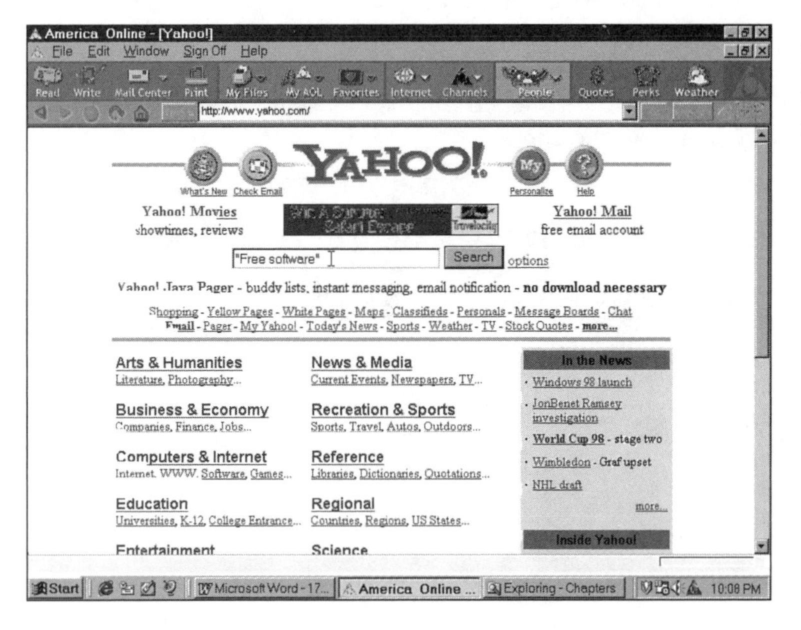

Be careful to put phrases in quotes to control the number of sites in your results list.

To find software, use the search engine's Computer or Software category, start there, and proceed to search. Type the name of the specific program you need, or a general type, such as "antivirus software". From the list of sites that meet your criteria, click the links and check the sites for downloadable programs and files.

Downloading is normally done by clicking a Download (or similarly named) button or link text within the site, as shown in the following figure. You select the program or file, and then click the button. If there is a fee for the software, you have to provide your credit card number before the opportunity to download is offered.

Is It Safe?

Although making credit card purchases on the Web is generally safer than it was a year or two ago, it's still not safe at all sites. Use your credit card only with large or well-known companies, when you're sure it's a real site and not a fraudulent front. Some browsers help you tell a safe site from a dubious one with key or lock icons (Netscape and Internet Explorer, respectively). When in doubt, opt to send a check and wait for the program to be shipped on disk or CD. If something goes wrong, you can stop payment on the check.

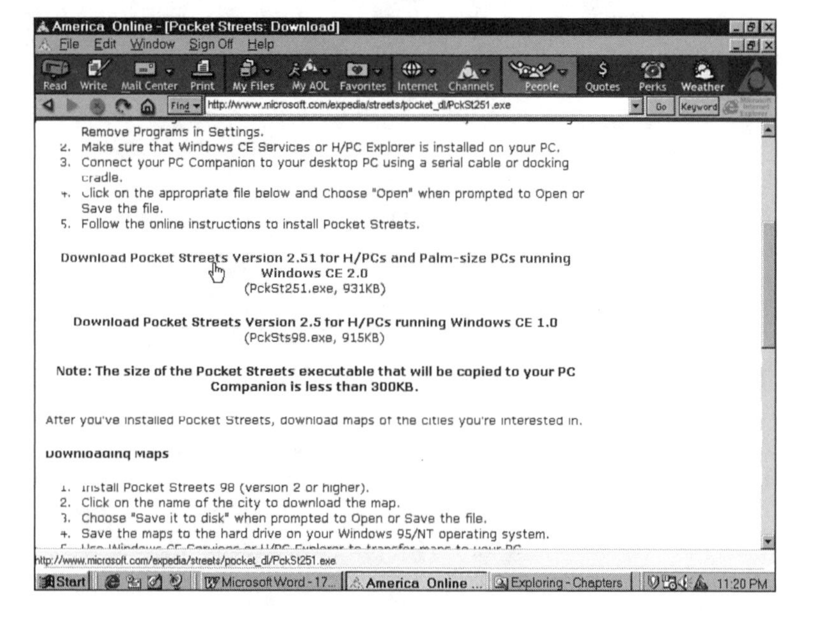

Even for free software, you may have to register before you get to the download page. Be prepared to tell them everything from your mom's maiden name to where you went for summer camp.

Some sites list the files in zipped format (you'll have to unzip and perhaps install them to use them later), and you can right-click them and choose Save (or a similar command) from the shortcut menu that appears. The following figure shows a site that offers free sound files.

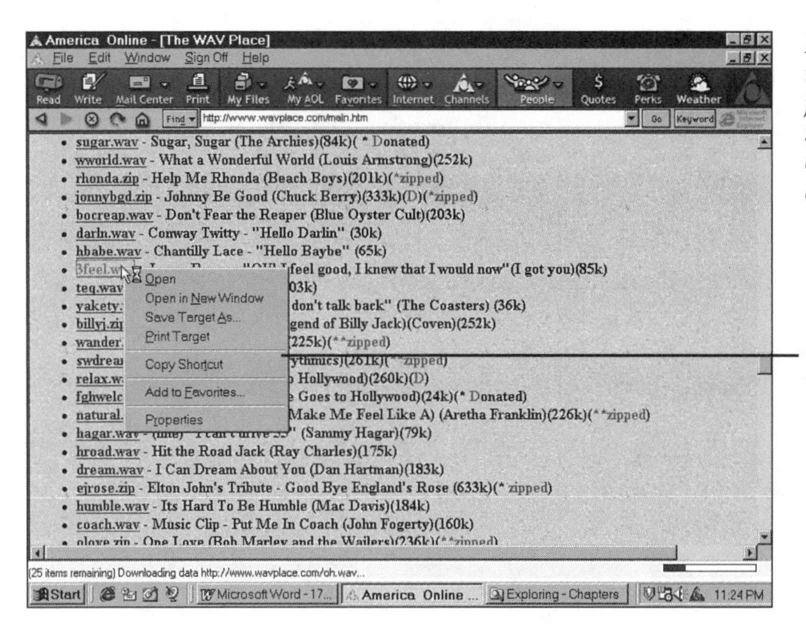

Download sound files for use in presentations or just for fun. My computer says "Doh!" every time I close a program, thanks to a sound file I downloaded.

Right click the filename to save (download) it to your computer.

Before the download begins, you'll be asked to select a folder into which the file should be saved. As soon as you select the folder, the download begins.

Had Your Flu Shot? Keeping Antivirus Software Up-to-Date

Hopefully you heeded my previous advice and have installed antivirus software on your computer. If you purchased your computer in the last few years, it probably came with the software loaded and set up to work in the background, testing your program files as you download them and before you run them. In either case, you can't rest on your laurels.

Some statistics tell us that as many as 1,000 computer viruses are being designed every week of the year. It's probably worse than that, according to some studies. Like human viruses, the inoculations are only as good as the timeliness of their antibodies. If a virus is new or has

You Don't Know Where That's Been!

Practice safe computing! Never use a downloaded program file without running it through an antivirus program such as Norton Antivirus or McAfee Viruscan. Without taking such a precaution, you run the risk that the file contains a virus that will infect your computer as soon as the program executes.

changed from a previous version, the antivirus software you bought two years ago may not find it, much less cure it.

How do you keep up? Hang onto the paperwork that came with your antivirus software (it will list a product key or license number that proves you paid for it), and take advantage of the manufacturer's offer to upgrade your software for some period of time for free. In most cases, if you can prove you bought the complete antivirus program, you can go to their Web site and download upgrades that update the software to look for and cure the latest viruses. Some manufacturers will send you periodic upgrades (via email or on CD) if you register the software.

It's a good idea to upgrade your antivirus software at least every six months. If the manufacturer of your antivirus software doesn't offer upgrades or their upgrades are few and far between, switch brands to one that stays on the cutting edge. Check out **http://www.symantec.com/nav/** for Norton AntiVirus (from Symantec Corporation) or **http://www.mcafeemall.com/mstore/avprod.html** for a complete list of McAfee antivirus products.

Click Here: Technical Support Online

Whether you need help with the file you just downloaded or you have a question about any software or hardware, the Web can be a great place to find it. From live chat rooms to help articles in a database you can search by topic, the Web contains many help resources.

Most software and hardware manufacturers' sites have a search engine within them that enables you to search for help and product information. These sites rarely offer any live help, although a phone number to reach a live customer service person will probably be provided.

Contact Them

If you're having trouble with software or hardware, and you go to the manufacturer's site, look for a Contact us or Write to us link that will open a mail message window. Many times your emailed question will result in a personal response from a technical expert from the company. You'll not only get an answer from the best resource possible, but you'll have a future resource to contact directly the next time a problem comes up! Copy their email address to your Address Book for safe keeping.

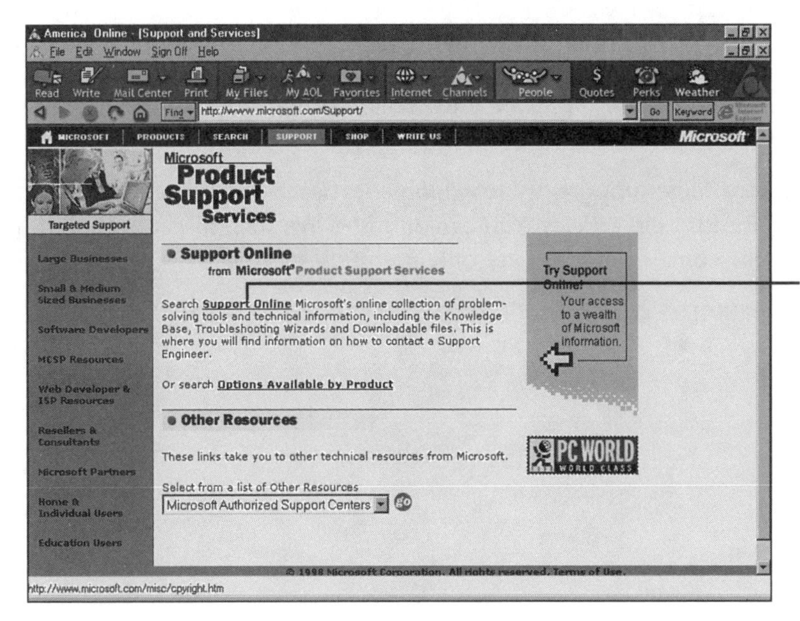

*The Microsoft site (**www.microsoft.com**) contains links to support for all its products, from Windows 98 to the full suite of Office programs.*

Yak, Yak, Yak: Chat Rooms and Forums

For live assistance, check chat rooms by using IRC (Internet Relay Chat), or through an online community such as America Online. Chat rooms are listed by topics ranging from general to specific, and depending on the number of people in the room, you should get some help in a relatively short time.

Does this sound too good to be true? In many cases, it is. How do you know if the help from fellow chatter PCDOC4U is legitimate? Is he or she a real expert or just some geek with a dangerous smattering of knowledge? You can only guess. You don't want to resort to this type of help for an emergency, because you can't be sure the advice will work. Better to call an actual customer service rep or use help articles on the manufacturer's site than rely on help that could make matters worse. If you're just looking for ideas or people who might have had a similar problem, the chat rooms can be a useful resource.

To find help on virtually any computer topic, check out **http://www.pchelponline.com**. This site lists the available help (online help, forums, live chat) on virtually any software or hardware topic.

The Least You Need to Know

- You can find free and not free software and computer files (sounds, movies, templates, clip art) on the Web, and access it through various search engines.
- When looking for online support, try searching a software or hardware manufacturer's Web site for help articles. You can also find live help in chat rooms, but that help may come from someone only pretending to be an expert.

Chapter 6

Understanding Your Microsoft Office Options

In This Chapter

- Four applications plus Outlook make the Office Professional Edition tough to beat!
- Are you small enough for the Small Business Edition?

Microsoft Office comes in four flavors—the Professional, Standard, Small Business, and Home Essentials editions. The two editions of Microsoft Office that most businesses prefer using are the Professional Edition or the Small Business Edition. The Professional and Small Business editions are the most comprehensive packages, offering the most effective tools.

If you already have any one of the four editions of Microsoft Office, it may be easier to stick with what you've got. After reading this chapter, if you see that the grass is truly greener in another edition, go for it. We're talking about your business here, savings for your college fund, and making your boat payment. For some of us, we're talking about groceries or no groceries. Choosing the edition of Office that gives you the tools you need is an important decision.

The Basic Four: Microsoft Office Professional Edition

This edition got its name from its intended audience, the professional business user. It's great for a business because it has the four major business applications, plus a program for email and scheduling. Through the software included in this suite, you've got a word processor (Word), a spreadsheet program (Excel), a presentation package (PowerPoint), a database (Access), and a way to send email and maintain your calendar (Outlook). Sing with me now—who could ask for anything more?

Well, maybe you can, because sometimes less is more. If you find that you need a full-fledged accounting system or a custom program written for you, having a powerful database program like Access may be overkill. Chances are, you may never use it. If you absolutely, positively never need to create a presentation, you may not want to waste hard drive space on PowerPoint. No one ever said that any edition of Microsoft Office was going to solve all your computing needs. The Professional Edition does, however, give you some powerful weapons for your business software arsenal:

- **Word** We all figured this out in high school: Being popular didn't necessarily mean you were a good person. For Word, however, popularity is borne out of greatness. Word is the best-selling (and most pirated) software for word processing on a Windows platform, and it is much loved by most of its users. It's powerful, efficient, and friendly.
- **Excel** Flexible, easy to use, and full of features that its closest competitor can't match, namely in the database area. Try doing a quick filter of your list with Brand X. You'll come running back to Excel.
- **PowerPoint** Fun, powerful, and jam-packed with animation and sound features to make a presentation both high-tech and entertaining. Even if you only use it for transparencies, you'll be amazed at all you can do. PowerPoint can also be used for simple flyers and announcements, covering basic desktop publishing needs as well.
- **Access** With a little help, even a database novice can use Access to keep track of data. Any database needs that exceed the capabilities of Excel are easily handled in Access, such as the need to relate several data tables in one report, or the capability to both *sort* and *filter* data and save the setup for future use.
- **Outlook** Send and receive messages via the Internet, and keep track of your schedule, contacts, and to-do lists with Outlook. With such a program, you'll never be late again. Who are we kidding? Of course you will be. But now you'll be able to send an apologetic email message.
- **Internet Explorer** You get version 4 of Internet Explorer with Office 97, enabling you to browse the Internet. Search for Web and FTP sites, and mark the ones you use often as Favorites so you can get to them quickly in the future.

Sort This, Filter That

Sort and *filter* are terms that refer to the manipulation of data. Sorting changes the order in which the records in the database are displayed. Filtering only shows the records that meet your criteria, sort of like playing 'Go fish' with your data—'Gimme all your records for people living in New Jersey!' Want to know more? Check out the section entitled "Creating and Maintaining a List Database" in Chapter 9, "Mass Hysteria: Marketing with Form Letters."

For a business that plans to grow, not only in size and scope but in computer savvy and level of automation, the Professional Edition is the way to go. Rather than stick with the Home or Small Business Edition that may have come with your computer, if you're serious about really using the tools in Microsoft Office, don't be an amateur, be a professional.

Picky, Picky, Picky

You don't need to install everything in either the Professional or Small Business Edition. You can pick and choose the programs you want (and the features within them) during the first steps of the installation process. Choose the **Customized** installation path if you want to install just one or two programs or to reduce the number of features you install with your applications.

Sometimes the best place to find out about Microsoft programs is at the Microsoft Web site. I say 'sometimes' because I usually prefer to ask people who use a product what they think of it rather than ask the company that sells the product. Honesty is the best policy, but sometimes it isn't the most profitable. If you want to check the Microsoft site to find out more about the Professional Edition of Office, use your Web browser to go to **http://www.microsoft.com/office/default.htm**.

At the site, you can read an overview of the product, get more information about the latest release of Office, and download files to add to your Office toolkit.

The Small Business Edition: Help or Hype?

The title of this section sounds like I'm not a fan of the Small Business Edition. Don't you believe it. That picture of me with my arm around the Professional Edition was doctored—they took my head and pasted it on another person's body. The Small Business Edition contains Word, Excel, Publisher, Financial Manager, and Outlook. Not too shabby! As proof of my impartiality, see Table 6.1. You can circle the YES responses that are important to you.

Table 6.1 Comparing Editions

Software Need	Professional Business	Small Business
A powerful word processor, with templates, wizards, and a full set of tools for a variety of documents.	YES	YES
A spreadsheet program with power and flexibility for creating financial reports and maintaining lists of data.	YES	YES
A powerful relational database program for creating a variety of tables, queries, and reports.	YES	NO
Ready-made or easily created reports for business accounting.	NO	YES
A presentation program for creating electronic slide shows, slides, and transparencies. Has animation and sound capabilities, and great automatic features.	YES	NO
A simple desktop publishing program for creating flyers and greeting cards. Easy for a new user to learn.	YES	YES
Scheduling and email capability.	YES	YES

If this table doesn't clear things up for you, try this. You'll really like the Small Business Edition if you see yourself in this list:

Check all that apply—the more you check, the more likely you'll like the Small Business Edition.

- ❑ You don't have the need for any relational database, or the need for fancy reports based on more than one database. A list database in Excel suits you just fine.
- ❑ You have a custom program running your business, and other than word processing and a little desktop publishing, you don't need a big, powerful suite of programs.
- ❑ You like a little hand-holding. Publisher and Financial Manager give you a lot of it. Publisher makes desktop publishing easy by providing a group of friendly tools that do the basics, plus Cue Cards, a helpful tool to take you through the most basic process. Financial Manager adds some quick reporting tools to Excel, making that program somewhat easier for the financial rookie.

No one will judge you if you don't need or want Access and PowerPoint. Most people also need some helpful tools that make getting started easier, which is what the Small Business Edition gives you.

To find out more about the Small Business Edition, go to the Microsoft site. Using your Web browser, type this URL: **http://www.microsoft.com/office/sbe/**.

It's also a good idea to poll any people you know who are using Office and get their feedback.

The Least You Need to Know

- ➤ The Professional Edition has the big programs that you can use to fully automate your business—from word processing to email. If you want to roll up your sleeves and get everything you can from Office, the Professional Edition is for you.
- ➤ The Small Business Edition cuts back on the big programs, excising Access and PowerPoint in favor of simple Publisher and helpful Financial Manager. If you need simplicity and friendliness, you need the Small Business Edition.

Part 2

Mastering Business Communication

No office is an island—you eventually have to share your thoughts with the outside world! Whether you're sending a letter to your landlord, a list of expenses to your accountant, or writing a message to your new client via email or fax, you need to know the proper and most efficient ways to build a document, a financial report, or a simple note that says exactly what you mean.

Chapters 7 through 11 take you through the nuts and bolts of business communication—from To Whom It May Concern to Very Truly Yours! Even the most accomplished letter-writers will find tips and new ideas that make business communication faster, easier, and more effective.

Chapter 7

Business Correspondence: It's Not Just for Secretaries Anymore

In This Chapter

- Learn to construct and proofread great correspondence
- Make sure your business letters and proposals are up to snuff
- Don't seal it with a kiss, use a label

The reason people ask "Can I get that in writing?" is because when something is written or typed on paper, it automatically seems more definite, more important, than if it has merely been spoken. In the past, people made deals and sealed agreements with a handshake. Although that still occurs in some cases, most people want to cover themselves by having every detail spelled out in black and white—the written word is powerful.

Whether you're writing a letter or building a complex proposal, how clearly you express yourself is essential to the success of your document and the ideas or goals it represents. I can't teach you to spell or use proper grammar—you either learned that in school or you didn't—but I can show you how to put what you do write into the proper format and take advantage of Office tools to improve the appearance, content, and accuracy of your business communications.

Put It in Writing: Making a Good Written Impression

When you put something in writing, you're committing to whatever you've said in the document. If you're expressing your opinion, or issuing a command, er, I mean request, you have created tangible evidence of your words. Unlike a spoken statement, which you can claim not to have made or not to have meant, when you write something down, you're stuck with it. But hey, that's why we have shredders—to get rid of the documents that we don't want to be stuck with!

The key to successful written communication in business—or in your personal life, for that matter—is clarity and organization. Plan what you're going to say, and then decide the best way to say it. When we're having a conversation, we often don't have time to plan. Things just pop out of our mouths, usually in the order they come into our minds, and typically without much editing. Written communication, on the other hand, has the benefit of the time allowed for planning, editing, and even re-editing, before the document is presented to the intended recipients.

Ready, Set, Go!

Word is already set up to provide you with a good basic font for your letters (10 point Times New Roman), left-alignment, single spacing, standard margins, and tabs every half-inch across the page. This enables you to concentrate on your content and worry (if at all) about changing fonts or document layout later.

Take advantage of this time. Don't just sit down at your computer and whip up a letter without organizing your ideas, at least in your mind. Use the following checklist to plan your next letter. Repeated use of this list will make building a great document second nature.

- ❑ What is the main message of this document?
- ❑ What is the best order for my topics?
- ❑ Does each paragraph lead into the one that follows it?
- ❑ Does this document answer all the questions that the reader will have?
- ❑ Have I provided all the necessary background information (if any) that the reader will need?
- ❑ Have I made my point effectively?

Does This Make Sense?

As soon as you've written the first draft of your document, proofread it. If the document is long or you've been working on it for some time, it can be a good idea to get someone else's input—a fresh pair of eyes can spot problems you might not see. By problems, I mean things that might not be worded clearly or that you've covered in an illogical order in the document. You can proofread onscreen or print out a copy and edit that. In either case, you'll probably find something that needs to be reworded or text that should be somewhere else in the document. Don't worry about spelling or minor grammatical issues yet—you'll get to them later. Only concern yourself with clarity and making your point effectively.

To reorganize your text, use Word's Cut and Paste commands. Select the text that needs to be moved, and choose **Cut** from the **Edit** menu or press **Ctrl+X**. The selected text will vanish. Click to place your cursor where the text belongs, and choose **Paste** from the **Edit** menu or press **Ctrl+V**. The text reappears in the new spot.

Shortcuts for Moving

If you only need to reorganize your words in a sentence or shuffle sentences within a paragraph, use drag-and-drop. Select the word or sentence you want to move, and then point back to the selected text. When your mouse turns to a left-pointing arrow, drag the selected text to where you want it. When you release the mouse, the text is repositioned. Drag-and-drop works best when you're dragging within a small area—within one screen-full of text at most.

Whaddya Mean I'm Not a Good Speller?

After you've written and proofed your document's organization and content, use Word's spelling and grammar-checking tools. Word checks your spelling as you type, underlining misspelled words (or words that it doesn't recognize) with a red wavy line, and any grammatical errors with a green wavy line. You can ignore them as you type and then fix them all later, or fix them as they occur.

To fix individual spelling errors, right-click the red-underlined text, and choose an alternative spelling from the shortcut menu that appears. You can also choose to **Ignore** the word if you know it's spelled correctly (for example, names, jargon) or **Add** it to Word's custom dictionary.

Never Assume

Don't assume the grammatical "error" that Word has underlined is really incorrect. You'll find many suggested changes that don't make any sense or aren't appropriate in context. You can fine-tune the way Word checks your grammar by choosing **Options** from the **Tools** menu. In the **Spelling and Grammar** tab, choose the writing style that matches yours. This can prevent strident rules from being applied to your more casual documents.

You can fix individual grammar errors the same way—right-click the green underlined text, and choose the corrected text, or **Ignore** the sentence.

You can also check your entire document's spelling (and your grammar, too) when you've finished typing. Choose **Spelling and Grammar** from the **Tools** menu, or click the **Spelling and Grammar** button on the toolbar.

When you use the Spelling and Grammar feature to check your entire document, it stops on each word that isn't found in your Office dictionary, and offers alternative spellings, or the opportunity to **Ignore** or **Add** the word to your custom dictionary. If you're in an industry with its own jargon, such as the legal or medical fields, you'll want to add all the esoteric terms that you use in your documents so the spell check won't stop on these words in the future.

By default, the grammar in your document is also checked during a spell-check session, displaying each questionably structured sentence.

The Key to Spell Check

If you're a fan of the keyboard shortcut, you can press the **F7** key to open the Spelling and Grammar dialog box and begin checking your document.

They're Just Little Red Lines

Although you can (and may be tempted to) turn off the spell check that underlines your spelling errors in red, the feature does serve to remind you that you need to make some corrections. Some users find the red underlines annoying, but it's much more annoying to find you've sent out a letter that makes you look like an idiot. If you feel you *must* turn the feature off, choose **Tools**, **Options**, and click the **Spelling and Grammar** tab. Remove the check mark next to **Check spelling as you type**. But don't say I didn't warn you...

Don't Hesitate to Proofread!

No matter how short or casual your document, don't forget to proofread it yourself. Better yet, have someone else check it for you. I once sent over 100 letters that ended with the sentence, "If you have any questions, please hesitate to call." Now, this was probably a Freudian slip on my part, but proofreading would have caught the error. I had run spelling and grammar checks, neither of which caught it. The sentence wasn't technically wrong, it just wasn't what I should have written.

Although Word's internal dictionary is comprehensive, it doesn't contain all the words in an unabridged dictionary. If you don't have a copy of such a book on your desk, try this Web site:

http://www.onelook.com/

You can type any word at the site and it will look it up for you. Use wildcards (***** for sections of the word, **?** for individual letters you're not sure of), or type the entire word as you know it.

If you want to look up a medical term, try the following Web site. Click the **Search OMD** button to enter your term and check it's spelling and definition.

http://www.graylab.ac.uk/omd/spell.html

Constructing a Proper Business Letter

"Proper Business Letter" sounds like we're going to go to charm school, and you'll be balancing books on your head and drinking tea with your pinky extended. Nope, we're just going to make sure you know how to build a business letter with all its components in the right place, with the right number of spaces between components, and an overall professional look.

Does all this really matter? Who cares if your letter's layout adheres to some silly rules? You do! If your reader opens your letter and thinks "this person doesn't know how to write a letter!," you're already starting off on the wrong foot. If your letter looks sloppy or like you didn't pay attention to details like spelling, maybe you'll let details slip in other areas. We all know you're a hard-working genius. Don't let your correspondence convince anyone otherwise.

Ask More of Yourself

Don't set your own expectations for the quality of your written communications based on your "average" customer. Although you may typically write to people who wouldn't know a well-constructed letter from a note scrawled on a napkin, you will have to write a serious letter or proposal one day. It's worth the effort to learn to do it correctly, even if it's not required day to day.

You can avoid negative impressions by following some simple rules for letter construction. Two types of business letter layouts are used—block style and traditional (you may also hear traditional referred to as "indented"). Block style is more popular, and requires little formatting for indents and alignment, so it makes writing a letter a faster, simpler process. Some conservative firms still use the traditional format, but their numbers are shrinking. The following is a list of the parts of a business letter, in the order they should appear:

- **Date** In block style, the date appears on the left, five lines from the top of the document. In a traditional letter, it is right-aligned.
- **Recipient Address** In both block and traditional style letters, the recipient address is found two lines below the date, and is left-aligned.
- **Salutation** Whether it's Dear or To Whom it May Concern (note the capitalization there!), the salutation appears two lines below the last line of the recipient address, and ends with a comma or a colon.
- **Body** The body of your letter starts two lines below the salutation. In traditional style, the first line is tabbed one half-inch. No indents are used in block style (each paragraph looks like a block—get it?). The body may be one paragraph long, or may go on for several pages.
- **Closing** Choose Very truly yours, Sincerely, Regards, or whatever seems appropriate for the relationship you have with the recipient. The three listed here are best for people you're not related to or not likely to have over for dinner. The closing appears two lines below the last line of the body. Leave this item on the left margin for a block style letter, indent to the horizontal halfway point in a traditional letter.
- **Your name** Your name appears two or three lines (depending on the size of your signature) below the closing. You can follow it (on the next line) with your title or the name of your company. In a block style letter, this text is left-aligned. In a traditional letter, you must indent the name to the horizontal halfway mark on the page so it appears under the closing.
- **Initials** If someone else does your typing (you lucky dog), his or her initials should appear four lines below your name. The initials should be in lowercase, followed by a slash, followed by your initials in uppercase.
- **Carbon copies** If people other than the direct recipient of the letter received a copy, list them two lines below the typist's initials. For example, "CC: Jill Byus, Macmillan Computer Publishing." This is a courtesy for the recipients, so they know whether what you've sent to them was shared with anyone else.
- **Enclosure** If there is anything enclosed with the document, the abbreviation "encl." should appear two lines below the carbon copy information. After encl., type the name or nature of the enclosure, such as "photocopied checks from 2/5/98."

The following figures show the same letter—in block style and again in traditional style.

A block style letter is fast and easy to create, and allows less margin for error if you're new to Word's formatting tools.

October 28, 1998

Dr. Marion Haste, PhD.
Communication Strategies, Inc.
1405 Chestnut Street
Suite 500
Philadelphia, PA 19103

Dear Dr. Haste:

I must thank you for the tremendous seminar you performed for our sales staff last week. I was very impressed with the amount of preparation you had obviously done, and your examples and role-playing exercises were very appropriate for our sales force.

Enclosed you'll find a copy of a letter I received from one of our regional sales managers. She was so pleased with the seminar, that she would like us to send you to her offices in Dallas to repeat the event for her entire staff of support and administrative personnel. This particular manager has also voiced her comments to our President, William Miller, and he wanted me to tell you that we're all very happy with the seminar and all of the services you have provided for us.

You'll be hearing from us soon to schedule another seminar.

Very truly yours,

Bob Frapples
Human Resources Director

lu/BF

CC: William Miller, President

encl. letter from Leva Malone, Regional Sales Manager

Pages by the Numbers

Don't forget to number your pages. If your letter exceeds one page, start numbering on the second page (no number on page one). Choose **Page Numbers** from the **Insert** menu and choose the location for your numbers (top, bottom, left, right, or centered).

Want to know more about letter writing? Check out these Web sites for the latest from the experts:

- **http://www.wisc.edu/writing/Handbook/BusinessLetter.html**
- **http://www.austin.cc.tx.us/lrs/wr_bus.htm**

Learn by example! Check out the templates that Word provides, and follow the instructive sample text that is inserted in each one. You'll replace the sample text with your own letter content, but look at the layout and read the instructive text—it gives you valuable insights into the process of building a business letter.

October 28, 1998

Dr. Marion Haste, PhD.
Communication Strategies, Inc.
1405 Chestnut Street
Suite 500
Philadelphia, PA 19103

Dear Dr. Haste:

I must thank you for the tremendous seminar you performed for our sales staff last week. I was very impressed with the amount of preparation you had obviously done, and your examples and role-playing exercises were very appropriate for our sales force.

Enclosed you'll find a copy of a letter I received from one of our regional sales managers. She was so pleased with the seminar, that she would like us to send you to her offices in Dallas to repeat the event for her entire staff of support and administrative personnel. This particular manager has also voiced her comments to our President, William Miller, and he wanted me to tell you that we're all very happy with the seminar and all of the services you have provided for us.

You'll be hearing from us soon to schedule another seminar.

Very truly yours,

Bob Frapples
Human Resources Director

lu/BF

CC: William Miller, President

encl. letter from Leva Malone, Regional Sales Manager

A traditional style letter requires use of indents and alignment, and in many industries, looks dated. Some businesses, primarily legal firms, still cling to this format, and probably will for some time to come.

To access these templates, choose **New** from Word's **File** menu. In the New dialog box, click the **Letters and Faxes** tab. Double-click any of the letter templates—Contemporary Letter, Elegant Letter, or Professional Letter.

Stand Out Text

Another benefit of the Word letter templates is the graphical content they include—shading behind text and clip-art images. To find out more about creating your own letterhead (with graphics and cool stuff of your own), see Chapter 12, "Keep Moving with Business Stationery."

Your Proposal: The Offer They Can't Refuse

A proposal in business is nothing like a marriage proposal. First of all, your customer will look at you funny if you drop to one knee. Second, diamonds are really overkill. Your product or service and the quality thereof should do the selling for you. A proposal merely puts the particulars in writing, in a format similar to a letter. You start with the date, recipient address, and a salutation, and the body of the letter becomes the proposal—what products or services will be provided, at what cost, with what guarantees, and so forth. The content of the proposal is determined by what the particular deal you're proposing contains, and what the customer wants to know about it—that's where the differences between effective proposal layouts come in. It's your job as a salesperson to know what's important to the customer and how to present it in the most attractive light.

In some cases, proposals are in response to a customer's RFP (Request For Proposal). These requests are submitted in writing to the firms that the customer is considering for the product or service. This may be part of a bidding process—the customer puts the work out for bid to at least two suppliers. If your customer is a publicly held company or works with government contracts, the law may require that a certain number of bidders be considered. If you're one of these bidding suppliers, the RFP tells you how to build your proposal—topics to discuss, order of topics, and level of detail. Adhering to the instructions is essential; many customers disqualify you immediately if you don't follow the RFP's instructions to the letter (pardon the expression).

If you're sending a proposal as a result of a phone conversation or a less formal written request from your customer, you can design the proposal yourself. This allows you to cover the important points in the order you think is best. Normally, you'll want to start with a description of the products or services you're selling, followed by pricing, followed by delivery dates, and any extra information, such as free services that come with the product or warranties that set your product/service apart from the competition.

Read It from the Customer's Point of View

Remember, you're selling here! When you proofread the proposal, ask yourself—would you be sold by this document? You'll want to call on the customer after they've received the proposal and close the sale in person or on the phone, but let the proposal do as much of the sales for you as possible.

Round and Round Again: Don't Reinvent the Wheel

If you find yourself writing the same (or similar) proposals over and over again, many of them identical to each other except for the customer name or some minor product-related particulars, you can alleviate the redundant effort by creating a proposal template. A template is like a cookie cutter for your proposals—you type the proposal once, and then you can use it over and over for all your similar proposals.

You may be thinking that you could just reopen an old proposal, change what's needed, and then print it with the changes. Well, yes, you can. But if you do that, you risk saving the changes and overwriting the old proposal (and you want a copy for reference), or forgetting to remove or add something for the current proposal. It would be pretty embarrassing if a proposal to someone named Susan ended with the line "Thank you, John, for the opportunity to offer our products." Susan would know she wasn't important enough to warrant you writing a proposal just for her.

A proposal template consists of no specifics—no customer name, no product names, no prices, just the content that appears in every proposal. Instructive or sample text can indicate where the customer-specific information should be inserted, as shown in the following figure. Each time the template is used, you'll insert the customer-specific information—names, their order, special pricing—creating a proposal that looks like you wrote it for one particular customer.

October 28, 1998

Insert Recipient Name Here
Recipient Company Name
Address
Address
City, State Zip

Dear Insert Customer Name:

Thank you for your interest in our training. Our task-oriented training programs are designed to meet the needs of growing companies such as yours, and we look forward to working with you.

After our meeting on [Insert Date here], I prepared the following list of classes for your staff. I am basing this on your total number of employees and their indicated areas of interest. Prices include a 15% discount.

TRAINING

- Type list of classes here

SERVICES

- Type list of services here

These prices include the instructor, manuals for each student, and access to our hotline support for six months after the date of the class. Additional hotline access can be purchased at $25 per call, with discounts for volume purchases. Call our Hotline administrator, Wendy Derby, at 800-555-2323 for more information.

If you have any questions regarding this proposal, please call me immediately. We look forward to scheduling this training, and to the beginning of a long and productive relationship.

Very truly yours,

John Kline
Director of Training

A simple one-page proposal template can be used over and over again for different clients.

Automatic Dates

Want the date to appear automatically on your proposal every time you use the template? When building your template, choose **Date and Time** from the **Insert** menu. Choose the format you want, and make sure to turn on the **Update automatically** option so that every time you open the template the correct/current date is inserted.

After creating this cookie cutter, the way you save it makes it a template. Choose **Save As** from the **File** menu, and choose **Document Template (.dot)** from the **Save as type** list box. Word automatically opens the Templates folder (a subfolder of Office). Save it to the Templates folder (or one of its subfolders, such as Letters & Faxes) so the next time you need a proposal, you can choose **New** from the **File** menu, and select the proposal template from the New dialog box. The New dialog box tabs correspond to the Template folder and its subfolders.

When you use your template, you'll notice that the filename on the title bar is Document1 (or some other number). This is because you aren't opening the template directly—you're opening a new document *based* on the template. This allows you to use a template over and over again without fear of accidentally changing the template's content.

Highlight and replace all the instructive text with your own, and insert any additional text that pertains to this particular proposal—perhaps this customer had extra concerns about product testing or service plans. After making these minor customizations, you can print and save the file as a regular Word document (.doc extension), saving it with any name you choose, to any folder you choose.

If you later feel that your template isn't meeting your needs or requires corrections, you can reopen it from the Templates folder (or whichever Templates subfolder to which you saved it), and make your changes. As long as you save it as a template (.dot) and leave it in the Templates folder (or one of Templates' subfolders), the edited template will appear in the New dialog box, ready for use in building a document.

...And Everything in Its Place

If you save your template to any other folder (other than Templates or one of its direct subfolders), the template will not be available when you choose **New** from the **File** menu.

Tables: Document Building Blocks

Proposals are highly structured documents, listing prices along with products and their descriptions, and showing different warranty options and their costs. Building these elements into a proposal or proposal template can be tricky and time consuming for even a veteran Word user.

You can get around this problem with tables. Tables give your document structure by providing boxes to type in. The following figure shows a proposal with a table to control the placement of product names and pricing.

October 28, 1998

Insert Recipient Name Here
Recipient Company Name
Address
Address
City, State Zip

Dear Insert Customer Name:

Thank you for your interest in our training. Our task-oriented training programs are designed to meet the needs of growing companies such as yours, and we look forward to working with you.

After our meeting on [Insert Date here], I prepared the following list of classes for your staff. I am basing this on your total number of employees and their indicated areas of interest. Prices include a 15% discount.

TRAINING

ITEM	Duration	Students	PRICE
TOTAL			

SERVICES

These prices include the instructor, manuals for each student, and access to our hotline support for six months after the date of the class. Additional hotline access can be purchased at $25 per call, with discounts for volume purchases. Call our Hotline administrator, Wendy Derby, at 800-555-2323 for more information.

If you have any questions regarding this proposal, please call me immediately. We look forward to scheduling this training, and to the beginning of a long and productive relationship.

Very truly yours,

John Kline
Director of Training

A simple table can help control a list of single-line items or a series of parallel paragraphs.

To create a table, click the **Insert Table** button on your toolbar. A grid appears, as shown in the following figure. Drag through the cells in the grid—across to choose the number of columns, down to choose the number of rows. When you release the

Use tables to build a solid foundation for lists and paragraphs within your proposal.

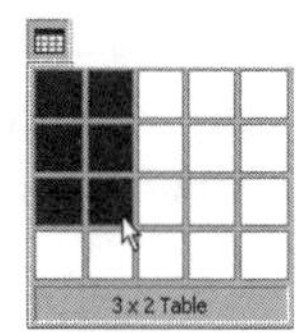

mouse, the table appears in your document.

To move forward from cell to cell, press **Tab**. To move backward, press **Shift+Tab**. Type single words, short phrases, or whole paragraphs in each cell. Paragraphs wrap within the confines of the cell. If you want to add a blank line or new paragraph, press **Enter**.

Something's Happening Here

You can sum the numbers in a column or row of your table by choosing **Formula** from the **Table** menu. Word assumes you're summing the cells above or to the left of the current cell. Click **OK** to insert the result. If the numbers in the column or row change, click in the cell that contains the total and press **F9**. The result updates to reflect the changes.

What if your text doesn't look right? If a table cell is too narrow, text wraps (even a single word may do it, and not at a natural hyphen point). You can adjust column width and row height by pointing to the gridlines and dragging (drag right to widen a column, drag up to make a row taller). You can also adjust the alignment of the text within the cells by clicking in the cell (or selecting a series of cells), and using your alignment commands (see Table 7.1).

Table 7.1 Alignment Keyboard Shortcuts

Shortcut	Alignment Result
Ctrl+E	Center alignment
Ctrl+L	Left alignment
Ctrl+R	Right alignment
Ctrl+J	Full, left, and right alignment

Most tables need a little tweaking before they look just right—remember that if you're creating the table in a template, you only need to do most of that tweaking once. When you use the template, the table will be ready to go, with only minor adjustments for text that is vastly different than the "normal" situations that you designed the template to accommodate.

The Urge to Merge?

If your table has, for example, three columns and you need one row to be a single cell (instead of three cells), merge them. Select the cells in the row, and choose **Merge Cells** from the **Table** menu. This is especially useful for table titles or conceptual breaks throughout your table.

Borders On and Off

If you don't want the structure of the table to show, turn off the borders on the table cells. You can turn them off for the whole table, or only for specific cells. After selecting the range of cells you want to border or unborder, choose **Borders and Shading** from the **Format** menu, and add/remove borders from one or all four sides. Choose line styles and colors for the borders you want to keep.

It's in the Mail: Envelopes and Labels

All the effort you put into creating your business letters and proposals isn't worth much if the document is never received. Not only is a properly addressed envelope or label essential to the document's delivery, it is also the recipient's first impression of you. Make it a good one!

Different types of mail require different addressing techniques as described in Table 7.2.

Table 7.2 Appropriate Addressing for Business Documents

Document Type	Method
Letters, business or personal, to a specific person	Printed envelope.
Mass mailing of a form letter to people you don't know	Printed envelope (preferably), or clear labels (easier than printing envelopes, but less tacky than white or colored labels).
Proposals	Printed envelope.
Announcements, cards, invitations	Printed envelope, or if card or flyer heralds a social or elegant business event, calligraphy by a real calligrapher.
Brochures, product samples, coupons	Labels, clear or white/colored to match the envelope. Folded brochures can be mailed without an envelope, with the label placed on an outside panel.

If you don't see the type of document you're mailing in the previous table, just apply this rule of thumb: The tone of the mailing should match the package it comes in. Word makes it easy to print envelopes and labels for your mailings, so whichever method is appropriate for your document, you can make it happen without trying too hard.

With your letter or proposal open onscreen, choose **Envelopes and Labels** from the **Tools** menu. Click the appropriate tab (**Envelopes** or **Labels**), and if the delivery address box is blank or the address in it isn't correct (Word picks the address from your letter/proposal's recipient address), edit it as needed. You may want to add additional text such as "Personal" or "Dated Material" to assist the recipient's mailroom staff in distributing your mail.

In the **Envelopes** tab, type a return address if you'll be using a blank envelope, or click the **Omit** option if you'll be using preprinted stationery. Click **Print** to generate your envelope, and then follow your normal procedure for your particular printer and printer tray to send the envelope through properly.

When printing labels, if you're printing to a laser or inkjet printer, Word assumes you're using a sheet of labels. You must tell word which label you want to print on (maybe you've already used the first two in the top row), or choose to print an entire sheet of labels with the same address. Like envelopes, Word takes the address from the active document, although you can edit it. Click the **Options** button to choose a label by Avery product number (to establish the dimensions and the number and layout of labels per sheet), and then click **OK**. Back in the Labels Envelopes and Labels dialog box, click **Print**.

Testing Labels 1, 2, 3

If you've never printed labels before or if you're using a particular label for the first time, it's a good idea to do a test page first. Print a sheet of labels on a sheet of regular paper, and then hold it up to the window with a blank sheet of labels on top. Make sure the addresses are within the boundaries of each label without being too close to any of the labels' four sides.

If your label text isn't in the right place on each label or if you don't like the label text, you can start over and make adjustments as needed. That's another benefit of doing a test page—you get to see how your labels will look, but you don't waste a sheet of labels doing it.

To adjust your label selection, start the whole procedure over, this time selecting a new label product number. To reduce the size of your text so your entire address fits properly, regenerate your labels and then click **New Document** instead of **Print**. Press **Ctrl+A** to select your entire sheet of labels (it's actually a big table), and then change your font size accordingly. You can then **Print** the document from the **File** menu or press **Ctrl+P**.

The Least You Need to Know

- Organization and planning are the keys to a great letter or proposal. Use Word's proofing tools to check your spelling and grammar.
- A business letter, in block or traditional style, should be properly constructed if you want to make a good impression. Show that you care about the tiniest details.
- Proposals should sell you and your product or service, and prepare the customer for your dynamic closing technique. Make sure you've covered what's important and what's important to the customer (sometimes not the same thing).
- If you create similar proposals repeatedly, build a template to speed and simplify the process. You'll be able to add just the things that apply to the current customer, relying on the template for standard text and layout.
- You can judge a book by its cover or a letter by its envelope. Don't send an important letter with a tacky label slapped on the envelope. Use the appropriate addressing method for each type of document you send.

Chapter 8

Playing the Numbers: Designing Your Own Financial Reports

In This Chapter

- Calculate sales to project your company's success
- Track expenses to see where your money's going
- Use Excel's Expense template and Financial Manager for fast reports
- Turn boring numbers into bar, pie, and line charts

If you're running a small business, you or your accountant probably spotted the need for an accounting program, and hopefully you're using one for billing, payables, and payroll, if you have a staff. For most businesses, this covers the financial basics—the data you need to pay bills, invoice customers, and report to the IRS. If you're undecided about which accounting package to use, ask your accountant, other business owners, or office managers in your line of work what they use. A recommendation from someone who is familiar with your particular situation can be more valuable than reading a catalogue listing or online sales pitch.

Although accounting software is thorough and detailed, it may not do everything you want, and you probably wouldn't want to take the time to customize it yourself. For the bright financial ideas that strike you in the middle of the night, and other types of number crunching, you need a spreadsheet program. The spreadsheet program in Microsoft Office is Excel—a powerful and (best of all) flexible program for playing with and tracking numbers. You can design a spreadsheet in just about any way you can imagine. As you test different ideas, you may find that some don't work as you intended—don't worry! Because you're only playing with the numbers (and not using your accounting software), it's no problem to start over and try a new approach.

This chapter shows you how to put Excel to work in several ways in your small office.

Fortune Telling: Calculating Sales Projections

Your sales numbers are one of the primary indicators of the health of your business. Are sales rising? Did you sell as much as last year? Have you met your goals? Although your accounting package may give you some of the answers to these questions, it may not be able to calculate a particular figure that you need.

The ability to play with numbers is important, because as you make business decisions, it's helpful to see what you're tossing around in your head in black and white. Are you considering buying a new copier? Will a 35% increase in sales enable you to do it? How much in outside copying expenses would a new copier save? If you create a report that projects sales and then you deduct projected expenses (based on numbers you can pluck from your past accounting software reports) less expected photocopy savings, you can figure out what it will take to make the copier affordable. Projections aren't real—you can't turn them into the IRS, because they frown on creativity. But you can use them to plan, to demonstrate your intentions to the bank or your accountant, and most of all, to keep you thinking and excited about the future.

Accounting's in the Bag

If you're still considering some manual method of tracking your income and expenses, consider this sad little saga. One of my clients maintained a bag, yes a bag, of receipts and deposit slips and handed it to her accountant every April. Hundreds of dollars later, her taxes were prepared, usually with bottom lines (the amounts owed to the feds and state) that curled her hair. Had she maintained a computerized accounting system and kept track of her money, she'd have cut her accounting expenses in half (at least) by handing a report to her accountant instead of a bag. In addition, she would have been able to see that tax bill coming and saved enough money to pay it, or found ways to creatively avoid at least some of it. Forewarned, as they say, is forearmed—get some accounting software and supplement the tracking of your financial comings and goings in Excel.

How do you create these fancy-schmancy calculations? Each new Excel spreadsheet is a blank grid, awaiting your text, numbers, formulas, and ideas. Excel's files are workbooks, made up of individual worksheets, each containing over 16 million cells! Although chances are you won't use 1% of them, you obviously have plenty of room to play.

Getting familiar with Excel first makes playing with your numbers easier. You'll spend less time figuring out how to do something and more time figuring out cool new ways to look at your financial data. One of the first things to master is workbook navigation. How do you move around in Excel? Practice using the keyboard shortcuts listed in Table 8.1 to get from place to place.

Table 8.1 Keystrokes for Moving in Excel

To Move	Press This Shortcut
To the next cell to the right	Tab or the right arrow
To the next cell to the left	Shift + Tab or the left arrow
To the cell below the current cell	Enter or the down arrow
To the first cell in the spreadsheet (A1)	Ctrl + Home
To the next screen-full of rows	Page Down
To the previous screen-full of rows	Page Up
To the beginning of the current row	Home

You can also click anywhere in the spreadsheet to activate a particular cell. To select a block of cells, click in the first cell in the range and drag through the remaining cells.

After you're comfortable moving around, you can start entering the numbers and formulas you need. To build a sales projection, gather your latest real sales numbers (you'll be projecting numbers based on them), and as much detail as possible—do you have more than one salesrep? Do you want to project sales by item? By product? By customer? Like many things we'll discuss in this book, you need to do some planning, some thinking ahead. Sketch your ideas on paper and write down the real numbers you want to start with. Similarly, look at your copying

Go There Now

To go to a particular cell from anywhere in the spreadsheet, press **Ctrl+G** and enter the cell address. Click **OK** or press **Enter** to go to that cell.

Shift into Selection Gear

While selecting cell ranges, you may select more cells than you wanted or not enough. Don't bother redragging with your mouse. Instead, press the Shift key and click in the cell that should be the end of your selected range. This either shrinks or adds to your selected block of cells, and allows for greater accuracy.

expenses over the last several months, and use the spreadsheet to calculate an average monthly expense. Then, you can factor that monthly savings (as well as revenue you get from charging clients for copies) into your projections.

When you have your numbers ready, you can start building the spreadsheet. The following figure shows a simple sales projection spreadsheet—it contains a title, a list of sales categories (products), and real numbers for the last quarter. Projections for the next quarter are based on a multiplier stored in one cell: H1. The formula bar shows the formula in cell F4 that calculates a projection, by multiplying (the * in the formula is the multiply sign) the prior month's projected sales by the amount in cell H1. The dollar signs in the reference to cell H1 in the formula (H1) indicate an *absolute reference.*

Keep your first attempts at financial reports simple. As you master the software, your reports can become more complex.

Formula for projection

Absolute reference cell

Report title 1

Microsoft Excel - Book1

E4 = =D4*H1

	A	B	C	D	E	F	G	H	I	J
1	Sales Projections							1.35	1.4	1.45
2		Actual			Projected					
3		January	February	March	April	May	June			
4	Training	4250	5680	5420	7317	10244	14854			
5	Consulting	8500	7850	8275	11171	15640	22678			
6	Documentation	6525	7520	6500	8775	12285	17813			
7	Presentations	750	850	725	979	1370	1987			
8	Web Page Design	2500	3000	2870	3875	5424	7865			

Sheet1 / Sheet2 / Sheet3

Real numbers from last quarter

Projected sales

Reference Only This Cell

When you use an *absolute reference* for a cell reference in a formula, the formula always refers to that cell, no matter where in the worksheet you may move or copy the formula. Usually the cell addresses referenced in a formula update to match the formula's new location when you move or copy the formula. By using an absolute reference, however, you can specify that one or more of the cell addresses in the formula remain unchanged, no matter where the formula is copied. Still foggy? Read along to the next section, where formulas are explained in more detail.

Mathspeak: Understanding Formulas

You could design a spreadsheet that didn't have any formulas, but it wouldn't be very useful. Formulas are needed to sum up a column of numbers or average a series of totals. Formulas also enable you to play with your numbers by calculating projected sales based on real sales numbers. Let's talk about the formula for that using real numbers.

If your sales for last month were $50,000 and you want to figure out what your sales would be with a 35% increase, you could probably do the math in your head: 50,000 × 1.35, right? Right. Now to do the same calculation in Excel, you need to replace the number 50,000 with the cell address for the cell where that number is stored. You also need to store 1.35 in a cell so that you can change the number at any time and see your answer change, too. By storing your multiplier in another cell (rather than typing it directly into the formula), you can change it to 1.50 or 1.25 to see a higher or lower projection appear automatically.

To enter a formula, click in the cell that contains the formula result, and press the equal sign (=). This tells Excel that you're starting a formula. After that, click in the first cell that will be part of your formula. For example, if you are multiplying the number in cell D7 by the number in F8, click in D7, then type the operator (*), and click in cell F8. The formula appears as =D7*F8. If the cell containing your multiplier needs to be an absolute reference (so that you can copy the formula to other places in your worksheet), press the **F4** key after you type that cell address into your formula. Pressing this key adds the dollar signs, and makes sure your cell remains static through all repetitions of your formula.

Formulas can be simple (=A5+B5), complex (=B5*(C5+D5)/3), or contain functions, such as SUM or AVERAGE. Functions are formulas that are built-in to Excel, making it simpler for you to build complex formulas.

Not So Average

We all know that if you average a series of five numbers, you take the total of the five numbers and divide by five. If you type that formula into Excel, you have to count the number of cells you are adding and then insert that number after a division operator, as in =(F5+F6+F7+F8+F9)/5. To make life easier, Excel has an AVERAGE function that does it for you. Type **=AVERAGE(F5:F9)**. The sum of the range of F5 through F9 is calculated, and the number of cells summed is used as the divisor. Neat, huh?

To find out more about functions, click the **Paste Function** icon on the Standard toolbar. A dialog box (see the following figure) shows you a list of categorized functions and their descriptions.

Your supporting totals also require formulas, but for those you can take the easy way out. The following figure shows the formula for totaling a column of numbers, and the toolbar button you use to get it. Yi-hah! No typing required!

The PMT function calculates monthly payments on a loan.

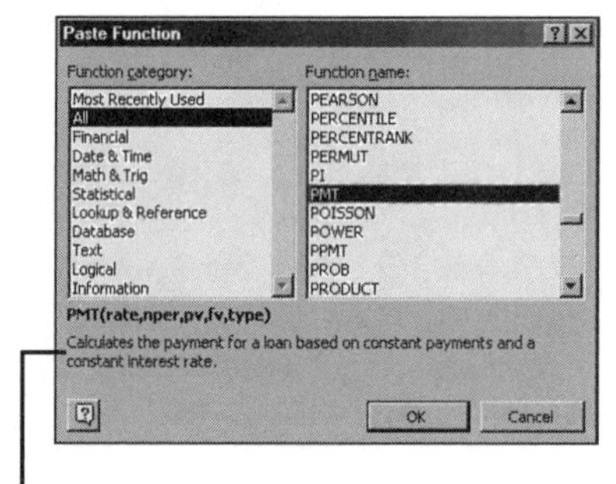

Description of function's use and operation

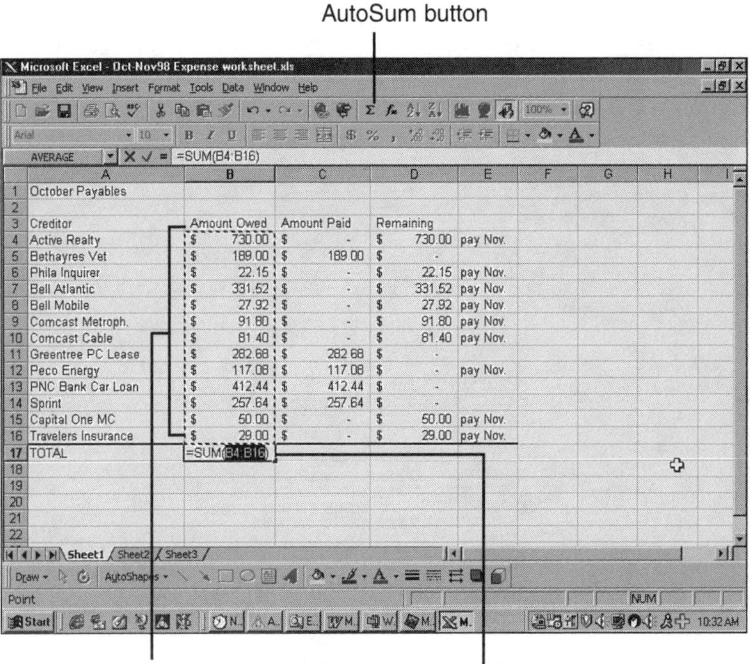

*Click the **AutoSum** button to select the column (Excel selects it for you) and then press **Enter** to insert the formula that displays the result.*

As time goes by, you can adjust your numbers to match reality, and continue adding columns of projected sales numbers. Because your formulas use cell references, when you update your numbers, all formulas based on the cells you edit are automatically changed to reflect your updates.

Sumtimes, Once Is Enough

Don't be redundant. If you're totaling a series of columns, total the first one and then copy that formula across the remaining columns. Point to the Fill Handle (the small black square in the lower-right corner of the active cell) and drag across the cells that will contain the remaining columns' totals. Release the mouse, and the totals appear.

All Dressed Up: Formatting Your Report

After you've created your sales report (or any other spreadsheet you might build), you may want to snazz it up a little. Maybe you intend to show it to your accountant to get some advice, or you need a bank loan to expand your business, so the report will be given to the loan officer. Reports that will be seen by anyone other than yourself can stand some formatting, if only to make them look more substantial, more serious <yawn>.

Excel gives you several tools to format your numbers, to apply borders and shading to your cells, and to change the appearance of your text. The following figure shows the sales report we saw earlier, but this time it's all dressed up. How was all this fancy stuff applied? See Table 8.2 for the buttons to use!

Got somewhere to go? Get all dressed up with centered titles, borders, shading, and number formats.

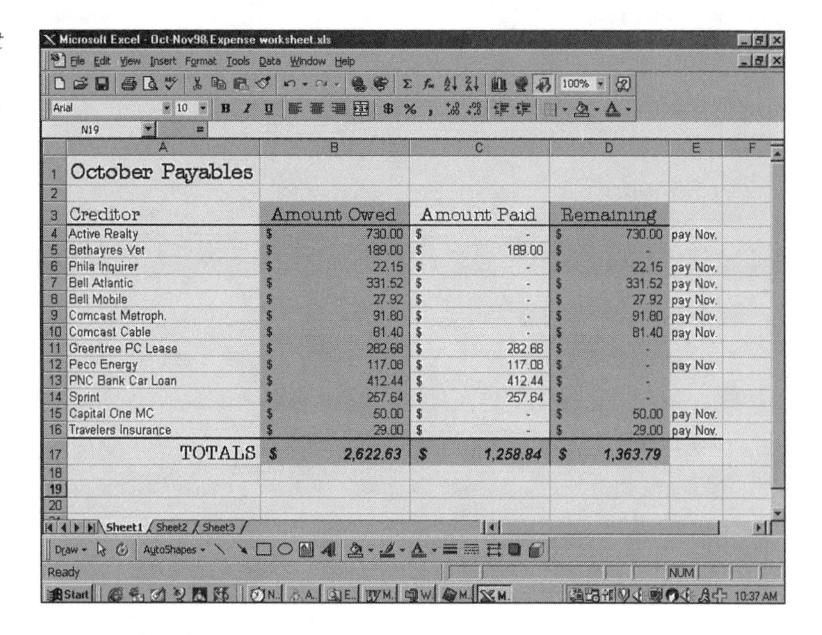

	A	B	C	D	E
1	October Payables				
2					
3	Creditor	Amount Owed	Amount Paid	Remaining	
4	Active Realty	$ 730.00	$ -	$ 730.00	pay Nov.
5	Bethayres Vet	$ 189.00	$ 189.00	$ -	
6	Phila Inquirer	$ 22.15	$ -	$ 22.15	pay Nov.
7	Bell Atlantic	$ 331.52	$ -	$ 331.52	pay Nov.
8	Bell Mobile	$ 27.92	$ -	$ 27.92	pay Nov.
9	Comcast Metroph.	$ 91.80	$ -	$ 91.80	pay Nov.
10	Comcast Cable	$ 81.40	$ -	$ 81.40	pay Nov.
11	Greentree PC Lease	$ 282.68	$ 282.68	$ -	
12	Peco Energy	$ 117.08	$ 117.08	$ -	pay Nov.
13	PNC Bank Car Loan	$ 412.44	$ 412.44	$ -	
14	Sprint	$ 257.64	$ 257.64	$ -	
15	Capital One MC	$ 50.00	$ -	$ 50.00	pay Nov.
16	Travelers Insurance	$ 29.00	$ -	$ 29.00	pay Nov.
17	TOTALS	$ 2,622.63	$ 1,258.84	$ 1,363.79	

Table 8.2 Formatting Tools for Reports

Click This Button	To Apply This Format
Arial	Change font
10	Change font size
B I U	Make text or numbers bold, italic, or underlined
	Align text or numbers to the left, center, or right side of the cell
	Center your title across selected columns
$	Apply dollar signs, commas, and decimals to numbers that represent money
%	Convert decimals to percentages
+.0 .00 / .00 +.0	Increase or decrease the number of decimals displayed
	Apply borders from the palette
	Choose a fill color for your selected cells
A	Change the color of your cell's content

The key to applying any format is to select the cells to which you want the formatting applied. Creating a border under a series of numbers? Select the cells and apply a bottom border. Shading a column of cells? Select the column first, then pick a color.

If you want to seriously simplify your life, Excel provides a great tool for formatting your worksheet report. Choose **AutoFormat** from the **Format** menu, and check out the 17 different table formats you can apply to your cells. You can apply the format to the entire report (by selecting the whole worksheet first) or to a section of it (by selecting one range of cells within the worksheet).

Voilà! Painted Formats

Use the Format Painter to apply your formats from one part of your worksheet to another. Select the part of your worksheet report that looks the way you want it to, and click the **Format Painter** button. Then click and drag through the cells that you want to look like the first group of cells. The formats (not the content) are pasted from the first selection to the second. If you want to apply your formats to several places throughout a large report, double-click the **Format Painter** before applying the formats—the tool stays "on" until you click it again to turn it off.

Another quick format that you'll want to apply is currency. If your numbers represent dollars, you'll want to make that clear, right? Don't waste time typing dollar signs when you enter your numbers. Type the numbers without anything but decimals (55.00, for example) and after the numbers are in, select their cells. Then click the **Currency Style** button on the toolbar. The selected cells are automatically formatted with dollar signs and commas. For more cell formats, choose **Cells** from the **Format** menu and check out the various formats you can apply—for money, percentages, dates, times, and text.

Where Does It All Go? Tracking Your Expenses

Many accounting programs allow you to categorize your expenses by storing the information about each check you write—if you write a check for your electric bill, the amount of the check goes into your Utilities category or a numbered General Ledger account. You can run these reports at the end of any billing cycle—the end of a month, quarter, or year—or on an as-needed basis.

But what if you want to isolate your expenses incurred for a specific project or period of time? Or create your own report to show how much you're spending on your car as a way to show your business partner that it's time to get a new company car? Or, tally your travel expenses for a trip using your notebook, while you're still on the plane, so that you can later enter the actual expenses in your accounting program? This type of flexibility is rarely found in an accounting package for small businesses. You'll have to build your own solution. You can start from scratch for a totally customized report or take the easy way out and use Excel's Expense Statement template. Easy is a good thing, despite what your parents told you.

Quick and Easy: Using Excel's Expense Template

Excel is a great tool for playing with expense numbers, and although you can design your own expense report, it's worth checking out Excel's expense template.

To access the template, choose **New** from the **File** menu from within Excel. In the **Spreadsheet Solutions** tab, double-click the **Expense Statement** template icon. If your interface is configured to show your file extensions, you'll see an .xlt at the end of the filename.

WATCH OUT!

But My Macro Didn't Look Sick!

As soon as you open the Expense Statement template, Excel warns you that you are about to open a file that contains macros. This template's macros are safe (they came from Microsoft), so you can click **Enable Macros** to open the template with the macros in place. If you're opening an Excel file or template that's not from a trusted source, click **Disable Macros** to open the file without the macros, which may include macro viruses that could damage Excel files on your system.

As soon as you open the template, your boring old Excel grid takes on an entirely new look. The following figure shows the blank expense statement form, complete with a floating toolbar that gives you the ability to insert and edit comments, insert sample data to show you how to use the statement, or apply a statement number automatically. To see which button does what, point to each one without clicking—the name/function of the button appears in a yellow ScreenTip.

And a Macro Would Be...?

A *macro* is a program that runs within a document, performing a series of tasks. You can record your own Office macros by recording any series of steps you perform—opening a file, inserting a graphic, or running a presentation. After the macro is recorded, the steps can be performed automatically when the macro is invoked, from a keyboard shortcut or toolbar button you assign to it. Macro commands are found on the Macro submenu of the Tools menu in Word, Excel, and PowerPoint.

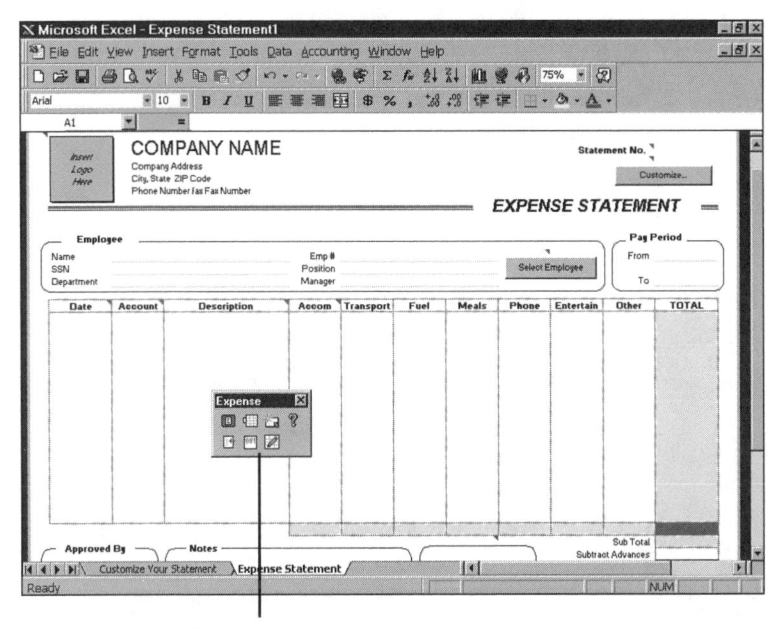

Replace instructive or sample text with your own, and begin entering expense data for yourself or an employee.

To use the template, insert your business information where indicated—the company name and address text at the top of the form, the logo (if you have one), and the text box that says "Insert fine print here" (for disclaimers, legal statements, and so on). After entering your company information, you can enter the information specific to this form by typing in the boxes that ask for employee information and dates. To enter your specific expense records, type in the columns (Date, Account, Description) and break down your expense by type (Fuel, Meals, Phone, and so on). As you type each expense record (press **Enter** and then **Home** to begin the next line item), a total appears for each expense accrues in the far right Total column and at the bottom right of the form for the entire list of expenses.

Unlike most spreadsheets, when you save your expense statement, you are prompted to save the expense record to an expense database. If you want to do so, click the **Create a new record** option. The data that you typed into the form is automatically updated to a file named expdb.xls, and stored in your Microsoft Office Library folder. If you want to treat this expense statement as an isolated spreadsheet with no connection to the database, click the **Continue without updating** option. In either case, the save procedure ends with you entering a name and folder for saving the workbook file and its contents.

What if you saved it to the database? What does that get you? Open the expdb.xls database and see that the line items from all your expense statements have been stored automatically in this spreadsheet, showing which employee incurred the expense, and in what category. This spreadsheet can be printed, sorted, filtered—in short, treated like any other Excel spreadsheet. Just don't change any field names or move the file from that folder, or you'll have to update the expense template's settings to find the right file and update properly when using the template in the future.

Make It Yours

Want to tweak the template so it works better for you? Click the **Customize Your Statement** tab and change the defaults for your company name and address (saving you the trouble of typing it in each time) and your mileage reimbursement rate. Although I don't advise it, you can also change the location of your database file.

You can find more Excel templates (to do a variety of things) at the Microsoft Web site:

http://officeupdate.microsoft.com/downloadCatalog/dldExcel.htm

Click the various links for templates, add-in programs, and utilities that enhance the way Excel works for you.

The Balancing Act: Your Checkbook and Expenses

If you have more customized or specific needs for an expense report, you can design your own. The appearance of the report and what information it contains is up to you—you can keep as much or as little information on your expenses as you need to, and you can make the report fancy or keep it bare bones.

The sample I'll be showing here demonstrates an expense report that does two jobs—it not only keeps track of expenses, it can be used to balance your checkbook. I've found that in addition to the checkbook feature in my accounting software, if I keep an additional checkbook spreadsheet in Excel, I can play with the numbers I've stored in many ways that the accounting software won't let me. I can track expenses for which I've written a check, or break down cash withdrawals (from a cash machine) into the specific expenses that the cash was used to pay. The following figure shows my checkbook/expense analysis spreadsheet, with the balance formula displayed in the Formula Bar.

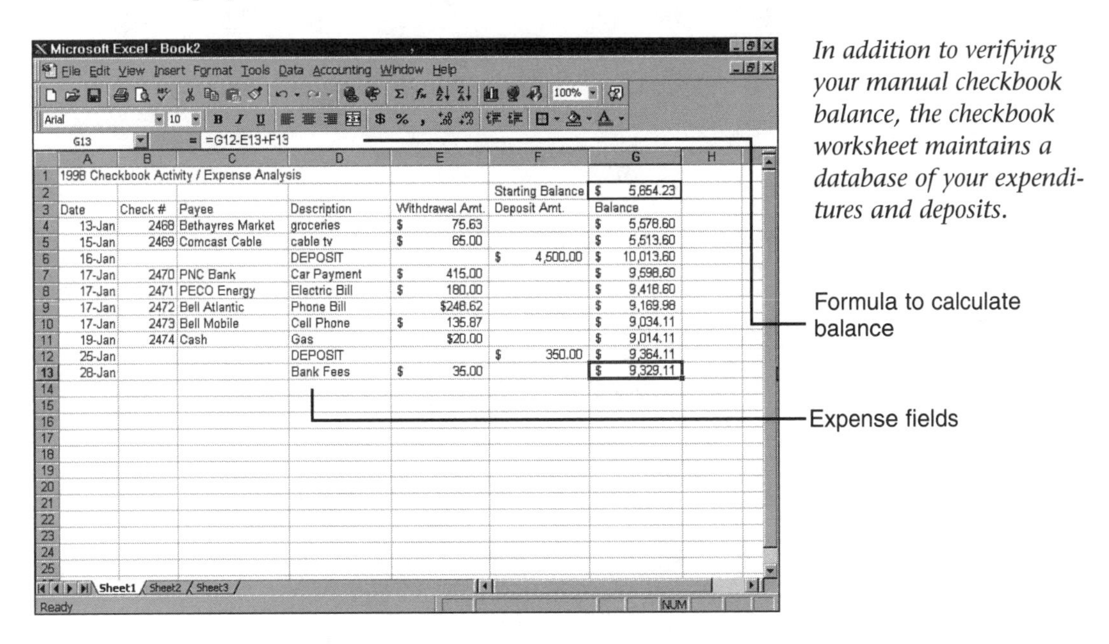

	A	B	C	D	E	F	G
1	1998 Checkbook Activity / Expense Analysis						
2						Starting Balance	$ 5,654.23
3	Date	Check #	Payee	Description	Withdrawal Amt.	Deposit Amt.	Balance
4	13-Jan	2468	Bethayres Market	groceries	$ 75.63		$ 5,578.60
5	15-Jan	2469	Comcast Cable	cable tv	$ 65.00		$ 5,513.60
6	16-Jan			DEPOSIT		$ 4,500.00	$ 10,013.60
7	17-Jan	2470	PNC Bank	Car Payment	$ 415.00		$ 9,598.60
8	17-Jan	2471	PECO Energy	Electric Bill	$ 180.00		$ 9,418.60
9	17-Jan	2472	Bell Atlantic	Phone Bill	$248.62		$ 9,169.98
10	17-Jan	2473	Bell Mobile	Cell Phone	$ 135.87		$ 9,034.11
11	19-Jan	2474	Cash	Gas	$20.00		$ 9,014.11
12	25-Jan			DEPOSIT		$ 350.00	$ 9,364.11
13	28-Jan			Bank Fees	$ 35.00		$ 9,329.11

In addition to verifying your manual checkbook balance, the checkbook worksheet maintains a database of your expenditures and deposits.

The concept is simple. Put everything you want to know about each expense across the top of the spreadsheet, creating fields. Fields break down data into digestible parts. In my sample, I have date, check number, payee, description (what you paid for), withdrawal amount, deposit amount (only if you'll be using this to balance your checkbook), and balance. Each one is a field (stored in a single column on the worksheet), and each row of the spreadsheet will be used for one expense, either a check or cash payment. Note! If you want to use this for balancing your checkbook, you can include cash expenses only if they equal (when grouped) the total of one or more cash withdrawals.

To play with your numbers after you've entered them, use Excel's Data menu commands to sort and filter your expense records. Sorting is the simplest process, allowing you to change the order in which your transactions appear. The following figure shows expenses sorted by amounts, so the highest amounts are first on the list.

Sorting can be done on one field or many. When sorting by more than one field (by payee and date, for example), choose **Sort** from the **Data** menu and then choose the first field in the **Sort by** box, and the second field in the **Then by** box. When sorting by more than one field, be sure to sort first by the field with the most common entries, and choose fields with more unique records for your second and

View your list of transactions in order by date, amount, or payee—you can sort by any column heading.

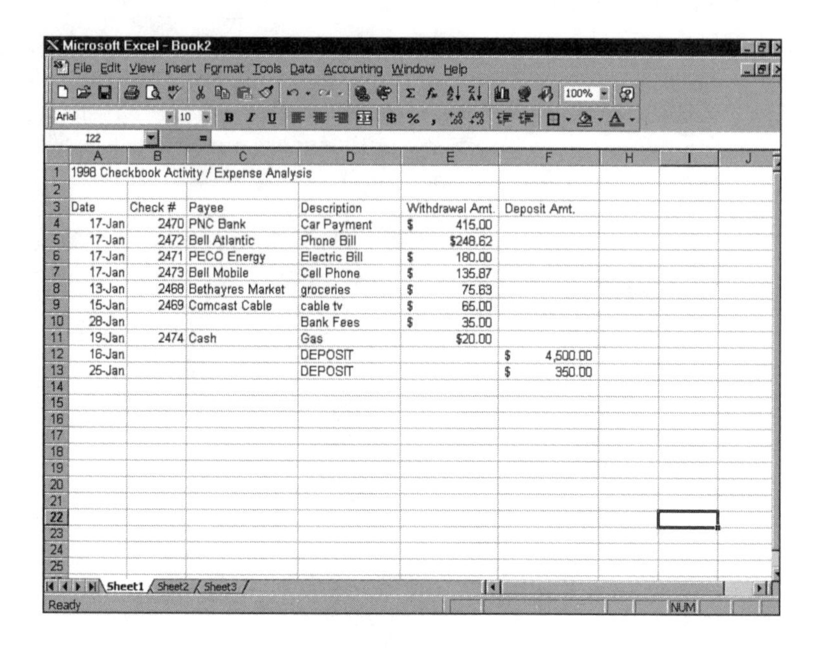

	A	B	C	D	E	F
1	1998 Checkbook Activity / Expense Analysis					
2						
3	Date	Check #	Payee	Description	Withdrawal Amt.	Deposit Amt.
4	17-Jan	2470	PNC Bank	Car Payment	$ 415.00	
5	17-Jan	2472	Bell Atlantic	Phone Bill	$248.62	
6	17-Jan	2471	PECO Energy	Electric Bill	$ 180.00	
7	17-Jan	2473	Bell Mobile	Cell Phone	$ 135.87	
8	13-Jan	2468	Bethayres Market	groceries	$ 75.63	
9	15-Jan	2469	Comcast Cable	cable tv	$ 65.00	
10	28-Jan			Bank Fees	$ 35.00	
11	19-Jan	2474	Cash	Gas	$20.00	
12	16-Jan			DEPOSIT		$ 4,500.00
13	25-Jan			DEPOSIT		$ 350.00

Sort by up to three fields in the Sort dialog box.

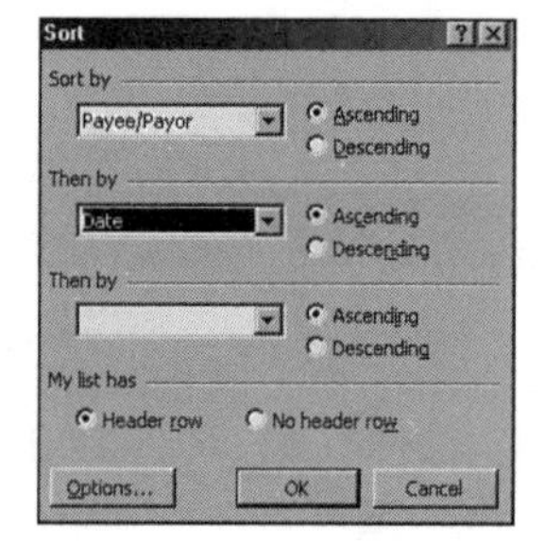

Sorting, A to Z

To do a quick sort by one field, click any cell in the column on which you want to sort, and click the Sort Ascending or Sort Descending button on the Standard toolbar.

third-level sorts. Why? Because if you sort first by a field that has mostly unique records, the second and third-level sorts won't work. The following figure shows a two-level sort setup for the checkbook worksheet.

Filtering your data is like playing Go Fish—"Gimme all your twos!" Instead of asking for a card, however, you're asking for data. Gimme all your checks for more than $50. Or gimme all your transactions for car-related expenses. Get the idea? You're presenting your database with criteria, and asking that only the records that meet that criteria be shown onscreen.

If you want to see only some of your expenses (your car-related expenses, for example), you can filter your list. Choose **Filter** from the **Data** menu, and select **AutoFilter** from the submenu. Click the drop-down list arrow next to the field you want to filter (such as Description), and then choose the entry you want to filter for, such as "Car repair." Your non-car repair items will disappear temporarily, and you can print your list of car repair expenses. You can even total them.

After you've filtered your records, you can bring them all back to the screen by choosing **Filter, Show All** from the **Data** menu. By the way, your records were never really gone, just hidden so only the records meeting your filter criteria would show.

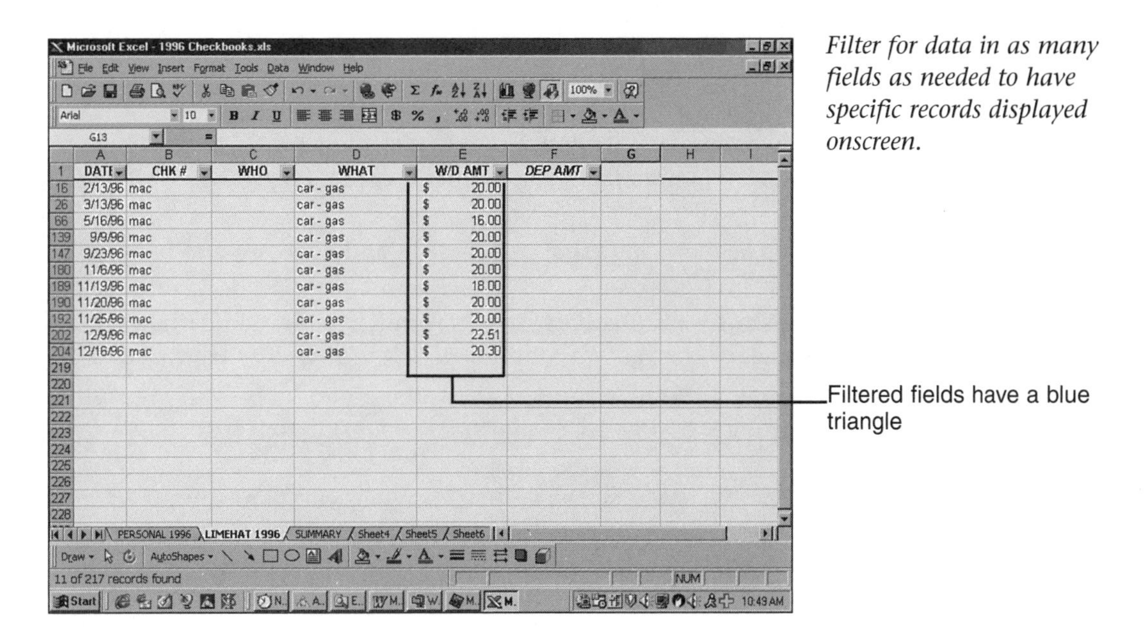

Filter for data in as many fields as needed to have specific records displayed onscreen.

Pick and Click: Financial Manager Reports

The Financial Manager is a program that comes with the Small Business Edition of Office, enhancing the use of Excel by offering seven different types of financial reports. The Small Business Edition was designed for novice users and for small businesses—perhaps like yours. If you don't have time to learn to use Excel thoroughly (and therefore create your own elaborate spreadsheets) or if you don't have an accounting program, you'll like the Financial Manager. Reports that you need for documenting the money your business makes and spends are just a few clicks away.

Financial Manager can be started while you're in Excel or from the program icon that installation places on your desktop. If you're starting from within Excel, select the **Accounting** menu, and choose **Report Wizard**. A program starts, helping you through the process of choosing and customizing the type of report you want to run. The following list shows the seven financial reports you can run with the Financial Manager. Which reports do you need? Check all that apply. Some may be more than you need or require information that your business isn't big or complex enough to track at this point. Try the Small Business Association in your area for advice if you're not sure. Your accountant (if you have one) can probably help, too, although he or she may want to create these reports for you and bill you for the privilege.

- **Trial Balance** Provides a full audit trail of your company's balance (assets less liabilities) for each of your accounts.
- **Balance Sheet** Creates a clear picture of your company's health—your assets, liabilities, and stockholder's equity at a specified point in time.
- **Income Statement** Summarizes your company's profits (or losses) through a list of your revenue and expenses.
- **Cash Flow** Looks at the money that has come in and gone out and helps you spot any big leaks.
- **Changes in Stockholder's Equity** Sees how much of the company you and your other stockholders (if any) own and how much is owned by your creditors (if any).
- **Sales Analysis** Analyzes your sales and expenses for different parts of your company.
- **Ratios** Compares your company's numbers to accepted standards for a business of your size. Uses the Altman-Z scale to see whether you're in danger of bankruptcy. Don't run this one if you're feeling depressed.

After completing a short series of dialog boxes (click **Next** to move forward through the steps and **Back** if you want to return to a previous step), click the **Finish** button in the last step of the Report Wizard. The report you've selected, complete with sample data (to help you figure out where to put your real data), formatting, and formulas appears onscreen. The following figure shows a trial balance, a report that shows assets, liabilities, and expenses.

Poof! It's the Accounting Wizard

Import data from an existing accounting database by running the **Import Wizard** from the **Accounting** menu. Select the file and complete the wizard's steps to save yourself the trouble of retyping numbers you've already been storing in another program or spreadsheet.

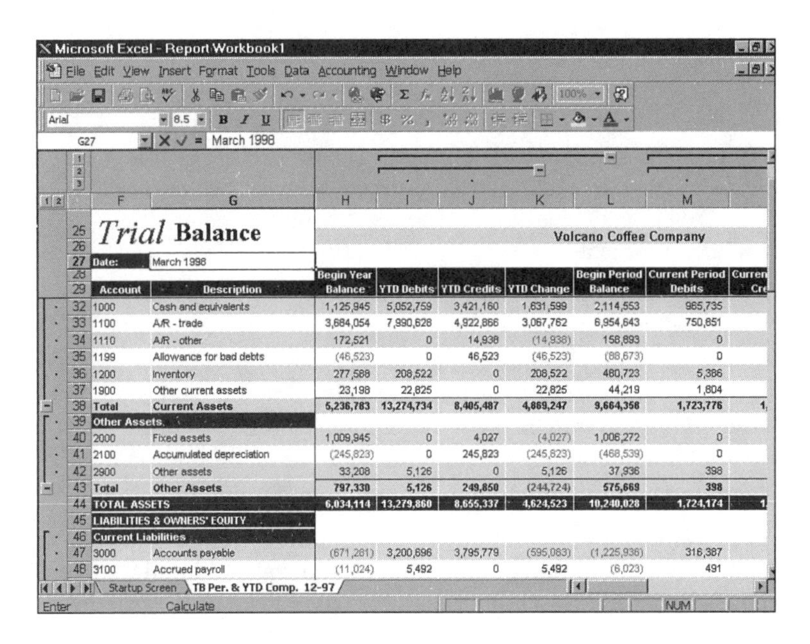

Trial **Balance**

Volcano Coffee Company

Date: March 1998

Account	Description	Begin Year Balance	YTD Debits	YTD Credits	YTD Change	Begin Period Balance	Current Period Debits	Curren Cr
1000	Cash and equivalents	1,125,945	5,052,759	3,421,160	1,631,599	2,114,553	965,735	
1100	A/R - trade	3,684,054	7,990,628	4,922,866	3,067,762	6,954,643	750,851	
1110	A/R - other	172,521	0	14,938	(14,938)	158,893	0	
1199	Allowance for bad debts	(46,523)	0	46,523	(46,523)	(88,673)	0	
1200	Inventory	277,588	208,522	0	208,522	480,723	5,386	
1900	Other current assets	23,198	22,825	0	22,825	44,219	1,804	
Total	**Current Assets**	**5,236,783**	**13,274,734**	**8,405,487**	**4,869,247**	**9,664,358**	**1,723,776**	**1,**
Other Assets								
2000	Fixed assets	1,009,945	0	4,027	(4,027)	1,006,272	0	
2100	Accumulated depreciation	(245,823)	0	245,823	(245,823)	(468,539)	0	
2900	Other assets	33,208	5,126	0	5,126	37,936	398	
Total	**Other Assets**	**797,330**	**5,126**	**249,850**	**(244,724)**	**575,669**	**398**	
TOTAL ASSETS		**6,034,114**	**13,279,860**	**8,655,337**	**4,624,523**	**10,240,028**	**1,724,174**	**1**
LIABILITIES & OWNERS' EQUITY								
Current Liabilities								
3000	Accounts payable	(671,281)	3,200,696	3,795,779	(595,083)	(1,225,936)	316,387	
3100	Accrued payroll	(11,024)	5,492	0	5,492	(6,023)	491	

Replace the sample data with your data, leaving formulas and formatting intact for the simplest use of this report.

Subtotal Your Report

After you feel comfortable with building databases (like the checkbook worksheet) and creating formulas, try creating a Subtotal report. After sorting your data, choose **Subtotals** from the **Data** menu. At each change in the content in the field you sorted, ask for a sum, a count, or an average to be inserted. A report that subtotals each group of like records in your database is created, saving you hours of worksheet structuring and formula-building.

Picture This: Turning Numbers into Charts and Graphs

We're all thinking it, so I'm going to just say it: Numbers are boring. Looking at sheets of numbers is dull, dull, dull. Even accountants admit that numbers are dull. You may have fun playing with them, manipulating them, seeing what happens to them in different scenarios—that's fun. But looking at them is *boring*, especially if they're someone else's numbers.

One way to make numbers less boring is to convert them to a chart. Your sales projection report is a likely candidate for this process, because a simple chart can show your hopefully increasing sales as a series of bars, increasing in height as time goes by. You can chart your expenses, expressing them as a pie chart, showing the percentage of the total expenses that each type of expense represents.

Charts help make your numbers more interesting, and can show the "big picture" faster than reading the numbers themselves. When you go to the bank or meet with your accountant to discuss expanding your business, take a chart with you—just throw one in with all the boring reports. The person reading the chart will be impressed by your initiative, and the chart will make it easier for them to interpret your numbers at a glance. Of course, they'll want to also read the boring report that supports the chart, but the chart itself is a nice touch.

You can also use charts for sales purposes. The next time you're visiting a client, take a chart that shows your product's performance or the amount of sales that come from repeat business (happy customers who keep coming back). The saying that a picture is worth a thousand words was never more appropriate—don't sit there telling someone how wonderful you are, show them a chart that proves it!

Excel gives you a friendly tool for building charts from your data. First, select the cells you want to convert to a chart (be sure to select your column headings and row labels if you want them to be part of your chart), and click the **Chart Wizard** button on Excel's standard toolbar. Follow the wizard through the process of selecting a chart type, adding titles to your chart, and positioning your chart's legend.

If at all possible, try to print any charts that you'll be giving to the bank or any other important resource in color. If you don't have a color printer, many printing and office service stores (like Kinko's) have the ability to print your chart in color for you. Although the following figure is in black and white, imagine how much more dramatic and polished it would be if it was printed in color!

If you're still not sure how or when you would use charts, check out the following list. The three most common chart types are listed. It's important to choose the type of chart that turns your data into an appropriate message.

A Legend in Your Own Mind

Your chart's *legend* helps the reader interpret your chart's colors and patterns. Usually found in bar and line charts, the legend tells us which color bar goes with which numbers. Are your sales of Widgets represented by the blue bar or the red bar? Check the legend.

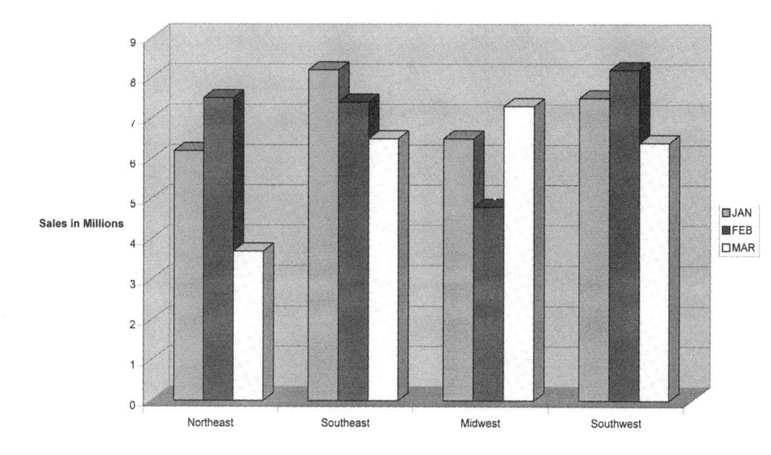

Compare this chart with the boring sales report earlier in the chapter. You can immediately see sales trends by looking at the height of the bars.

- **Bar/Column** Shows comparisons, and if the bars/columns are shown in chronological order (left to right) they can show trends.
- **Pie** Pies show comparisons only and can show only one series of data at a time.
- **Line** Line charts show trends over time or comparisons between categories, although trends are their primary use.

The Least You Need to Know

- Supplement the reports your accounting software provides by creating your own in Excel. Sales reports, expense analysis, even a quick checkbook balancing spreadsheet can be created quickly and easily.
- Excel's formula and function tools makes manipulating numbers much simpler, even for the mathematically challenged.
- Use Excel's Expense template to keep track of the money you spend. You can also download more templates from the Microsoft Web site.
- Convert your numbers to charts when presenting a proposal to the bank or anyone else you're working with to get financing or other assistance for a project. The chart makes it easier to interpret your numeric data, and it shows you took the time to make your data accessible and interesting.

Chapter 9

Mass Hysteria? Marketing with Form Letters

In This Chapter

- Find your perfect mailing list
- Get the skinny on your competition and potential customers by surfing the Web
- Build a cheap and easy home for all your data
- From Occupant to Dear Bob, learn all about form letters and how to give them your personal touch
- Print your own labels and make addressing your mailings less of a sticky situation

Short of shouting from the rooftops, mass mailing is the most efficient way to make contact with your potential clients. Print ads in a newspaper or magazine can be hard to target—you have little control over who picks up the magazine, and even less control over whether he or she will even see your ad. Cold calls (you showing up, propaganda and hat in hand) are nobody's idea of fun, and unless you happen to show up at the client's door on the day he needs exactly what you're selling, you'll feel like a nuisance (and you probably are). So, mass mailing is an attractive alternative, and an effective way to get your message out. It's easy to do, relatively inexpensive, trackable (you know whom you mailed to and when, and you'll know if they call you). After you've built your database of recipients, you can easily mail to them over and over until you reel `em in!

Find Your Target Audience

When you send your mailing to a wide selection of people, you can expect about 1% of them to contact you or respond in any way. For the mathematically challenged (hey, I used my calculator!), that's 10 responses for every 1,000 pieces mailed. The percentages go up (to about 5%) if your mailing is targeted to a specific group with specific interest in products or services such as yours.

Over and Over Again

In marketing, there is a rule known as the Nine Times Rule. It's based on the idea that your marketing materials must cross a person's desk nine times before they act on it. Of course, you hope they'll respond sooner than that, but it makes a good point: Don't give up too soon!

The Microsoft Office suite offers two packages that can be used quickly and easily to build a database of contacts and to generate form letters. Word and Excel can be used together to take you through the entire mass mailing experience—from the first name and address you type into the computer, to the labels that make sure your missive hits its mark.

Taking Aim: Targeting Your Audience

A mass mailing shouldn't go out blindly to every Tom, Dick, and Harriet, unless your product or service is usable by everyone, such as carpet cleaning (even if they don't have rugs, you can do their upholstery) or flowers (everyone is eventually in the doghouse and needs to send flowers). For most businesses, however, a targeted audience is required to make the most of the mailing.

How do you target your mailing? Research. Find out which people and businesses typically use a product or service such as yours, and add the local ones (or those in your serving area) to your list. You'll find out how to make and maintain that list later.

In theory, you should already know who your potential customers are—if you sell copier supplies, small businesses are your bread and butter. If you sell bread and butter, restaurants are probably a good contact for you. The key is finding the names and addresses of businesses in your area and finding out the name of each company's decision maker. The better researched your mailing is, the more responses you get, and the more bang you get for your mailing buck. Some ways to research your list:

- **Visit your library** Either in person or online, check out a business firm's directory. Most counties publish one, and believe it or not, it lists every business in the county. Some businesses willingly list themselves and give a lot of information about their directors and officers, and others appear as just a company name, address, and phone number. These are the companies that also have the receptionist that never puts your calls through. The listings in these books are generally in alphabetical order and/or by SIC (Standard Industrial Classification) code. There is also a code system called NAICS, which is relatively new.

- **Call your Chamber of Commerce** They publish a directory of their members and will sell you a copy, usually close to the cost of joining the chamber for a year. Because you're already forking over for the book, why not join the chamber, and go to meetings? The guy next to you gagging on rubber chicken might be your next big client.

But I'm Not Feeling SIC!

A *SIC code* is a number assigned to a business, such as 0721 for Crop Planting. If you plant crops, 0721 is your SIC code. You can get a complete listing of both SIC and NAICS codes by going to the government census Web site, at: **http://www.census.gov/epcd/naics/naicstb2.txt**.

Beware the List Police

Check the fine print before you buy a list. Many times the list provider puts a limit on the number of times you can use the list—allegedly to keep the people on the list from being deluged with mail—but for you that can mean limited return on investment potential. How do they know if you've used it more than once? They stack the list with dummy addresses, and if one of them gets your mail twice, you're busted! Their recourse is fairly limited, but you could find yourself blacklisted in the mailing list world!

- **Read the Yellow Pages** They took out an ad, so you'll send them yours. Actually, because it lists businesses by their product or service, if your target audience is businesses, this is a great place to find people.
- **Contact local organizations** Do your potential customers have a professional organization? If your prospects are lawyers, check the Bar Association. They'll have a list of their members, including addresses and phone numbers, which you can purchase for anywhere from $50 to $150, depending on your location. Other professions that have their own organizations include doctors, plumbers, electricians, nurses, computer programmers, and teachers.
- **Buy a mailing list** Contact two or more companies that sell mailing lists (find them in the Yellow Pages or online) and ask for a quote. You can tell them what SIC codes you're looking for to make sure you're targeting the right group. Make sure you can specify zip codes so your mailing goes to the area you serve, and that the list can be sorted by zip code to make your bulk mailing easier. Most of all, make sure the list includes phone numbers! You want to be able to follow up on your mailings by phone. Your per-listing price should fall in the 5-cent to 12-cent range, depending on how much information about each listed person or business you need. You can get simple address and phone listings or find the name of the decision maker and the company's income data, but you'll pay more for it.

Formats You Can Use

When buying a list, make sure you get it in a format you can use with your preferred software. In this book, I'm suggesting Microsoft Excel for list databases. Make sure your list comes in .TXT, .DBF, or .XLS format so Excel can read and open the file.

Yahoo! A List of Mailing Lists!

To find firms that sell mailing lists, go to Yahoo.com or any other large search engine, and type (in quotes) **"Mailing Lists"**. Check out the Web sites for the firms you find, and make a few calls. It pays to shop around for the best per-listing price, and the greatest level of flexibility on the part of the list supplier. Ask about a sample list that you can use at will, to test the accuracy and appropriateness of their listings. If they're not willing to give you a few names (about 5% of the total names you intend to purchase), go elsewhere.

You Get What You Pay For!

The Magic Carpet, a carpet-cleaning firm, tried to get along with a very old computer (bought for $150) and a word processor. Unable to do more than send preprinted postcards with labels that a friend (guess who) had to make on her computer because Magic Carpet only had a ratty dot matrix printer, they couldn't creatively or proactively market to their existing or potential customers without great effort. Consequently, they only did one or two mass mailings a year. If your company needs a new computer or better software to get the job done, it's worth the investment.

Gotcha! Searching the Web for People and Businesses

Another way to use the Web to facilitate your mailing (or any other communication) is to use the various people-searching tools available. All the major search engines (Yahoo!, Altavista, Lycos) boast a tool for finding lost loves and distant cousins. You can use these tools for finding information (missing phone numbers, owner's name) about people and businesses to supplement your mailing.

The Ethics of Internet Information

You may be treading on legal or ethical toes if you try to use a Web people-search tool to find hundreds of names to build your mailing list. The only efficient and ethical way to use one of these search tools is to look up missing information—you know their address, but what's their phone number?—or to find a business that sells something you need, like mailing lists or postcards for your mailing. These companies *want* to be found! Many of the business-search tools list companies by SIC code, making the search that much easier.

Most people-finding tools require a last name (or a business name) to do the search. The more information you have in addition to that (first initial, name, or city), the narrower the search criteria. This is especially helpful if the last name or business name is generic, like Smith or American. The following figure shows the Yahoo! People Search screen and some search criteria entered.

Remember that these listings generally come from the phone company. If you can't find the person, he or she may be unlisted and technically, they *shouldn't* appear. Because businesses are rarely unlisted, if you can't find them, either they're out of business or you entered something incorrectly in your search fields.

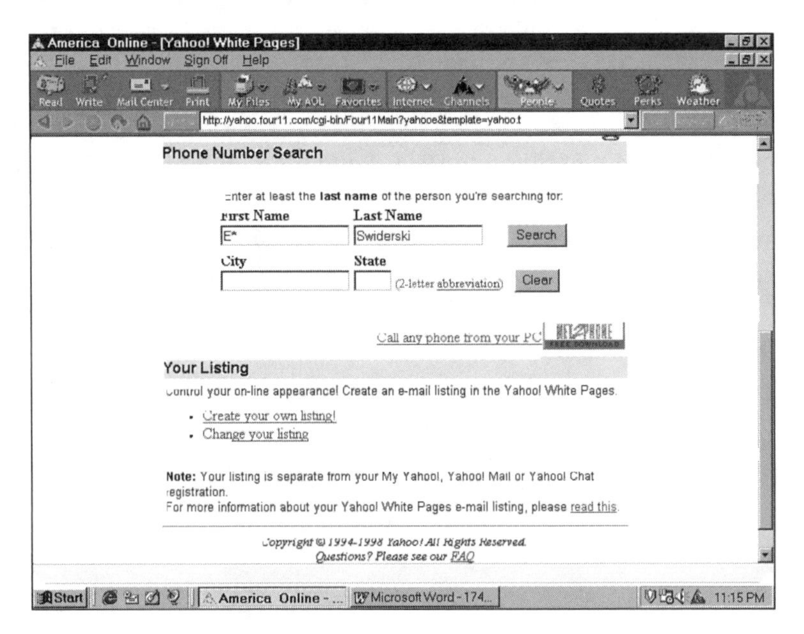

*If you're not sure how to spell the name, use the first letter or two and then the * wildcard to represent the rest of the name.*

Seek and Ye Shall Find

If your research has only netted you the company address and you need to know more about the firm before you fire off that mailing, check to see if they have a Web site. Many Web sites contain the names of the firm's major players. You may also be able to find out how many employees they have so you know how much potential business they represent! Don't hesitate to look up your competitor's Web site, either. See what they're offering, check out the overall look of their site. Although you don't want to copy it, you do want to make sure yours is even better!

Creating and Maintaining a List Database

So you've found the people you want your mailing to go to. If you purchased your mailing list and it arrived on disk, you can import that list into your computer, thus saving you a lot of typing. If your list is on paper from one or more resources, you have to create a database and enter the records.

Data, Fields, and Records

A *database* is a collection of information. If you've ever used the phone book, you've used a database. Each listing is a *record*, and each record is broken up into *fields*, such as first name, last name, address, city, phone number, and so on. The collection of records is the database. Got it? Good!

Setting up your database, however, is just the beginning. For your list to remain useful, it must be continuously updated. If you want to be a successful mass marketer, you must resign yourself to being in continuous sales mode (sigh), always looking for people to contact, groups to speak to, addresses to mail to. No one's suggesting you become obnoxious about it, but you have to be wearing your sales hat a lot of the time.

Now if all that sales stuff sounds like fun, here's the not-so-fun part: as you gather these contacts, you need to enter them into your database so your next mailing includes them. This can be a lot of work, especially if you're keyboard-challenged. But you only need to enter the records once, and they're in there for life. It's worth the effort to be up-to-date and actively looking for leads.

Maintain Your Status

When you're building your database, add a field called Status. For each record, add a P for prospect, C for current, X for inactive, and so on. You get the idea. Later, you can run a report that shows just the Currents, or just the Inactives, and decide how to best market to them and them alone.

Wait a minute, did she say "in there for life"? Well, sort of. Part of the maintenance program includes getting rid of the dead wood. Got prospects that you've written to several times and they've never responded? They don't return your calls? Delete them! Better yet, move them to another database that you might call "Dead Wood." That way, they're not really gone, and they can be recycled if they ever do call you or you think your most recent offering will finally catch their eye.

Importing an Electronic Database

The firm from whom you purchased the mailing list should provide instructions for its use, but in the event that these instructions are missing or unclear, you can use the following steps for taking your list file from the disk you bought and getting it into your computer. We'll be using Microsoft Excel to house the database:

1. Place the disk or CD that you bought into the appropriate drive on your computer.
2. Open Microsoft Excel from the **Start** menu, under **Programs**.
3. From Excel's **File** menu, choose **Open**.
4. Click the **Look In** list box, and choose the drive that contains your mailing list file.
5. Click the **Files of Type** list box, and select the file format of the mailing list file. If you don't know what format it's in, choose **All Files**.
6. In the large white box that contains the list of files on your disk (floppy or CD-ROM), double-click the mailing list file.

Assuming that Excel can convert the file format of your mailing list, your mailing list opens in a new spreadsheet onscreen.

If you're an Access user, you can use that program to open your mailing list file, too. The process of using the data after it's in Access isn't as simple as it is in Excel, but you have more power to create fancy reports or query specific information in Access. It's your choice.

To open your mailing list file in Access, open Access and choose **New Database** from the **File** menu. Give it a name, and choose where to save it. Choose **Table** from the **Insert** menu, and choose **Import Table** from the list. After you click **OK**, you can look on your floppy disk or CD-ROM drive for the mailing list file and import it. You're ready to go—the mailing list is now part of an Access database. You're a genius!

Building a Database from Scratch

If you did the legwork and gathered your contacts from one or more manual sources, you have to create a database to house them. Doing this properly requires planning. Boring, you say? You're more of a fly-by-the-seat-of-your-pants type? Well, good luck. If you don't plan your database, you'll spend a lot of extra time fixing it up when you realize you forgot things. Either plan for it now or smack yourself on the forehead later.

First of all, decide what fields you want to have. You obviously need fields to accommodate the information you have in your mailing list—first name, last name, title, company name, address (add two address fields for the companies with long addresses), city, state, zip, phone, fax, email, and so on.

The less obvious fields you may want to add are for the subjective information you normally keep in your head—customer status (new, prospective, current, dead), credit history (good, deadbeat), even memo fields to type things like "sounded interested last time" so that you know this person may roll over soon.

That's Mr. Letterman, to You

The "Mr." is only possible if your database includes a Title field. It's a good idea to include such a field, because it enables you to filter out males or females (should a particular mailing be directed at one gender more than another), and it gives you the ability to create a more formal salutation (Dear Mr. Letterman instead of Dear Dave).

Why break a record down into so many pieces? Breaking it down gives you the power to make more creative use of the data and to get more information out of the data. If, for example, you had one field "Name" instead of two, "Last Name" and "First Name," you could only address a letter to "John Smith," and your form letter would start "Dear John Smith." By breaking the name into two fields, your letter can start with "Dear John" or "Dear Mr. Smith."

Breaking your data into smaller pieces also gives you more ways to look at the data—if you have a status field (current, potential, and former customers) or a field that contains the date of last contact, you can run a report that shows, for example, only current customers who you've been in touch with in the last six months. A well-designed database can be used not only for the mailing list, but to plan your future mailings.

Microsoft Excel has a few rules of its own. Following these rules will make it easier for you to fully use your records later, so it's a good idea to play along:

- Database records go in the rows on your spreadsheet, never the columns. Remember you're maintaining a list.
- Each column in your database is a field. The column headings are your field names.
- Don't leave any blank rows between your field names row and your first record. Don't leave any blank rows between records, either.
- Keep any abbreviations consistent. For example, if you have a Job Title field, don't enter Mgr. in one record and Manager in another. Consistency gives you more options for using your database effectively later.

If you keep these basics in mind as you build your database, you'll be much happier with your results. To get started building the database, open Excel and make sure you're in a blank workbook. Choose one of the sheets in the workbook and begin typing the following items:

- **Database title** Usually placed in cell A1, and it's okay if it spills over into A2, A3, and so on. You can skip this step, but adding it here can make it easier to identify your data without having to create a long filename.

Show Me the Way to Go Home

At the end of your first record, press **Enter**. This moves you one cell down. Then press **Home**. This takes you to the first cell in the next row, and you can begin your second record.

- ➤ **Field names** Go to row 1 (or 2 if you're inserting a title) and type the field names, one in each cell. Don't skip over any columns. If you have 8 fields, make sure they're in cells A1 through H1, with none missed.
- ➤ **Your records** Starting with the first blank row under your field names, begin typing the information for your first record. Don't worry about alphabetizing the list, you can do that later.

If your number of records exceeds the length of one screen (about 25 records on an average monitor), you may want to keep your field names fixed at the top of the screen so you can tell which field you're filling in as you move through the list. You don't want to find out, 150 records later, that you've been typing phone numbers in the zip code field. To prevent this, select the row below your field names (click the row number to select the whole row), and choose **Freeze Panes** from the **Window** menu. You can **Unfreeze** them later as needed. The following figure shows a list of mailing list contacts.

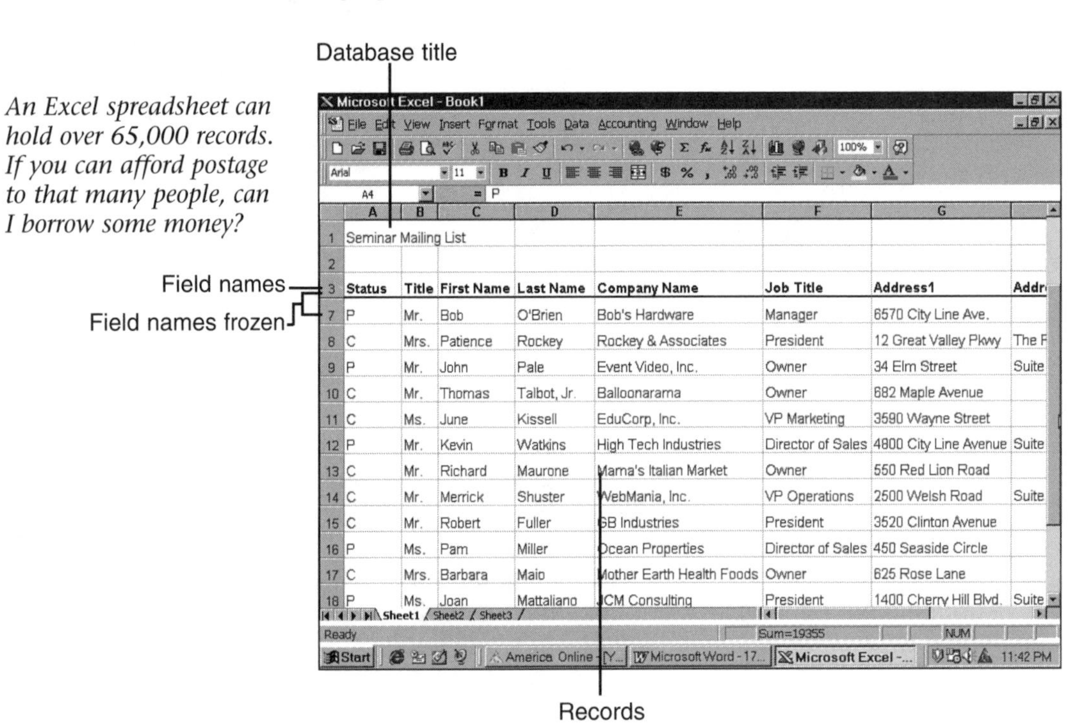

	Status	Title	First Name	Last Name	Company Name	Job Title	Address1	Addr
7	P	Mr.	Bob	O'Brien	Bob's Hardware	Manager	6570 City Line Ave.	
8	C	Mrs.	Patience	Rockey	Rockey & Associates	President	12 Great Valley Pkwy	The F
9	P	Mr.	John	Pale	Event Video, Inc.	Owner	34 Elm Street	Suite
10	C	Mr.	Thomas	Talbot, Jr.	Balloonarama	Owner	682 Maple Avenue	
11	C	Ms.	June	Kissell	EduCorp, Inc.	VP Marketing	3590 Wayne Street	
12	P	Mr.	Kevin	Watkins	High Tech Industries	Director of Sales	4800 City Line Avenue	Suite
13	C	Mr.	Richard	Maurone	Mama's Italian Market	Owner	550 Red Lion Road	
14	C	Mr.	Merrick	Shuster	WebMania, Inc.	VP Operations	2500 Welsh Road	Suite
15	C	Mr.	Robert	Fuller	GB Industries	President	3520 Clinton Avenue	
16	P	Ms.	Pam	Miller	Ocean Properties	Director of Sales	450 Seaside Circle	
17	C	Mrs.	Barbara	Maio	Mother Earth Health Foods	Owner	625 Rose Lane	
18	P	Ms.	Joan	Mattaliano	JCM Consulting	President	1400 Cherry Hill Blvd.	Suite

An Excel spreadsheet can hold over 65,000 records. If you can afford postage to that many people, can I borrow some money?

Great. Now you have hundreds of records, and you're staring at the screen, perhaps scrolling up and down, admiring your future sales. Although you may look busy, you're not fooling anyone. Get to work:

Ascending or Descending Order

If you want to do a quick sort on just one field, click any cell in that column and click the **Sort Ascending** or **Sort Descending** icon on the Standard toolbar.

➤ **Sort those records!** Sorting changes the order that the records appear in your database. If you want to see your list in Company Name order, you can sort it by that field. To sort your Excel dialog box, choose **Sort** from the **Data** menu, and choose the fields (from one to three of them) to sort by. When sorting by more than one field, start with the field that has the greatest number of duplicate records, and work down to a field containing unique data in each record, as shown in the following figure.

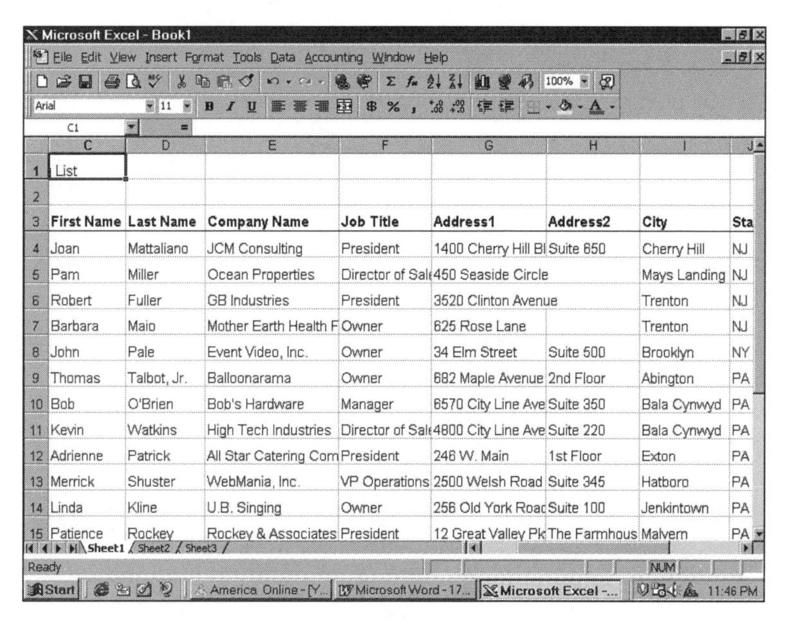

	C	D	E	F	G	H	I	J
1	List							
2								
3	First Name	Last Name	Company Name	Job Title	Address1	Address2	City	Sta
4	Joan	Mattaliano	JCM Consulting	President	1400 Cherry Hill Bl	Suite 650	Cherry Hill	NJ
5	Pam	Miller	Ocean Properties	Director of Sal	450 Seaside Circle		Mays Landing	NJ
6	Robert	Fuller	GB Industries	President	3520 Clinton Avenue		Trenton	NJ
7	Barbara	Maio	Mother Earth Health F	Owner	625 Rose Lane		Trenton	NJ
8	John	Pale	Event Video, Inc.	Owner	34 Elm Street	Suite 500	Brooklyn	NY
9	Thomas	Talbot, Jr.	Balloonarama	Owner	682 Maple Avenue	2nd Floor	Abington	PA
10	Bob	O'Brien	Bob's Hardware	Manager	6570 City Line Ave	Suite 350	Bala Cynwyd	PA
11	Kevin	Watkins	High Tech Industries	Director of Sal	4800 City Line Ave	Suite 220	Bala Cynwyd	PA
12	Adrienne	Patrick	All Star Catering Com	President	246 W. Main	1st Floor	Exton	PA
13	Merrick	Shuster	WebMania, Inc.	VP Operations	2500 Welsh Road	Suite 345	Hatboro	PA
14	Linda	Kline	U.B. Singing	Owner	256 Old York Road	Suite 100	Jenkintown	PA
15	Patience	Rockey	Rockey & Associates	President	12 Great Valley Pk	The Farmhous	Malvern	PA

Sorting shuffles the deck and lists your data in any order you choose. In this case, I've sorted by State.

➤ **Filter those records!** Filtering is like playing the kid's card game, Fish. You're essentially saying "Gimme all your…" to the computer, and it shows only the records matching what you asked for. Occasionally, you'll be told to "Go fish!" when nothing matches your criteria, but in general, the records you ask for (everyone in New Jersey, all companies in Philadelphia, anyone with "Director" in their title) will come out.

Filtering doesn't remove the records that don't meet your criteria from the list; it temporarily hides them. To filter your records, choose **Filter** from the **Data** menu, and then select **AutoFilter** from the submenu. List box arrows appear next to each of your field names. Click the arrow to the right of the field (or fields) that you want to filter, and choose the value you want the filter to look for, as shown in the following figure. When you're ready to end your AutoFilter session and have all your records return to the screen, choose **Filter** from the **Data** menu, and choose **Show All** from the submenu.

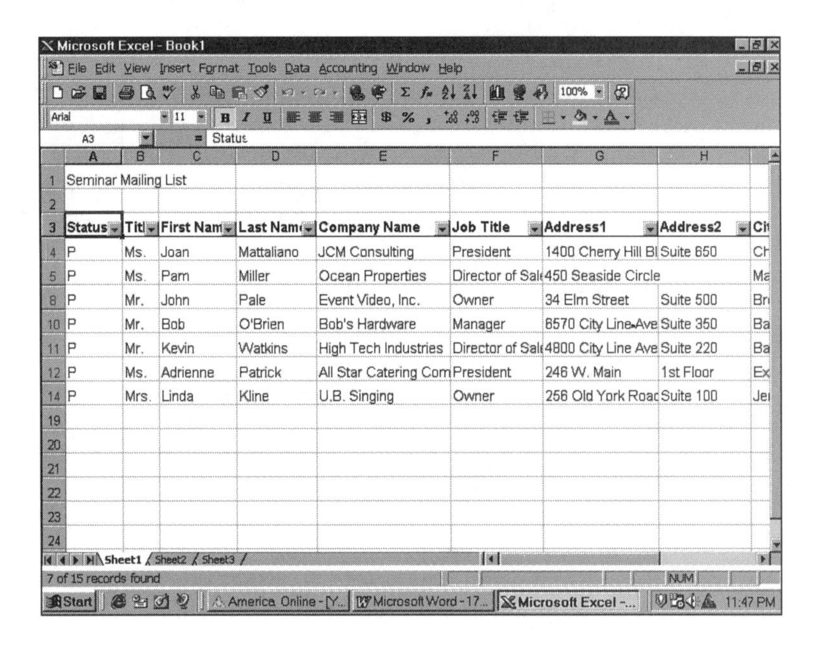

After filtering status for Ps, the records with a status of P (for Prospect) are the only ones showing.

Writing a Personal Form Letter

Form letters. We've all found them in our mailbox, telling us we may have already won. In addition to never winning, we never seem to get off the mailing list.

No matter how personal a form letter appears, each form letter is the same, no matter who it goes to, except for the address, salutation, and the occasional reference to your city or first name in the body of the letter. These references are supposed to make you feel cozy with the sender, like he or she really *knows you*. Nobody falls for this, but it is nicer than To Whom it May Concern, isn't it?

Heeeeee's SAFE!

Save your database file before starting your Mail Merge process. Leaving the file unsaved risks damage or changes to the data which can mess up the records that are merged with your form letter.

The term Form Letter is a generic one, meaning any document that contains data from a database, inserted for the purpose of sending the document to a large group of people. In addition to the traditional letter format, your data can be pulled into other types of documents, such as these popular and effective mass marketing pieces:

- **Postcards** Sheets of preperforated postcards (with or without artwork on them) can be sent through your inkjet or laser printer, each one coming out with an address on it, inserted from your database.
- **Catalogues** This requires a two-step process that brings in data from a product database and places it on the pages, and then from a mailing list database and places the address on the back cover.

Whichever type of mailing you decide to create, the process of creating it requires merging a document that you type and format in a word processing program such as Microsoft Word, and a database you build in a program like Excel. The process of bringing these two things together is called a Mail Merge—document and data are merged for the purpose of a mailing.

Doing a Mail Merge in Word is a three-step process:

1. Choose a type of document and build its basic text.
2. Choose or build a database and relate it to the document.
3. Merge the two items, printing the document, which now includes insertions from the database.

Pretty simple, no? Yes, if you've done your homework ahead of time. Do you have a database set up? If not, you'll have to detour out of the process to build one. You can build a database in Word, but it's not a good idea if you want to be able to easily use and add to the database for future mailings. Sorting and filtering the database is also much easier in Excel, so you want to avoid using Word for your data if at all possible.

We'll forge ahead, assuming you have a database all set up, records entered, and are ready to go. Your records are sorted in the order you want them to print out, and you've checked the accuracy of your records, filtering for and filling in any blank fields. Ready? Let's go.

From Word's **Tools** menu, choose **Mail Merge**. A large Mail Merge Helper dialog box opens, showing you those three steps I told you about. The following figure shows you the dialog box. Click the **Create** button, and choose the type of document you want to create.

Next, decide where you want to build this document—in the Active Window or in a New Main Document. If you're on a blank document, choose **Active Window**.

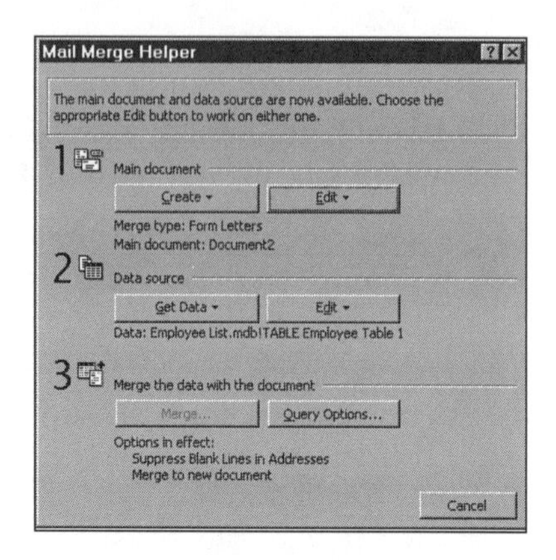

Merging a document with your database is as easy as one, two, three.

Having a Wonderful Time, with Labels

If you want to print your own postcards, you must pretend to create labels. The only way to get several addresses per page (in blocks) is to choose a label that matches the dimensions of your postcard. Check out the next section in this chapter for more information on creating labels and envelopes.

Click the **Get Data** button. Assuming you have a database already, pick **Open Data Source** from the menu. You can then browse to the database you created in Excel. Double-click the file when you find it. This creates a relationship between the data and your soon-to-be document. You'll be able to insert *merge fields* into your letter (or other type of document), and they'll match the field names from your database.

Go back to the first step and click the **Edit** button. The Mail Merge Helper dialog box disappears, and a new toolbar (shown in the following figure) appears onscreen. At this point, you can begin adding your two types of content—the generic content that will appear on every page, and the merge fields that tell Word where to insert your data.

I'm assuming you know how to type and create a basic letter. What I figure you don't know is how to insert merge fields. If you already know, forgive me and skip this whole paragraph! If you aren't sure how, read on.

To add a merge field, click the **Insert Merge Field** button. A list of fields drops down. Whaddya know? They're the same ones you had in your database! Click one, and see it appear in your document with pairs of greater than and less than symbols around it. Note that you cannot take what seems to be the obvious shortcut and type these in—you can only insert these fields by clicking the Insert Merge Field button.

When you've finished building your text and fields, click the **Mail Merge Helper** button on the toolbar. The three-step box reopens, and you're ready to click the **Merge** button.

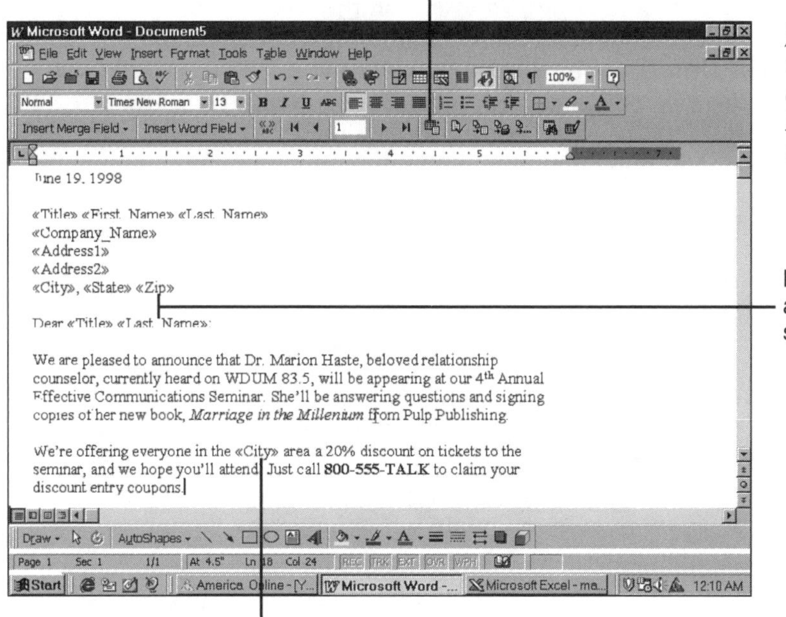

Just what you wanted—more buttons that you don't know how to use. Don't worry, you only need to use one of them.

As soon as you click Merge, the Merge dialog box opens. The default settings in this box are your best bet—merge to a **New document** (don't go right to the printer), merge **All the Records**, and **Don't Print Blank Lines**. Click **Merge** to bring your document and your data together. You'll get one letter for each record in your database.

WATCH OUT!

Ssssh! Keep Merge Errors a Secret!

Why print to a new document and not directly to the printer? Because if you messed up, you'll waste your letterhead or other stationery. Now I *know* you never make mistakes, but if you've accidentally added a field twice or missed something important, merging to a new document gives you a chance to spot your error and start over before you commit to paper. It also keeps the error a secret between you and your monitor.

You may have noticed a Query Options button in the Mail Merge Helper dialog box. I skipped over it because for most mailings, you want all the records, and you've already sorted the database in your database program. If, however, you want to choose specific records (by filtering the database) or want to print them out in a specific order (by sorting them in a different order than you sorted them in Excel), click the **Query Options** button before you click the **Merge** button. The Query Options dialog box appears in the following figure.

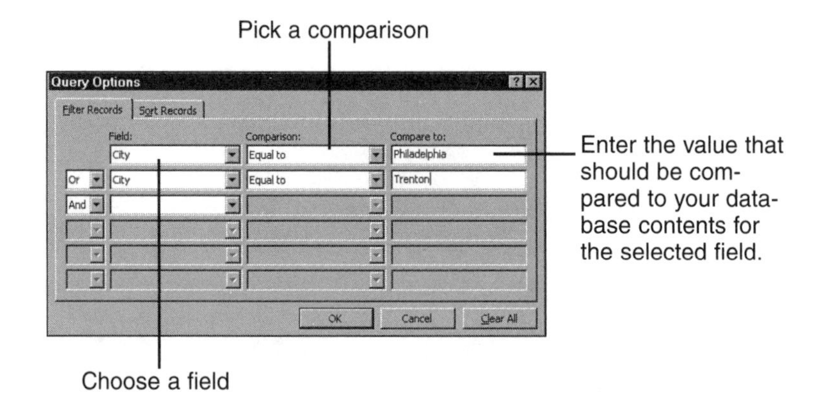

Filtering your records creates a smaller, more focused mailing.

Filtering records requires that you select a field to filter on. Want all your New Jersey customers to get a special mailing? Choose the **State** field, and set your Comparison to **Equal To**. In the Compare To box, type **NJ**. You can filter on more than one field, linking each level with And or Or.

If your records are not in the order you want them in, click the **Sort Records** tab. You can sort by up to three fields. For example, you might want to see all your clients by State, and within each State by City. For each City, you might want them in order by Last Name. A three-level sort is set up in the following figure.

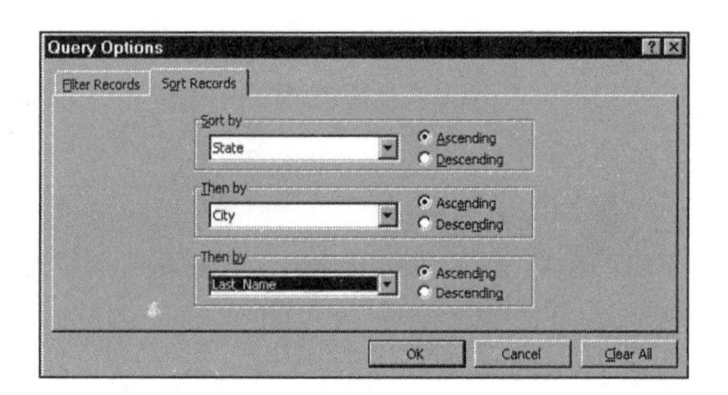

Sort by the fields that will help you proof and distribute your mailing.

The Offer They Can't Refuse: Creating an Effective Mailer

We've talked about who to mail to, how to mail it, and later, we discuss how to get it delivered. But for now, before you slap the label on or lick that envelope, how about some ideas for making what goes in the envelope really great?

First of all, don't go cheap if you can avoid it. If you have to go cheap, don't look cheap. For example, if you can't afford a two-color mailing, use colored paper, and not that day-glo purple stuff. Use a dignified shade of moss green or sunset orange. Don't use 25 different fonts and 18 pieces of clip art. Keep it simple and professional but use cool visual effects like drop shadows behind text and graphics, and borders around the card or page.

Give the recipient a job to do. Don't just send your sale announcement or a list of your services. Give them a call to action! Tell them to call you back to hear about a discount or a special offer. Give them a card to fill out and return, one that will qualify them for a drawing for some gift. (Remember, there must really be a gift—the authorities call it fraud if there's no gift!) Hold a seminar at a local bookstore or library (only if it's free), and make your mailer a way to sign up.

Imitation, the Sincerest Form of Flattery

One way to make sure your mailing is effective is to keep a file of the mass mailings you receive. Keep the ones that you hated in one file, the ones that grabbed you in another. Although you don't want to copy anything outright from the good examples, you can learn from them and try your versions of what worked.

Going Postal: Addressing Your Mass Mailing

Your mailing is printed, and now you need to get it into the mail. Depending on the time-sensitivity of your mailing, you may be able to save money by mailing your letters as bulk mail (about 19 cents per one-ounce piece). If you need to have this letter in people's hands in a day or two, First Class (32 cents for one ounce) is your best bet.

If you decide to go with a bulk mailing—hey, it's not glamorous, but it's cheap!—you need to understand a few things:

- You can't send bulk mail unless you have a bulk mail permit, and you have to apply for and purchase one. The cost depends on how many pieces you'll be sending, roughly 19 cents per piece. You'll be assigned a number that must appear on your mailings. Either get a stamp made or have the permit number imprinted on your mailing where the stamp would go. Check out the U.S. Post Office Web site (**www.usps.gov**) or call the post office nearest you—they have pamphlets and yards of red tape you'll want to read.

Dated Material: Do Not Delay

Wanna save money by using bulk mail? Don't wait too long to send your mailing. One of my clients ended up using First Class because their mailer (advertising a seminar) was going out too late. Realize that people don't always grab the phone the minute something hits their desk. Some people need time to open the mail, read it, put it in the In bin, and look at it again a few days later before they act on it. Maybe they have to get an okay to attend the event. Allow that time in mailing anything time-sensitive. Don't let procrastination increase your mailing costs and decrease your response rate.

- Your bulk mail must be sorted and bundled by zip code. If you're printing your own labels or envelopes, set your Query Options to sort by zip code, and nothing else.

Like Envelope, Like Letter

If you'll be printing form letters to go inside your bulk mail envelopes, merge them in zip code order also so that you can more easily match them with their labels/envelopes.

If your mailing consists of letters, you'll probably want to put them in envelopes, unless you like the folded-letter-with-a-label-slapped-on look. You can address your envelopes by hand, or to save time and the early onset of carpal tunnel syndrome, you can have the computer address them. This requires another pass through the mail merge process, merging your database with the envelopes. I only suggest you address the envelopes directly if you have a small database or a reliable envelope feeder on your printer. If neither of these apply to you, I suggest you print labels and put them on the envelope.

To generate labels, start the Mail Merge process again, with a blank document. Click the **Create** button, and choose **Mailing Labels**. After telling Word which document you want to work on (Active or New Main), click the **Get Data** button and choose your database file. Word's next concern is which label you want to use. Click the **Set up Main Document** button, and using the Label Options dialog box, pick the product number for your labels (the number is found on the side and front of the box your labels came in). If you aren't using Avery labels, look in the **Label Products** list box for another manufacturer.

After you've chosen your label, you're ready to build it. Click **OK** to close the Label Options dialog box, and the Create Labels dialog box opens automatically. Click the **Insert Merge Field** button to insert your name and address fields one at a time. You can also type any additional text you want to appear on each label, such as "Personal" or "Deliver to Addressee or Current Resident."

Click the **OK** button as soon as you've completed the content of your label. The Mail Merge Helper dialog box is again facing you, and you can click **Merge** to create your labels. It's a good idea to merge to a **New document**, in case you've made a mistake in your text or merge fields. After you've proofed the labels onscreen and you're sure they're okay, print the merge document by selecting **Print** from the **File** menu.

It's Clear, White Labels Can Be Tacky

Many users think that white mailing labels are tacky, and I agree. If you're mailing a proposal to a fancy new client, don't use labels. For mass mailings, however, labels are considered appropriate. Try clear labels (with a nice, subtle matte finish) to "hide" the fact that you've used a label. I use them for return address labels because I don't want to invest in preprinted stationery.

It's Faster with a Bar Code

Click the **Insert Postal Bar Code** button to have Word create a bar code and print it on each label. The bar code is created based on the address on each label. This can potentially speed your mail through the postal process, as your mail doesn't need to be bar coded by the post office equipment.

The Least You Need to Know

- ➤ A targeted mailing is the most effective, and you can find your best candidates by checking the library and the Web, or by purchasing a mailing list.
- ➤ An Excel database is a good choice for storing your mailing list, whether entered from scratch by you or purchased on disk.
- ➤ Word's Mail Merge feature allows you to combine a form letter (or any other form marketing document) and your database.
- ➤ Printing mailing labels is more convenient than printing directly on envelopes. Word contains all the standard Avery labels, so choosing the right label is easy.

Chapter 10

Email: Getting Connected and Staying in Touch

In This Chapter

- Choose an email connection that suits your needs and personality
- Use email to increase sales and improve business relationships
- Understand the do's and don'ts of email society
- Handle your incoming and outgoing mail traffic
- Always have the scoop on your favorite topic with newsgroups

Gone are the days when a phone call or a letter by mail could sustain a business relationship. Of course, businesses survived just fine before the advent of email, but no more. If you don't have an email address on your business card, people will assume you're somehow technically challenged or extremely cheap. Either or both of those things may in fact be true, but let's keep that our little secret.

Email is electronic mail, meaning mail sent electronically. That's all there is to it—it's not some mysterious thing. Email software is very easy to use because it's been designed for people who may use a computer only for email and nothing else. It's easy, it's relatively inexpensive, and it's essential for communication with the outside world. If you don't have it already, why on earth not?

Do I ISP? Choosing an Email Connection

One of the primary reasons many small businesses don't have email is that they're intimidated. If you've never used it before, it can seem like it's complex and it requires a lot of setup. It's not and it doesn't.

Email is conducted via the network of computers that make up the Internet. Your office may also have an internal email network, allowing you to send and receive messages within your office, with no connection to the outside world. If that's the case, you're probably already familiar with the sending and receiving part. What you may not know is how to extend your reach and communicate with the rest of the planet.

Email that reaches anyone, anywhere (provided they, too, have an email address) requires a connection to the Internet, and that costs money, though not a lot. You can establish this connection in one of two ways—through an online community (such as America Online or the Microsoft Network) or through an ISP (an Internet service provider). Which one is best for you? Read on, and then use the handy checklist in Table 10.1 to help clarify which suits you. Circle each YES that matters to you, and see which column has the most circled.

Table 10.1 Compare Online Communities to ISPs to Determine Which Environment Suits You.

Feature	**Online Community**	**ISP**
Simple to set up on your own	YES	NO*
24-hour phone support and online help	YES	MAYBE**
One rate for unlimited access	YES	YES
Chat Rooms and a social environment	YES	NO***
Offers Website setup and maintenance	NO	YES
Offers the ability to set up your own domain name	YES	YES
Multiple email addresses available	YES	YES
Requires use of Internet Explorer or Netscape	NO	YES

**You can set up the software on your own, but only after calling an ISP, sending them money, and setting up an account with them.*

***Many large or nationwide ISPs have the resources to provide 24-hour support. Many small or local ISPs don't.*

****You can chat through the use of IRC (Internet Relay Chat), but this isn't part of the ISP's services.*

Choosing an online community needn't preclude your use of an ISP's other services. If you think you'd like an online community for the social aspects but you also want a real Web presence, you can still hire an ISP to host your Web site and register your domain name. You can have a social email address through the online community and a business email address through the ISP, using your domain name, such as **jdoe@businessname.com**.

Joining an Online Community

Many new email and Internet users choose to get started by joining an online community. An online community is a closed group of users who pay to belong to that group. The members of the group can email each other as well as people outside the group, and outsiders can also email members of the group.

The benefit of an online community is the simple access to services such as chat rooms, news, sports information, the latest weather data, and stock status from NASDAQ and other stock exchanges. The online community is designed to place this type of information at your fingertips through a series of buttons and menu choices, enabling you to access it without having to navigate the Internet to find it. The figure below shows the Welcome screen for America Online.

Click a button to see local weather, news, or pull down a menu to access sports or online shopping.

Of course, you can access the Internet through an online service such as America Online, the Microsoft Network, or CompuServe. Both programs contain a browser that enables you to check out both Web and FTP sites.

File This Please

FTP stands for File Transfer Protocol, meaning a system for sending files over the Internet. An FTP site is an Internet site that stores files for people to access. Many organizations use FTP sites to store documents that their members need, saving the cost of mailings or other methods of distribution. Your ISP or online community offers tools to search for an FTP site that stores documents that might be of interest to you.

The costs? America Online is currently charging $22.95 per month for unlimited access. This includes email, online services, and Internet access. Most of the other online communities (CompuServe, Prodigy, Microsoft Network) charge similar amounts and offer similar services. AOL has the largest membership, nearing 12 million.

Getting set up with an online community is simple—you install their software (it usually arrives for free on CD or disk in your mailbox, or you can call them to order it), and as the installation program nears completion, it dials the home server, using your modem. When it connects, it asks you to choose a name for yourself and asks for your credit card number so that you can be billed each month (they pluck that fee right out of your account). As soon as they make sure your email name isn't already taken and that your card is valid, you're set to go.

Pre-Installed?

If you've just bought a new computer, check to see whether any online services are installed. You'll have to do the setup—pick an email address and provide your credit card information—but you don't have to bother installing the software yourself. You may find three or four different services are installed—delete the ones you don't need, or keep them around so that you can test each service to find the one you like best.

To find out more about the online communities, check out their home pages:

- **http://www.msn.com**
- **http://www.aol.com**
- **http://www.compuserve.com**

Choosing an Internet Service Provider

In lieu of (or maybe in addition to) an online community for your email and Internet access, you might choose to hire the services of an ISP, or Internet service provider. Thousands of these firms exist in the world, hundreds in any city in this country. Some are large corporations with years of experience and lots of services. Some are small companies run by a couple of people out of someone's basement. Many ISPs fall between these two extremes. All ISP's fees are generally the same, normally from $10 to $50 per month, depending on what types of services you use. You can find them in the Yellow Pages under Internet, or in any computer newspaper, such as the Computer User, which is published in most major U.S. cities. If you're on someone else's computer and accessing the Internet, search for "Internet Service Providers +Your City" to find local ISPs.

Local ISP, Local Calling

When you choose an ISP in your area, they provide an access number that's a local call for you. If they don't have one that's not a toll or long-distance call for you, find another ISP! Even if you think you won't be spending much time online, you'd be surprised how fast the phone bill can get out of hand. Your phone time on the Internet should be free or as close to it as possible, depending on the local calling service plan you have through your phone company.

What are your choices? You can simply have an email address and the ability to browse the Internet, in which case your fees will be at the lower end of the range, closer to $10 per month. You may have to sign a three- or five-year contract to get such a low rate, however. You can also go for the whole enchilada, and have email, Internet access, your own domain name, and a Web site, stored on the ISP's server. That will cost you some upfront money (to set up the Web site and "buy" a domain name), and the monthly fees will be from $30 to $50.

What's in a Domain?

A *domain name* is the part of your email or Web address that comes before the .com. For example, when I write to my editors at Macmillan Computer Publishing, I address them by their email names (first initial, full last name), @mcp.com. MCP is their domain name. So John Smith's email address is **jsmith@mcp.com**. The Macmillan Web site's address (URL) is **www.mcp.com**.

Calling Earl

The term *URL* (some geeks pronounce it "earl", others say the letters, U-R-L) is an acronym for Uniform Resource Locator. This is a long name for a Web address. The entire URL for a Web site consists of the www (for World Wide Web), the domain name (Yahoo, for example), and the extension, such as com or org. Each section is separated by periods (**www.yahoo.com**).

What are the benefits of going for these extra services? Having your own domain name gives you a more substantial-looking email and Internet presence. Many ISPs give you several email addresses with your purchase of a domain name so that if you have employees, each one can have an address, such as jdoe@yourcompanyname.com. Domain names must be registered with the InterNIC, the governing body of the Internet. By governing, I mean they control domain names and the administrative side of things, making sure there aren't two identical Web or email addresses and that everybody uses the appropriate technology for transmitting data.

Why have a Web site? We'll discuss that later, in Chapter 17, "Should You Weave a Web (Page)?" Benefits are there for anyone who wants to use the Internet to advertise a business, and many companies actually conduct business over the net—people can order products directly from the business's Web site.

So what's the bottom line? An ISP isn't as warm and fuzzy as an online community. Many of them give you a copy of Netscape or assume you have Internet Explorer (if you have Windows, you have IE) and give you the phone numbers of their modems in your area so that you can log on. After that, you're on your own. This can be a good thing, especially if you have no interest in the social aspects of an online community and don't want to deal with a lot of the advertising and excessive hand-holding that an online community offers. If you want to get on the Internet and surf unhindered, a simple ISP connection is for you. If this libertarian existence has an appeal but you feel you're too new to the Net to make it work, start out with an online service and then cancel and switch to the more hands-off ISP when you feel you're ready. The following figure shows an Internet Explorer window, with my home page displayed.

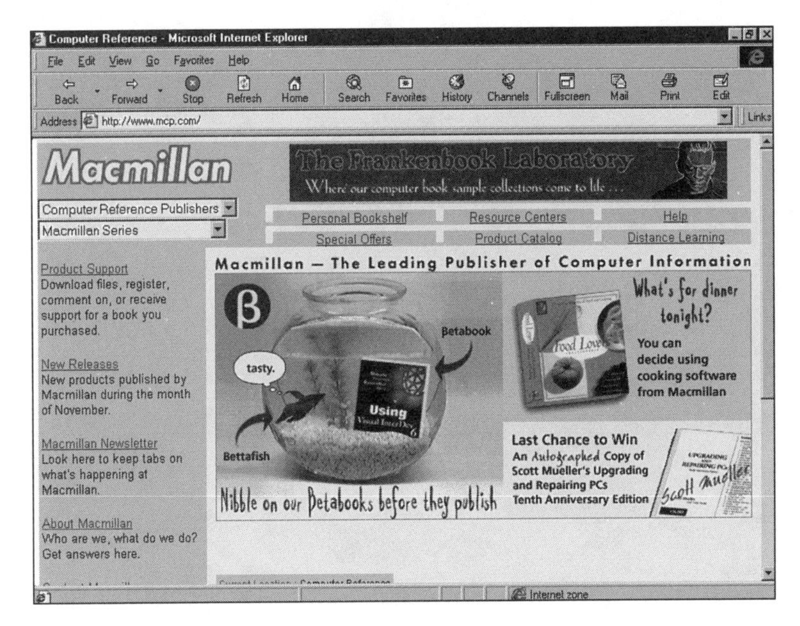

Jump right onto the Net through this uncluttered window.

Most ISPs offer some sort of technical support, though the smaller companies may not offer an 800 number or 24-hour access to that support. You can weigh your needs and skills against what each ISP offers and find one that suits your needs.

Free Email Account

You can also get free email from companies such as Hotmail, Angelfire, Yahoo!, and Juno. Go to their Web sites (**www.yahoo.com**, for example) and look for information on setting up a free email account.

Increasing Your Reach with Email

So you're set up. You have an email address through an online service or an ISP. Now what? What'd you do this for, anyway? To give yourself the ability to contact anyone, anywhere in the world and send them a note, a document, a picture, a video, or a program. Yes, you can do that with regular mail (now known as *snail mail)*, but it can take days to get there, depending on the distance between you and your recipient.

Email, on the other hand, can be received in seconds, anywhere on the planet, regardless of distance. The way the recipient's ISP or online service is set up to check the Internet for incoming mail (how often it checks) can be the only cause for any delays.

You can attach files to your email messages, meaning that along with your note, the recipient can also download a document, a program, a picture, a video or sound clip—anything that can be stored as a file on your computer. These extra items are called *attachments* because they're attached to your message.

Writing, Sending, and Responding to Email

The exact method you can use for creating, sending, and responding to email messages varies from program to program. The following figure shows the America Online window, and the Write button is indicated. You can also see the window into which the email message is typed.

Click the Write button and then type your message into the message window. You need to enter addresses for the recipient(s) and a subject so they know what your message is about!

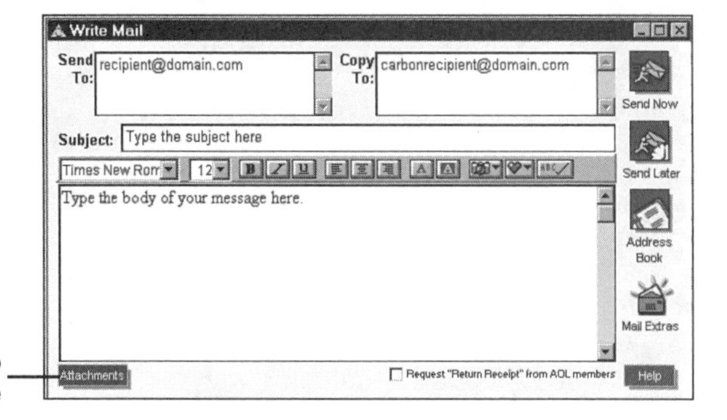

Click here to select files to accompany the message

When addressing a message, type the addresses of the people who'll receive your message. You can make them direct recipients (put them in the To: box), or send them carbon copies (put their names in the cc: box). Some email programs also allow blind carbons to be sent, which means the other recipients won't know that the bcc: recipient got a copy. This feature is mostly utilized for shifty reasons, as you can imagine! The figure below shows the Internet Explorer message window with a bcc: box for blind recipients.

Some email programs separate multiple names with a comma, others with a semicolon. Read your program's instruction manual or consult the Help files to find out.

Return Receipts—Friend or Foe?

Gone are the days that you could claim you never got a message! "That fax never arrived" is easy to get away with. Bill? I never got that bill. But many email programs allow the person to send their message with a return receipt—this means that when you get the message, they get a message from their email server indicating your successful receipt of the message. You're busted!

Targeted, Discreet Email Marketing

Consider using email for marketing your services. Although I'm not condoning anything pushy or intrusive, you can build distribution groups (groups of email addresses assigned a single name) through your email software's address book, and send periodic mailings to prospects, current customers, or randomly selected people or organizations to alert them to special sales or seasonal offerings.

Email Etiquette

Society has rules, such as using the salad fork for the salad and not for the entrée, or sending thank you notes to the people who brought gifts to your wedding. The world of email has similar rules:

- Don't use profanity, unless you know the recipient really well and know that he or she won't be offended. Avoid it all together in a business setting. Nasty emails that contain personal insults are called flames, and the sender is a flamer. Don't be a flamer.

- Don't click Send without thinking. My mom had a piece of advice for me that I've always remembered. "Never put anything in writing that you'd be embarrassed to hear read on the radio." This is good email advice, too. Before you send something that could have any conceivable negative fallout (hurt feelings, bruised egos, or misconstrued blame), read your email carefully. Trust me, I give you this advice from experience—many seemingly reasonable people turn out to be overly sensitive wimps.
- Don't send unsolicited emails—junk email is currently one of the most annoying aspects of having an email account. The act of sending junk email to many recipients is called Spamming. Considering Spamming? Think of canned luncheon meat and that should stop you.
- Don't use business email accounts for personal email unless you're the boss or it's been formally sanctioned. The email system belongs to the company, and your privacy is not assured. It can also be considered the equivalent of using their stamps for your Christmas cards.
- When replying to a message that was sent to people in addition to yourself, use the **Reply to All** option instead of simply **Reply**. If you don't send your reply to everyone, it's the equivalent of standing in a group at a party and whispering your responses in the ear of one person in the group, snubbing the others. The only time it's okay to exclude the other recipients from your reply is when the content is confidential and your not including them won't disrupt the flow of essential information through the group.

And You Thought Hall Monitors Were Bad!

Your online service probably has what it calls Terms of Service, or some behavioral standards for its members. If you violate them, you can be bounced—your privileges revoked or suspended. If your violation also violated any actual laws, you could be turned over to the police.

Birds of a Feather: Using Newsgroups

Newsgroups are groups you join to share information about a given topic. Newsgroups are there for just about any topic under the sun, from health problems to head shaving. Newsgroups can be helpful to your business if the information the group shares helps you expand your business, find out more about your industry, or share ideas with similar business owners. Also, newsgroups can be used for recreation and socializing, and as we know, many social contacts result in business. The following figure shows a list of newsgroups.

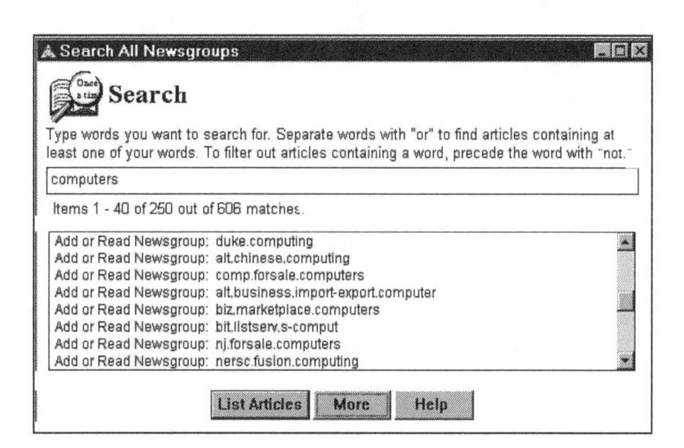

Newsgroups are divided into categories. Your newsgroup's category is the first part of its name, such as comp for computers or rec for recreational topics.

Newsgroups list their messages by topic, and messages often follow threads—you send a message, and someone responds to it. Someone else responds to the response, and so on. This message tree can be traced by other members who want to see who said what to whom. Hopefully, these messages contain useful information. Many times, however, newsgroups become social groups, and the messages are no more than personal notes. For this reason, many people choose to *lurk*, the term for reading newsgroup messages without formally joining the group.

What happens when you join a newsgroup? You receive email from the group, sending you the latest postings. Your responses are sent to the rest of the group. This is another reason to lurk and not join—your mailbox won't be full of messages you may not have time or the inclination to read.

Joining a newsgroup is called *subscribing*. When you join, you give your email address and check an option or in some way (depending on your browser) indicate your intention to join. If you attempt to post an article or respond to an existing article, you'll be asked to subscribe. You can unsubscribe if you find that the newsgroup no longer meets your needs.

'Tis Better to Lurk Than to Receive

Posting messages to newsgroups that don't relate to the topic can anger the hard core members of the group and result in nasty emails heading your way. Don't post anything that isn't salient to the topic, and don't join a newsgroup unless you want a lot of mail!

The Least You Need to Know

- Email is an essential part of your office life—sending, receiving, and responding to email from friends, professional peers, vendors, and anyone who can help you do business. If you don't have email, you're out of the loop.
- Choosing between an online community such as AOL or a local ISP is a matter of personal preference and often depends on what other Internet-related services and products you need. An ISP provides domain names, and many Web site services, such as setup, support, and maintenance. Choose an online community if you feel intimidated by the Internet or crave a social life online.
- It's not good to Spam, flame, or abuse your email recipients with nasty or useless email messages. If you use an online service such as AOL, you can be bounced from the community if anyone complains about your violations of these standards of behavior.
- Newsgroups allow you to share information with like-minded people. They can be a great resource for business, if you can find one that's focused and not too chatty.

Chapter 11

Just the Fax, Ma'am

In This Chapter

- Understand your fax software options
- Use Microsoft Office to send a fax
- Play by the rules and be a good faxing citizen

Can anyone remember how we survived before fax machines? I'm dating myself when I tell you that I remember a time in the past when people watched for the postman, perfectly happy to wait a day or two for a document to arrive by mail. If something was a matter of life and death, a messenger was hired to get a document delivered right away. Now, we have a fit if we can't fax something, even the least significant document, three seconds after we finish writing it. God forbid someone says "I'll send this over later"—we may call a few times to see where it is. Why hasn't it been faxed yet? I need it now!

With the immediacy that fax machines (and more recently fax modems in our computers) have afforded us, it's important to make the most effective use of the technology. You want to be sure your faxes get where they're going, are as legible as possible when they get there, and that you don't upset anyone in the process. Microsoft Office is a significant tool that you can use to make sure your fax arrives in one piece and on time.

Choosing and Using Fax Software

For those of you with fax modems on or in your computer, many fax programs are available, each one capable of the same set of tasks—taking a document from your computer and sending it to someone else's fax machine or fax modem. You can opt to add a cover sheet, perhaps created by the fax software. You can even schedule a time for the fax to go out, perhaps in an hour when you expect the fax line to be free, or at a time that the recipient requests the fax be sent.

If you have Windows 95, you have Microsoft Fax, and you can access it through Word, Excel, or PowerPoint. Microsoft Fax is part of the Windows 95 operating system, and through your Office applications, it uses a program called the Fax Wizard to set up your outgoing fax. Microsoft Fax is a simple program, with basic tools for selecting the recipients, choosing the documents that will be faxed, and creating a cover sheet. If you need to be able to schedule the fax to go out automatically at a specific time in the future, you need to use a different fax program, such as the programs discussed later in this chapter.

Why Didn't You Fax Before We Left?

I squeezed the following piece of information out of a Microsoft support technician (and then verified with a second Microsoft tech to make sure): If you've upgraded from Windows 95 to Windows 98 and never used Microsoft Fax while in 95, you won't be able to use it in Windows 98, even if you see it in your Accessories list. Why? Because Microsoft decided not to support it in Windows 98. You have to purchase another manufacturer's fax program if you want to send faxes from your computer.

Before running out to the computer store for fax software, do a little shopping online. Go to **http://www.computershopper.com** and search for Fax Software. You can also go to the Web sites of any large computer stores in your area, such as CompUSA (**www.compusa.com**), and search their inventory. Some products to consider:

- WinFax PRO from Symantec, list price $82.95
- Intelliquis Total Fax, list price $59.95
- Smith Micro Hot Fax, list price $99.95

When you install your fax software, you must know some things about your modem. Although the software may guess or assess some of this information on its own during the installation process, it pays to look these things up first. Use this checklist to make sure you're prepared:

- ❑ If your fax modem is internal, what speed is it?
- ❑ If you have an external fax modem, what is the manufacturer/model number?
- ❑ To which COM port is your external fax modem connected?
- ❑ What is your fax number?
- ❑ Are any prefixes required for dialing out? (Do you have to dial 9 to get an outside line or do you need to turn off Call Waiting with *70?)

Just Give Me the Fax!

A client of mine had a fax machine as well as a fax modem. With all that faxing equipment, sending them a fax should be a breeze, right? Wrong. Because they had their fax modem and machine going to the same phone line, as soon as they got online (to check email, surf the Web), they became incommuni-faxo. Because the office staff found the Internet rather compelling, they were rarely offline. After many complaints (from people like me), they finally wised up and got a separate phone line for their fax machine. Now when they're online, they're still reachable by fax, and at night (when no one's in the office), they can receive faxes on their computers as well. When they remember to leave them on, that is!

Sending a Fax with Microsoft Office

If you have Windows 95, you have Microsoft Fax. If your fax sending needs are simple, it's a great tool. You can access it by choosing **Send to** from the **File** menu in Word, Excel, or PowerPoint. Choose **Fax Recipient** from the submenu—this opens the Fax Wizard, which you can use to enter the names and fax numbers of your recipients, select the document to fax (it must be one of your open documents in the active application), and if desired, choose a cover page and enter it's contents.

Use What You've Got

When entering the names and fax numbers of your recipients, you can choose them from the Office Address Book, which saves you from typing them. Of course you must build your Address Book entries beforehand (names, addresses, phone and fax numbers), but after the names and numbers are in there, you'll never have to type them again—in the Fax Wizard or other tools such as the Envelopes and Labels dialog box in Word.

Play the Match Game

If you're using the Word letter templates (Contemporary, Elegant, Professional) for your letterhead, the Fax Wizard gives you a choice of the equivalent fax cover sheet styles—your cover sheet will match your letterhead automatically! If you've tweaked the installed letter template, make the same changes to the fax template for a perfect match.

If you're sending a fax cover sheet with your fax, what should it say? If you use one of the cover sheets that the Fax Wizard offers you, you can enter information about the recipient and the sender, and choose the status of your fax, such as Urgent, or For Review. The following figure shows a completed fax cover, using Word's Contemporary fax cover template.

A floating toolbar appears on your document (or cover sheet, if you're sending one), and when you're ready, click the **Send Fax Now** button. If Microsoft Fax is configured correctly (set to send through the internal fax modem or through the right port to your external modem), you're good to go.

If you're using another fax software program, you follow a similar procedure. You can access the software from your **Start** menu, a desktop icon, or if the software setup enables you to, from within your Office application (**File**, **Send to**, **Fax Recipient**). If you start the Fax Wizard as described previously, you can choose your fax software instead of Microsoft Fax. This activates your fax software, allows you to set up your cover sheet (if you're using one), and lets you enter your recipient information before sending the fax.

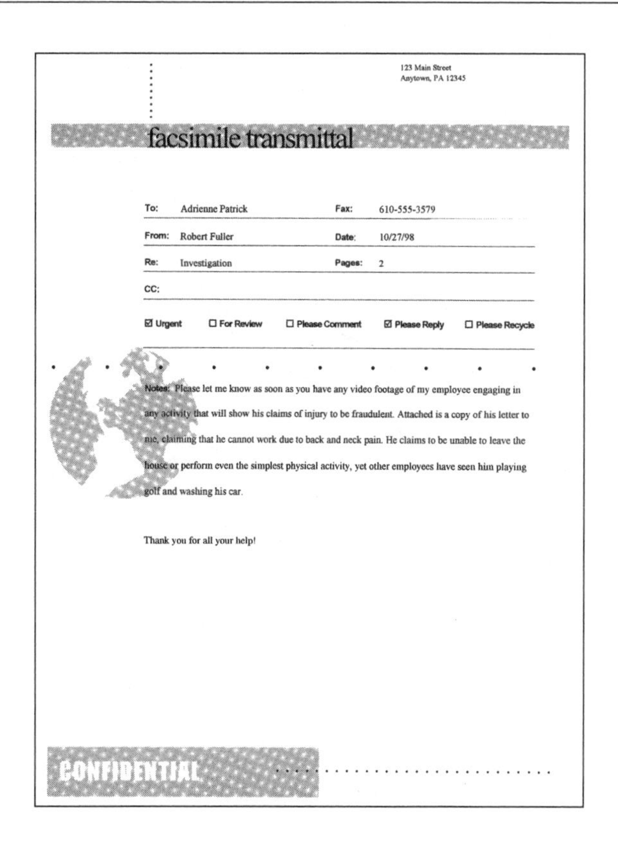
123 Main Street
Anytown, PA 12345

facsimile transmittal

To:	Adrienne Patrick	Fax:	610-555-3579
From:	Robert Fuller	Date:	10/27/98
Re:	Investigation	Pages:	2
CC:			

☒ Urgent ☐ For Review ☐ Please Comment ☒ Please Reply ☐ Please Recycle

Notes: Please let me know as soon as you have any video footage of my employee engaging in any activity that will show his claims of injury to be fraudulent. Attached is a copy of his letter to me, claiming that he cannot work due to back and neck pain. He claims to be unable to leave the house or perform even the simplest physical activity, yet other employees have seen him playing golf and washing his car.

Thank you for all your help!

CONFIDENTIAL

Keep your comments simple, and try not to be redundant with the information in the rest of the fax.

Hard Copy to Follow: Faxing Procedures and Etiquette

Faxing a document enables you to get a résumé, proposal, purchase order, application, or any important document into the hands of the intended recipient in just minutes. It's a good idea, however, to follow up your more important faxes with a hard copy by mail. You can speed up the hard copy's receipt by sending it overnight, using FedEx, UPS, or Express Mail from the post office. Hard copy follow-up is a good idea for two reasons: First, it gives the recipient another nudge—they get to receive your document again, reminding them of you. Second, if the fax doesn't come through clearly or completely, or has been lost at the recipient's office, the hard copy is your second chance to make sure the legible, complete document is received.

Other good ideas for faxing come from your desire to play well with others. You read in Chapter 10, "Email: Getting Connected and Staying in Touch" that sending unwanted email to strangers is called spamming, and that sending nasty messages is called flaming. We don't want to be Spammers or Flamers, and we don't want to be guilty of any similar offenses when it comes to faxing.

When It Absolutely Must Be Legible...

Many companies won't accept faxed invoices, contracts, or proposals. The more important the content of the document, the less likely a fax will be acceptable. This policy protects you, as well. How would you like to send an invoice for $5,000 that appears as $500 when faxed? When a check for $4,500 less that you billed arrives in your mailbox, you'll wish you had used "snail-mail" to send that invoice!

Most of the time, our business faxes are part of the ongoing task of maintaining a quality relationship with someone—a customer, a vendor, or someone else who wants something from us or provides something we need. Don't bite the hand that feeds you! How can faxing become biting? Think about some of these infractions:

- **Sending broadcast faxes to hundreds of recipients, most of whom have no interest in the content** Called junk faxes, pyramid schemers, telemarketing guerillas, and local luncheonettes do it all the time. Do you want to know that you could be making $10,000 a week in the comfort of your own home without a computer? No, I didn't think so.
- **Sending angry or indecent faxes** Even if the recipient deserves to hear how mad you are and see that drawing of what you want to do to him or her, the poor soul who takes it off the fax machine or opens the fax document onscreen doesn't. Remember, too, that anything you put in writing has twice the impact of the spoken word. Not to mention that your fax can be used as evidence against you if you actually do choke the guy.
- **Sending long faxes (10 pages or more) without calling first to see if the fax is wanted or if enough paper is in the fax machine** I once received a 30 page fax that used the last scrap of fax paper in the machine. After that, a fax I was waiting for couldn't be sent because I wasn't home to reload the fax machine. Oh, and don't think that sending to a fax modem makes it okay to send huge faxes. The recipient still has to open and read through the thing before they know its safe to toss it. Your ears will be burning as they curse your name.
- **Sending confidential information via fax** How would you like it if your accountant faxed last year's tax return to your office? If you aren't the only one who grabs stuff off the fax machine or reads incoming faxes on the computer, you won't like it one bit.
- **Sending messy, illegible faxes** If the paper's crumpled, folded more than once, or it's a faded photocopy, don't fax it without testing it (run it through your fax machine in Copy mode first to see how it looks). In some situations the original is unclear and it's the only one you have and you absolutely must fax it. If so, try one of the fine or high resolution modes on your fax machine to improve the output.

- **Sending a fax with no cover sheet** Whether done to save paper or through an innocent oversight, it's still annoying. If you're an eco-terrorist or just a tree-hugger like me, you can save paper while still letting people know who you are. Use those little fax Post-It notes that allow you to write the recipient and sender information on a 3″ × 1″ space note. At least you'll be letting the people at the other end know both whom the fax is for and from. Don't make them read the whole letter to figure it out.
- **Sending an anonymous fax** What did your mom tell you about being sneaky? If you don't want to reveal yourself, chances are the recipient doesn't want the fax in the first place. If your anonymity is accidental, remember to put your data (name, phone, and fax number) on the cover sheet or Post-It note next time.

Some of these infractions only apply to fax machines—sending an illegible fax (due to crumpling or photocopying) is hard to do with a computer-generated fax. You can, however, scan documents and images and then fax them, so if the scanned image is illegible, you can potentially fax something that can't be read easily. At least with a scanner, you probably have software for cleaning up the image.

The bottom line is to apply the Golden Rule when faxing. Fax unto others as you would have them fax unto you.

The Least You Need to Know

- You can use Microsoft Fax, part of Windows 95, to send faxes from your computer. If you want more power than that gives you, or if Windows 98 has rendered MS Fax unusable, you can buy fax software from a variety of manufacturers. These programs are simple to use, and can allow you to schedule your transmissions as well as create a cover sheet to accompany the fax.
- Microsoft Fax can be accessed from Word, Excel, or PowerPoint. The Fax Wizard takes you through the process of entering the names and numbers of your recipients and choosing a cover sheet format.
- People seem to forget many common decencies when faxing. Sending anonymous faxes, long faxes, or faxes that nobody wants in the first place is just the tip of the iceberg.

Part 3

Marketing: Cheaper and Safer Than Skywriting

As soon as you tell someone you're in business, they ask for your card. Got one? Even if you just had 500 of them printed up at the local copy place, you should know that when you run out, there are cheaper and easier ways to make your own. In addition, you can and should be cranking out your own flyers, brochures, and other types of sales and advertising stuff on your computer. You can even build a Web page with Microsoft Office and take advantage of the millions of potential customers on the Internet!

Chapters 12 through 17 show you how to create professional-looking, effective marketing materials on a small business budget, with software you already have. In addition, learn valuable public-relations tips to take advantage of virtually any situation to spread the word about you and your company!

Chapter 12

Keep Moving with Business Stationery

In This Chapter

- Save money by designing your own letterhead
- Make a great entrance with your own customized fax cover sheet
- Create your own business cards, one for each hat you wear

Keep moving with business stationery? Get it? Stationery sounds like stationary, which means to remain still. Like your business might if you don't have the right stationery to make a great impression. Ah, now it all makes sense.

Think about it. Your letterhead gets your marketing foot in someone's door every time they get mail from you—your logo and company name/address is on your preprinted envelopes, or perhaps your return address labels. Your letterhead reminds them of your company name, and hopefully lists your services along with your address and phone number. Never miss an opportunity to remind people who you are and what you do.

Designing stationery yourself is easy with Microsoft Office. Although a fancy graphical logo requires an illustration program, a scanned photo, or other type of image, the process of bringing it all together into documents that will be your letterhead, fax cover sheet, and business cards is simple with Microsoft Word.

Making a Statement with Letterhead

Your letterhead can set the tone for your company as well as your business documents. If you're a stock broker or a lawyer, you'll want a dignified logo and conservative fonts. If you're a landscaper, you'll want something rugged and natural-looking. If you run a night club, you'll want something exciting and cutting edge. Each time you send a letter, you're not just sending whatever information is contained within the text of the letter—you're sending yourself, your company.

Designing your own letterhead takes a long time for some people, because it can be hard to decide which logo you like best, and whether you like it at the top, on the side, or as a watermark, centered on the page. You should also list your services or major product lines, and place them on the page along with your address and phone number. Finding the most aesthetically pleasing place to put them takes some people a long time. It took me a few hours the first time I did it, and I've redesigned my letterhead three times in the eight years I've been in business for myself. The following three figures show a sample letterhead, with the components in different positions—you can see that it's a matter of taste and preference to choose the one that says you.

Go traditional with a centered logo and small fonts.

Technical Documentation – Software Training – Web Design & Hosting

123 Main Street – Anytown, PA 12345 – 215/555-1234 phone – 215/555-2468 fax

- Technical Documentation
- Training
- Web Design & Hosting

123 Main Street – Anytown, PA 12345 – 215/555-1234 phone – 215/555-2468 fax

Go a little wild with a right-aligned logo and bulleted items.

Pretty Fancy…and Fast!

Try buying paper with preprinted designs on it. Add your company name, product/service list, address, and phone number, and you've got instant custom letterhead! Check your local office supply store, or try Paper Direct—they're a great resource for preprinted business papers, and they have matching business cards and envelopes for most of their designs. Call 800-272-7377 for their latest catalog, or check their Web site at **www.paperdirect.com**.

Try a watermark that places a lightly filled copy of your logo behind your letter's content.

Getting Graphic: Adding Your Letterhead Logo

Word is your primary Office tool for the design of your letterhead (except for the actual creation of any complex logo). Start with a blank page, and reduce your top and bottom margins to a half-inch (choose **Page Setup** from the **File** menu, and click the **Margins** tab). This allows you room to place your graphics and text closer to the edge of the paper without having to use the header and footer areas, which can be difficult to work with.

If the graphic for your letterhead needs to be scanned, you can use your scanner with Word (if you're running Word 97 or 2000, choose **Insert**, **Picture**, **From Scanner** to open Microsoft Photo Editor) or the software that you installed with your scanner to capture the image. If you don't have a scanner, go to a copy service (such as Kinko's) and they'll scan the image to a floppy disk for you, assuming it's not copyrighted or you have written permission from the copyright holder to use the image.

To add your logo, choose **Picture** from the **Insert** menu, and choose **From File** from the submenu. Navigate to the folder that contains your logo (stored as a graphic file), and insert it. After the logo is inserted, you can move it and resize it as needed. To move the graphic, click anywhere inside the image to select it, and then drag it to a new location. If you need to make the image bigger or smaller, click the image to select it, and point to any of the four corner handles (the small boxes around the image). When your mouse pointer turns into a two-headed arrow, drag outward to increase the image size, or inward to make it smaller.

If you don't have a logo and don't fancy hiring a graphic designer to create one (or installing an illustration program and trying to create one of your own), use one of Word's many simple tools for adding a graphic image to your letterhead:

- Use the clip art that comes with Office (choose **Insert**, **Picture**, **Clip Art**), selecting one of the images in the Microsoft Clip Art Gallery. The clip art images are organized into categories, allowing you to view them in small groups. You can also see them all in one long scrolling array by choosing **All Categories**. If you want to manipulate the colors of your inserted clip art, display the Picture toolbar and use its tools for changing the color, contrast, and brightness of the image. Convert it to grayscale, black and white, or a watermark by using the **Image Control** button.
- You can also insert a symbol (choose **Insert**, **Symbol**) into a text box, and then increase the font size of the symbol to 72 points or more. For some interesting symbols, try the **Wingdings** or **Dingbats** font libraries. You can also buy fonts on CD-ROM at your local office supply or computer store, some of which are symbol libraries that provide animal, plant, and people shapes. Install these font libraries and then access them through the **Insert, Symbol** command.
- Draw geometric shapes and lines with the **AutoShapes** button on the Drawing toolbar. Use the **Fill Color** tool to apply solid, textured, gradient, and patterned fills to the shapes you draw. The Drawing toolbar also contains tools for rotating an image, inserting a drop shadow, and giving the image a 3D look.

Copyrighted Clip Art?

You can get a lot of clip art on the Web by searching for "clip art" or "computer graphics." When you find a site with clip art to download, be sure that it's not copyrighted before you use it in your letterhead. Not all sites specifically say their images are okay to use, but if the site suggests you use the images in your own work, you're safe to do so. One great site with hundreds of free images is

http://www.barrysclipart.com

Check it out!

Working with Letterhead Text

Adding your text (company name, products/services list, address, phone, and other contact information) is the next step in the process of building your letterhead. Depending on how much text you want to add, you may be faced with a dilemma. You don't want to have so much text that you leave no room for the body text of your letter, but you don't want to skimp on valuable marketing information or make the fonts so small they can't be read easily.

Don't Get Lost in the Translation

Always remember that your letters may be photocopied or faxed by the recipient, or you may need to fax someone a letter. Keep that in mind as you choose fonts, font sizes, and use any intricate designs. Tiny or ornate text and complex images are often lost on a photocopy or fax.

If alignment or placement of your text is a problem (it can be if you want to do much more than type a line of text above or below your logo), you can create text boxes for your information. To add a text box, click the **Text Box** tool on the Drawing toolbar. Drag to draw a rectangle the size you need to contain your text. When you release the mouse after drawing the box, your cursor appears, blinking in the text box.

Type and format the text inside the text box, and then move the text box into position. To create a good layout for your letterhead, try to balance the objects at the top and bottom of your page—if you have a large logo at the top of the page, put most of your text at the bottom of the page to balance it. If you need to align your text boxes and graphics (to center them or line them up across the top or bottom of the page), choose **Align or Distribute** from the **Draw** button on the Drawing toolbar. The following figure shows my letterhead. I used a scanned graphic and then placed my other text in text boxes at the top and bottom of the page.

Never Say Forever: Printing and Saving Letterhead

Although you can save the document as a template for all your new letters, I don't advise it. Why not? The file size for your letters may be huge because of the graphic elements. Also, it can take your printer longer to print your letters because it has to compile the entire image, not just the text. In addition, you have to divide your template into sections so your second and all subsequent pages will only contain page numbers and won't contain the letterhead's graphics and text. This approach requires too much effort and has too many drawbacks.

Instead, print one clean copy of your letterhead on clean white paper and take it to a printer. It shouldn't cost you more than $180 dollars for 200 copies (roughly $.89 per copy on 24 lb. paper), especially if you don't use more than one color. Printing your letterhead in two or three colors can be more expensive, perhaps as high as $300 for 200 copies, if your design requires a lot of setup (complex images with overlapping

Technical Documentatio
Computer Training
Web Design & Hosting

limehat@aol.com
www.limehat.com

123 Main Street - Anytown, PA 1234
215/555-1234 (phone) - 215/555-2468 (fax

A traditional layout with a somewhat larger graphic creates a conservative yet assertive look. At least, that was my intention!

Font Consistency

Try using the same font for your letterhead text, envelope delivery and return addresses, and the body of your documents. This makes everything match, giving your business documents a polished, pulled-together look. To set your default font in Word, choose **Font** from the **Format** menu. Select your font and size, and click the **Default** button. Click **Yes** to confirm that this is to be the new default font for all your new documents.

colors, for example). The quality of the paper can also bump up the price, although 24 lb. paper is perfectly fine for letterhead. Although printing in larger quantities doesn't really reduce the price (per sheet of letterhead), call around to different printers to get a cross section of quotes from small "mom n' pop" places and franchise stores such as Kwik Kopy or Sir Speedy. If your letterhead graphics are complex, it pays to show the printer your original before you ask them to give you a price.

Can Your Original Say, "Cheese!"?

If you use an inkjet or bubble jet printer, your output may not be suitable for use as an original. If you want to create "camera ready" copy (an original suitable for making many copies), take your file on disk to a copy service where you can output to a high-resolution laser printer (preferably 1200 dots per inch).

When deciding how many sheets of letterhead to have printed, base your order on your normal correspondence—don't bump the number up to accommodate any mass mailings you have planned. For your mass mailing, you'll probably want to use a lighter weight paper (to reduce mailing costs) and you may want to include more marketing information on the letterhead itself. Check out Chapter 9, "Mass Hysteria? Marketing with Form Letters" for more information on mass mailings.

If you don't want 200 or more copies (maybe you're not sure you love this letterhead or you don't send that many letters), print 20 to 50 copies on your printer and keep them aside for putting in the printer tray when you're printing a letter.

Create Your Own Fax Coversheet

Just as your letterhead is an opportunity to market yourself each time you send a letter, your fax cover sheet is a chance to remind people who you are and what you do every time you send a fax. A fax cover sheet is largely informative—who the fax is for, who it's from, how many pages it is, and any brief message from the sender. Microsoft Word even comes with a handful of fax coversheet templates that can be customized to include your company name, and with some additional effort, your logo.

To customize an installed template, choose **Open** from the **File** menu, and open the **Templates** folder. Change the **Files of type** to **Document Templates (.dot)**, and open the **Letters and Faxes** folder. Double-click the template you want to customize, and it opens onscreen.

At this point, you can reformat the text, add your company name, and insert your logo—a graphic file, clip art, a symbol, or a drawn AutoShape. Add your marketing text (in text boxes for easy placement), and save the file with the same name. The next time you start a fax cover sheet from this template, your changes will have taken effect.

You may find, however, that the installed templates don't provide enough room for all your marketing content or that the process of customizing them to the extent you require is too much trouble. If you find that you need to customize the installed template beyond simple changes, create your own new template. Your fax cover sheet can be a variation on your letterhead, and with the extra room available (you won't be typing an entire letter on the page), you can add even more information about your company—a slogan, some product or service information, anything to tell the recipient something about your company that he or she may not have known.

Use What You've Got

If you want to create a new version of an existing template (and maybe make minor changes to the template you already have), open the template, make your changes, and then save it with a new name by choosing **Save As** from the **File** menu. You save time by not starting from scratch.

After creating the document (be sure to insert only text that you want to appear on every fax), save it as a template by choosing **Save As** from the **File** menu, and switching the **Save as type** setting to **Document Template (.dot)**. The Templates folder opens, at which point you can double-click the **Letters and Faxes** folder, and name your template. Click **Save** to complete the process. The following figure shows a fax cover sheet created from scratch.

LIMEHAT COMPANY
INC.

TO:	
FAX #:	
PHONE #:	
DATE:	
PAGES:	
FROM:	Laurie Ann Ulrich
	Limehat & Company, Inc.
COMMENTS:	

555 West Avenue - Jenkintown, PA 19117 -
215/555-1234 phone - 215/555-2468 fax - limehat@aol.com

Using a table gives your cover sheet structure, and helps show the user where to put the information.

Store Only the Common Content

When building your fax template, be sure to include only the text you want to appear on all your cover sheets—leave the recipient information, comment, and number of pages boxes blank. If you want to have the date appear automatically, insert the date as a field by choosing **Date and Time** from the **Insert** menu. Choose a date/time format, and make sure to select the **Update automatically** option.

To find out more about the ins and outs of faxing, see Chapter 11, "Just the Fax, Ma'am."

A Business Card for Every You

I drive around with a big fish bowl in the back of my car. I use it at seminars to collect business cards, using a variety of ploys to get people to drop theirs in. Giveaways are the most effective, because everyone wants a free gift. People know their card will be saved and their contact information stored for future sales opportunities, but the chance to win something makes that seem worthwhile.

I give my card to just about anyone I meet in a business or potential business situation. I don't hand them out at parties, but I keep some in my purse in case a business conversation develops. It's a good marketing tactic to hand out as many business cards as you can. The following is a checklist of places your card can be used to advertise your services. (Most of these opportunities are free. If there's a charge, its a small one.)

- ❑ Bulletin boards in stores and businesses where your potential customers shop.
- ❑ Under glass-top tables and countertops in stores, hotels, and restaurants.
- ❑ In church and library newsletters (they photocopy a page-full of business cards, and charge a small fee to cover printing costs).
- ❑ Give them to your hairdresser, your accountant, your plumber, your doctor. Many service and professional people keep a business card file so that they can make referrals.

Be All That You Can Be!

A client of mine has four different cards—one showing him as president of his firm (which he is), and others showing him as a sales rep, the marketing director, and one that lists his job title as "Consultant." Depending on what type of event he's attending or customer he's visiting, he wears different hats, and has a card to match each one. He's not lying when he uses any of the cards—as the owner and only employee of his firm, he really performs all these roles. Having so many different cards would be way too expensive if he were having cards printed for him—creating his own on his laser printer enables him to afford having many different professional personas.

Not all of these sites will be appropriate for your business. If you're an undertaker, it may not be tasteful to ask your doctor to make referrals. If you sell adult videos, the church or library may not want to include your card in its newsletter. Think about where your customers are likely to shop, eat, or stay for the weekend. Will they think its tacky to see your card there? If not, go for it! If you're not sure, ask someone you trust to give you an opinion.

Creating business cards is easy, and can be done with Word. Buy sheets of 10 preperforated business cards, usually sold 25 sheets to a box. In case your calculator isn't on, this is enough to create 250 business cards, and the cost is usually under $20. When shopping for cards, look for terms like "microperf" or "disaperf" on the box to indicate that when separated, the individual cards won't have little tabs along the perforated edge. You want the cleanest edges so it isn't obvious that you printed your own cards.

Depending on the manufacturer, the box of cards may come with instructions for setting up a document to create your cards. If not, or if the instructions don't work or are too difficult (I've encountered both situations), feel free to wing it, measuring the cards and the strip around the edge of the paper, and design your own document from scratch. You'll need to create a table, and its cells should be the same size as the cards. The page margins should match the width of the strip on all four sides of the sheet.

Why use a table? Because you can build one that matches the dimensions of your sheet of cards, making it easy to place the card content within the boundaries of the individual cards. You'll design one card and then copy the content to the remaining nine cells in the table. The figure below shows a sheet of cards, created with a Word table. Each cell in the table is 3.5 inches wide, and 2 inches tall, with a half-inch margin all around.

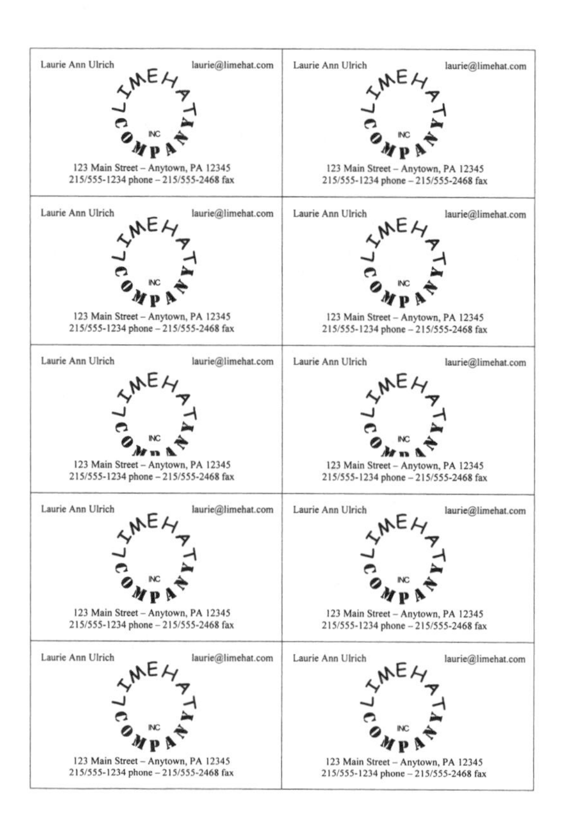

Place your logo and company name on the card, as well as your name and contact information.

You aren't restricted to white or even solid color cards anymore. Several manufacturers make sheets of cards with vivid colors and designs printed on them. All you need to add is your information, and even without a logo, you have a distinctive card. Be prepared, however, to have people recognize the card stock—your customers may shop at the same stores you do! You can also contact Paper Direct at 800-272-7377 for their catalog. They have hundreds of coordinated letterhead, envelope, brochure, and business card selections. Create all your stationery from a single design series, or just buy the cards à la carte!

Fun with Graphics

Placing graphics and paragraph text in table cells can be tricky—it's driven me to tears on several occasions before I discovered this trick. Place your graphics in text boxes that you've drawn inside the table cell, create additional small text boxes for your card text, and move them freely within the cell. Be sure to set the **Wrapping** options for your text boxes to **Tight** so the items can be placed close together.

Double Your Exposure

Don't waste the back of the cards. Set up another table with more information about you and your company—product/service lists, slogans, a short customer testimonial repeated in each cell. Then, before you separate the individual cards, flip them over and send them back through the printer. You'll have a two-sided business card with twice the information!

The Least You Need to Know

- Letterhead presents a marketing opportunity each time you mail a letter. Make sure it creates a good impression, and don't be afraid to include information about your products and your company—just be sure to leave enough room for the letter.
- Fax cover sheets are another chance to get your name and marketing information in front of the customer. Make sure that first sheet that emerges from the fax machine makes a positive statement about you.
- Many business owners wear different hats, performing different jobs and roles in their professional lives. Create inexpensive business cards quickly and easily with Word and a box of preperforated sheets of business cards.

Chapter 13

Printed Matter: Do-It-Yourself Marketing

In This Chapter

- Lay out your documents like a publishing pro
- Use different types of attributes to make a more powerful presentation
- Give your documents visual punch with clip art and digital photographs

A few years ago, before the company was purchased by Adobe Systems, Aldus Corp. got a lot of mileage out of the fact that the Russian government used the company's PageMaker desktop publishing software to produce various documents after the fall of Communism. Although I'm sure that it wasn't desktop publishing that struck the major blow for democracy in the former Soviet Union, desktop publishing (DTP, for short) really has revolutionized the world. Indeed, it's been said that the most amazing aspect of DTP is that it's put such incredible publishing power in the hands of the masses. On the other hand, it's also been said that the worst aspect of DTP is that it has put incredible publishing power in the hands of the masses.

It's true that DTP software—including the publishing features built-in to Microsoft Word—gives you the tools to publish like a pro. But stop and think for a second. It takes more than the right tools to make a beautiful garden grow, doesn't it? The same holds true for DTP. If you don't know what you're doing, the fastest computer and the snazziest DTP software on the planet won't save your DTP projects.

If you're new to the world of desktop publishing, you're probably a little excited at all the possibilities. The problem for many new desktop publishers is that they often become so excited, they try to use every possible desktop publishing gadget there is in every document they create. These documents end up loaded with dozens of fonts, hideous graphics, wild colors, and way too much information. In short, they may as well have "amateur" rubber-stamped across the top.

This version of the document uses about every trick in the book.

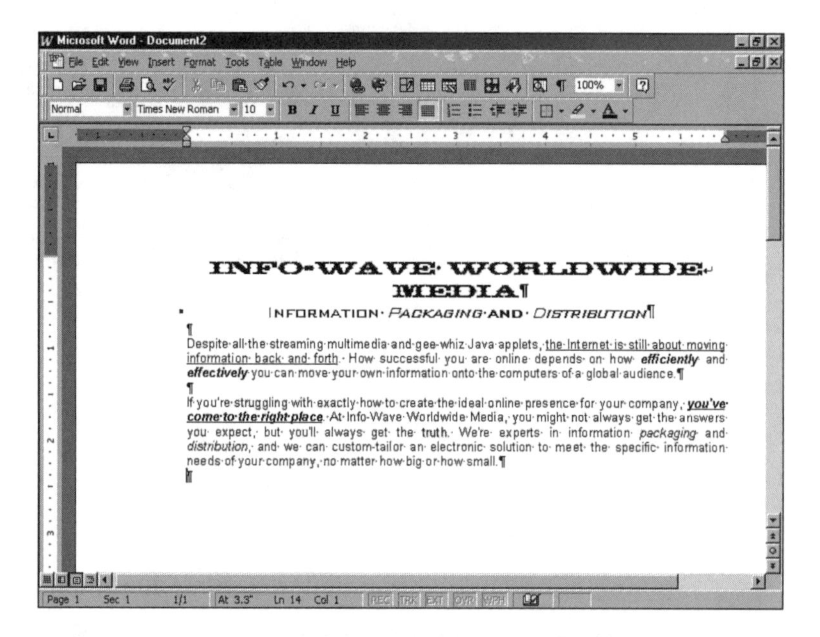

By using fewer special effects, you end up with a more professional look.

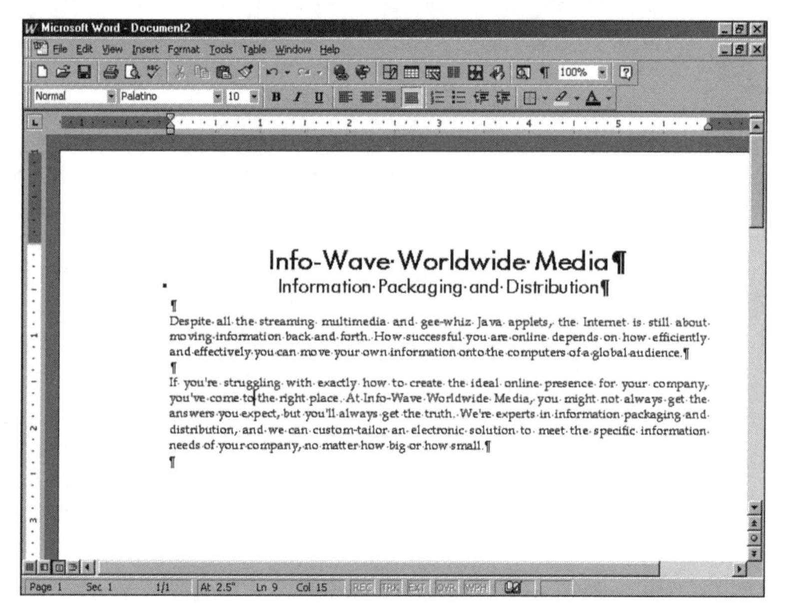

Nobody expects you to be a world-class graphic designer. On the other hand, your prospective clients don't know, nor do they care, whether you created your own brochure or paid a design house $10,000 to do the job. Although each of your DTP projects doesn't have to be a work of digital art, it absolutely must look professional. The good news is that a professional-looking design usually calls for less instead of more. If you don't believe me, just take a look at the preceding figures.

Sure, there's nothing flashy about the document in the second figure. But it beats the heck out of the first figure for a professional look. As the old saying goes, sometimes less is more.

Desktop Publishing Basics

No matter what type of marketing material you're creating—a brochure, flyer, an ad for the yellow pages—you need to realize one thing: The purpose of your marketing materials is not to sell your product or service; their only purpose is to spark interest in your product or service.

This is an important distinction because many new desktop publishers feel they must cram every possible bit of information into every document they create. Take a look at some of the marketing materials you encounter each day. If you study them, you'll realize that the trick is to provide just enough information, but not too much, all the time making sure that the document is also visually pleasing. That may sound like a major feat, but believe me, it's easier than you think.

Any marketing material can be broken down into two basic components: content and form. Content refers to exactly what you have to say—the words and images you choose. Form refers to how you elect to present that content. In other words, form refers to the layout of the document.

Content Do's and Don'ts

As a writer, I naturally believe that the best way to ensure top-notch copy for your marketing materials is to hire a professional copywriter to do the job. On the other hand, as the operator of my own small business, I understand that the budget is usually tight and we're often called upon to wear several hats.

One thing I've learned over the years is that most people are very sensitive about their writing skills, regardless of whether they're actually good writers. In fact, some of the worst writers I've encountered in my lifetime were absolutely convinced of their superior writing skills. This is not to say that if you think you're a good writer, you're not, or that if you're not currently paid to write you couldn't be any good. The point is, if you're interested in producing persuasive marketing materials, there's no room for ego when it comes to your writing skills.

I'm not trying to discourage you from writing your own copy. Instead, I'm trying to drive home what I consider to be the number-one rule of do-it-yourself copy writing:

No matter how good you think you are (or how good you may be—even professional authors have editors!), let someone else read your finished work. The more opinions you can get from friends and family, the better. Be sure to tell them (and mean it) that you want their honest opinions. Remember, you're not trying to appeal to yourself; you're trying to appeal to the world at large.

With that said, here are a few tips to guide you on your quest for perfect copy.

Avoid Flowery Descriptions

This is a classic example of less being more. You may feel that to create compelling copy, you need to use as many adjectives as possible. In fact, I've seen so-called professional copy that falls into this trap. However, in my opinion, you should use as few adjectives as possible and instead focus on the facts.

Think about it. If someone picks up your brochure, they do so because they're looking for information. Too many adjectives detract from the point your trying to make and likely cause the reader to lose interest in a big hurry. Another negative result of using too many adjectives is that you run the risk of looking like you're covering something up or that your product or service isn't worthy of a straightforward, just-the-facts description.

Be Honest

It goes without saying that you should never lie in your marketing materials. However, I'll go one step further and say that you should never even stretch the truth. In almost all instances, doing so eventually backfires.

Remember that consumers are constantly barraged by TV and print ads that lie to them, whether they're selling laundry detergent or a new senator. People are tired of being lied to, and as our society has matured in the glow of that TV, we've become pretty good at sniffing out a liar. If you claim to be "The Best," people don't buy it just because you said so. Everyone thinks they're the best, but by the nature of the word, there can only be one, so it can't possibly be everyone!

Don't Be Too Honest

When you're writing copy, you're not under oath. You have no obligation to tell the truth, the whole truth, and nothing but the truth. In other words, you should never make mention of any of your company's shortcomings.

Some people think that by noting some deficiency in the marketing material—for example, their product is better than ours in this area, but ours is better than their's in this area and that area—they appear more sincere and somehow endear themselves to their prospective customers. Wrong!

I can guarantee that your competitors will be more than happy to point out areas in which their product is better than yours, don't help them along. Instead, focus only on the positive aspects of your product.

Finest? Says Who?

A dear friend of mine (who will kill me upon reading this) records the answering machine messages for both her and her husband's small home-based businesses. In both messages, after the "Thank you for calling the...", she adds, "the finest in...", essentially claiming they're "The Best." I've told her that the person who's calling is already interested so there's no need to brag; no one will assume that she is an unbiased source for this information; and it makes her sound like a carnival shill. Don't get me wrong—they both run thriving businesses, so the self-aggrandizing hasn't hurt either of them. It does sound silly, however, and depending on the type of business you run, this sort of tagline could be a detriment.

Think Like a Customer

The best way to figure out what to write is to put yourself in your prospective customer's shoes. What information would you want to know about a product like yours? What information wouldn't interest you? This can be an important step. Sometimes, when you approach the matter this way, you'll realize that the information you're most anxious to convey isn't necessarily the information the customer is most interested in.

Issue a Call to Action

No matter how powerful and precise your words, you still need to get results. Just knowing about your product isn't enough if readers aren't also left with the idea that they should *do* something. It might be calling your 800 number to talk to a sales representative. It might be visiting your Web site for a free download. Or it might be visiting a local retailer to pick up a copy of your product. Whatever it is you want your prospective customers to do, just make sure you spell it out for them in no uncertain terms. Better yet, tell them they *need* to do it.

Furthermore, instead of just telling them what to do, tell them when to do it, too. Words like "now" and "today" can provide that extra little nudge some people need. Of the following two sentences, which seems more compelling?

"For more information, call 800-555-1234."

"For more information, call 800-555-1234 *today*!"

Adding one extra word to your brochure isn't likely to make or break a sale. On the other hand, every little bit helps.

It's More *How* You Said It...

It's important to remember that different businesses have different styles. If you're a birthday clown, you can be rambunctious, irreverent, and use lots of exclamation points and jumpy text. If you're a stockbroker or a lawyer, however, having "Call Today!" with a big, fat exclamation point at the end might be a bit too chirpy for your audience and their desired impression of you. Like your mother always said, "Don't use that tone of voice with me!" Be careful—use the right tone for the message you're trying to convey.

The ABC's of Layout

A little later in this chapter, I discuss design considerations for both text and graphics. But before I get into the specifics, I want to cover page layout in a more general sense.

If you expect anyone to read your marketing materials, you have to produce documents that look interesting and useful to the reader. In other words, before anyone has a chance to read a single word or identify a single graphic in your document, you have to give the visual impression that your document is worth reading. You have to make people want to read your document with just a single glance.

One of the most powerful design tools you have at your disposal is nothing—just plain, empty space. In publishing lingo, this is called whitespace, even if you happen to be printing on colored paper. This whitespace includes all your page margins, as well as any space you leave between various items on the page.

There's no perfect amount of white space for every document. However, if you don't have enough of it, your documents will looked cramped and cluttered. On the flip side, if you have too much of it, you might come off as frivolous and inefficient.

And of course, you have to consider your particular product. For example, a flyer for an art gallery may make ample use of whitespace, although a flyer for an auto repair center might use considerably less. To see for yourself how whitespace can be used as a design tool, take a look at the next two figures.

High Strung Productions

presents...

Cooking with Compassion

a night of vegetarian and vegan cooking
with world-famous chef *Trevor Constable*

Saturday, January 10, 1999
7 p.m. to 9 p.m.
at the Royal Philadelphian Hotel,
Philadelphia, PA

- Learn to prepare delicious meals with no meat or animal products
- Create healthy meals that will lengthen your life and delight your family and dinner guests!

Call 1-800-555-1234 for information and reservations for this elegant, enlightening, and educational evening.

Nothing is necessarily wrong with this version.

However, this one makes better use of white space.

The key to creating just the right amount of white space in your document is the ability to position different page elements independently of each other. Experiment with different layouts for the major components of your flyer or brochure, whatever the item might be. One good rule of thumb is to keep the "weight" on the page evenly distributed. If you have a large, bright item in the upper-left corner, put either another similarly-sized item in the opposite corner (lower-right), or put a block of text in that spot. Step back from the page and see whether it looks "even"—is your eye drawn to one spot immediately? That's good if that's the key to your ad. If it's just a piece of nonessential clip art you're drawn to, it's not good. You want the layout of your items (text, graphics) to move the readers eye from one important thing to another.

To make this experimentation easier, Microsoft Word lets you move graphics freely around your page. Paragraph text, however, just flows down the page in a linear fashion. If, however, you use the Text Box tool on the Drawing toolbar to create, as the tool name implies, text boxes to house your text, you'll be able to move both your text and graphic elements independently.

Earlier in this chapter, I suggested that you let your friends and associates read your copy before you finalize it. The same goes for your layout. You're not always the best judge of your own work and a second (or third, or fourth) set of eyes can often see little problems you may have missed.

It's Not Stealing, It's Flattery!

Although you'll get in hot water if you try to steal someone else's copyrighted words or graphics for your marketing material, no law exists against borrowing a design idea. I have a friend who keeps a design file. Every time he sees an interesting page design, he puts the document into his design file. Then when he needs to design a new document for his business, he goes to his design file and looks for something that will fit his particular needs. After all, they say that imitation is the sincerest form of flattery.

Working with Type and Color

In the good, old days of the typewriter, you didn't have to worry too much about what you did with your text—because you couldn't do all that much. Today, with programs like Microsoft Word at your disposal, you can do all sorts of crazy things with your text, but that doesn't mean you should. Just to make things easy, I'll start this section with a list of things you *shouldn't* do with text:

- Never capitalize entire words in your document (called all caps). Like email, that is not an accepted way to accentuate a word. You should accentuate words by putting them in italics or boldface.
- Never underline words. Underlining obstructs the decenders of some letters (for example, the part of the "y" that dips below the baseline). Again, the proper way to accentuate words is with italics or boldface.
- Going one step further, in most business documents, never use the Shadow, Outline, Emboss, or Engrave attributes that you find when you select Font from the Format menu in Word—at least not in the body of your document. These special effects may be okay for things like the main heading on a flyer, but that's about it.

- Never use more than one serif and one sans serif font in the same document. A serif font, such as Times New Roman, has little wings at the ends of the letters (the term "serif" comes from the word "seraphim" (angels), and refers to those little wing-like flourishes on the ends of the letters). A sans serif font, such as Arial, doesn't have the little wings ("sans" means "without"). Typically, use the sans serif font for headings and the like, and use the serif font for the document body. Professional designers can get away with extra fonts in their documents, but for the beginning desktop publisher, this is an excellent rule to follow.
- Use no more than two fonts in the same document. Ever had a flyer crammed under your windshield wiper? Most of the ones I get are a riot of fonts and graphics and it takes me five minutes to figure out what the heck they're selling. Not that I usually give it five minutes—I usually wad it up and throw it out—but the key here is to not distract the reader with fonts and other visual stuff. Get to the point, and do it simply. Don't detract from the message with a flashy messenger!
- Never use script fonts or long blocks of italics in the body of your document. These type styles are difficult to read. The more difficult you make your document to read, the more likely it is that someone will refuse to read it. To test your ad's overall legibility, put it down and walk away. Go do something else to get your mind off the ad. Then walk back, pick it up, and read it fast. Do you have to stop and focus? Do you have to read anything twice to get the idea? Did you have to squint or turn your head sideways to read anything? The answers should be "No" to these three questions. If not, back to the drawing board.

Did this list of don'ts scare you? It seems like a lot of things to remember not to do. It is, I guess. But it's easier to start a good marketing piece knowing what you don't want to do. Get all the stuff you shouldn't do out of the way, and concentrate on what you definitely want to say and the impression you really want to make.

And Justification for All

As you create your marketing materials, you have to decide how you want your text aligned. You can have text aligned on the left (sometimes called ragged right), aligned on the right (sometimes called ragged left), centered, or fully justified (meaning both the right and left sides are aligned). All four of these options are available from Word's Formatting toolbar.

According to studies on readability, people find it easier to read text that is left aligned over text that is justified. Apparently, the ragged right margins helps people keep track from line to line. You'll want to restrict your use of centered or right-aligned text—it's harder to read. It can have a visually pleasing affect, so don't rule it out, but use it judiciously.

Coloring Your Words

You can change the color of any text by first highlighting it and then clicking the **Font Color** button. Word lets you choose from 16 different colors for your text.

Just because you can change text color certainly doesn't mean you should. I've seen plenty of people go overboard on the good ship Colored Text. For example, you may be tempted to change every occurrence of your company name to a different color. But why? That's not just me asking the question. Your readers will be thinking the same thing.

Special text effects either make your document better or worse; there's no in between. In this case, a change in text color for no apparent reason only distracts your reader. Instead, use colored text only when it benefits the reader. For example, if your document includes important information on a sale or special service, draw attention to that bit of text by using color. If you use color everywhere, it reduces the effectiveness of color as an attention-grabber.

Feeling Fully Justified?

I just stated that whether you left align or justify your text is up to you. However, there is one exception: if your layout includes narrow columns of text (for example, the tri-fold brochure described in Chapter 14, "Three Folds, No Waiting: Brochures, Flyers, and Print Ads"), you should always use justified text. In those cramped quarters, left-aligned text just doesn't work as well.

A Cool Text Trick

If from my previous suggestions you think I'm steering you toward boring marketing materials, I'm not. I'm trying to save you from creating ads that look homemade, brochures that look too busy, and flyers that would be better used to advertise a circus. Sometimes, however, a snazzy graphic or text that looks cool (rather than sober and professional) has its place. Word has a great tool for creating snazzy graphic text, and it's called WordArt.

Select **Picture** from the **Insert** menu and then select **WordArt**, Microsoft Word displays a palette like the one shown in the next figure. This same feature is available by clicking the **WordArt** button on the Drawing toolbar.

Just Give Me the Highlights

Word's Highlight tool can be used to literally highlight your text as though you're using one of those florescent yellow pens. This highlighter is even better—you get a choice of 15 different colors. Apply it by choosing a color from the palette and then dragging through your text.

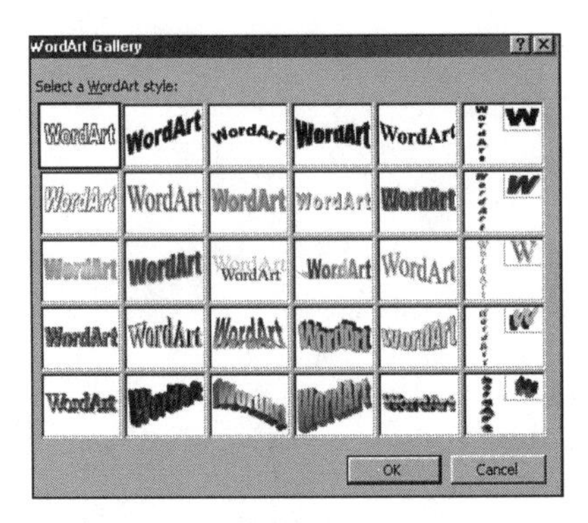

WordArt lets you choose from 30 different styles.

After you select a style, you're given the opportunity to type in your own text. One more mouse click and your text appears as a graphic in the style you selected. While the WordArt is active (selected onscreen), you can use the WordArt program tools to change the style, shape, and text attributes of your WordArt text. You can even rotate it!

An Excel-ent Idea

From time to time, you may discover that you need to use some information you've stored in an Excel worksheet in your marketing materials. Lucky for you and me, it's extremely easy to create a Word table from an Excel worksheet. In fact there are two ways to do it.

The first method is to select the range of cells you want to use by clicking and dragging through the cells in the Excel worksheet that you want to use in your Word document. Then select **Copy** from the **Edit** menu. Next, switch to your Word document and position the cursor where you want to create the table. Finally, select **Paste** from the **Edit** menu and your new table pops right in.

This copying and pasting is cool enough, allowing you to take work you've done in one place and move it to another. I wish I could do that with housecleaning—I'd love to vacuum the bedroom and have the living room be simultaneously cleaned, too. Well, you can realize this dream through Microsoft Office, by linking the stuff you copy to the place where it's pasted. What do I mean by linking it? I mean if you paste some cells from an Excel worksheet into your Word document, you can choose to have any future changes made to those cells in their home in the Excel worksheet reflected in the copy in the Word document.

To create such a link, choose **Paste Special** instead of Paste from the **Edit** menu when you place the copied material in your Word document. In the Paste Special dialog box, click the **Paste Link** button, and you've established your link. From now on, each time you open the Word document, it'll ask you if you want to update the linked table, meaning that if changes have been made to the Excel worksheet, those changes will be updated in the Word document, if you say Yes. (Pretty cool, eh?)

That's Right, Ignore Me

When you add a piece of clip art or a text box to your Word document, your Word paragraph text moves aside to accommodate it. When it comes to WordArt, however, your paragraph text ignores it (or is WordArt ignoring your text?) and the WordArt lands right on top of your paragraph text. To make your text wrap around the WordArt object, right-click it, and choose **Format WordArt** from the shortcut menu. In the dialog box that opens, click the **Wrapping** tab and choose the way you want your Word text to move around the WordArt.

Using Clip Art and Other Images

You don't have to convince me that words are the most important part of your marketing materials. On the other hand, the world would be a pretty boring place if marketing materials were all text and no graphics. Graphics give your marketing materials the visual punch they need to get noticed.

Microsoft Word gives you plenty of ways to insert graphics into your documents. You can insert

- Clip art from Word's built-in Clip Art gallery
- Other graphics that are stored on your hard drive
- Basic shapes called AutoShapes
- Images directly from your scanner
- Charts and graphs using Microsoft Office's built-in charting program
- Charts that you create in Microsoft Excel

The following section explains each one of these options.

Clipping Word's Clip Art

Microsoft Office comes with an okay (but not spectacular) set of clip-art images. These images are stored in the Clip Gallery. To insert one of these images into a Word document, select **Picture** from the **Insert** menu, and click **Clip Art**. If Clip Art isn't listed as an option when you select Picture, that means you didn't install the Clip Gallery when you installed Microsoft Office. If that's the case, you must run the Office setup program to install the Clip Gallery.

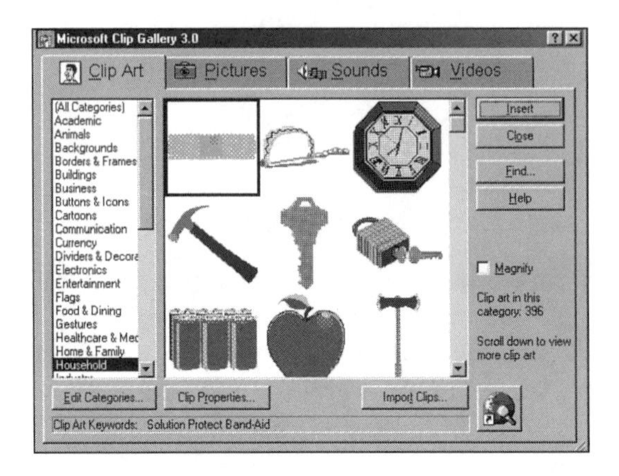

The Clip Gallery includes a wide variety of images.

After you click **Clip Art**, a Clip Gallery window pops up with four tabs: Clip Art, Pictures, Sounds, and Videos. Because you're out to create a printed document, you can skip sounds and videos. Under the Clip Art tab, you'll find images that were drawn or created on a computer; under pictures, you'll find digital photographs. To use one of these images, click it once and then click the **Insert** button, or double-click the image you want to use. The preceding figure shows the Clip Gallery.

Outside Artwork

You don't have to add an image to the Clip Library just to add it to your word document. As long as the graphic resides somewhere on your hard drive, you can get to it by selecting **Picture** from the **Insert** menu and then clicking **From File**. Word can import graphics in any of the following formats:

- Bitmap (BMP)
- JPEG and GIF (the two popular Web (formats)
- Windows Enhanced Metafile and Windows Metafile
- Portable Network Graphics (PNG)
- Tagged Image File (TIF)
- Macintosh PICT
- A variety of other formats

Picture THIS!

The Clip Gallery window includes a button marked Import Clips. Suppose you already have images on your hard drive that you use on a regular basis. To make life easier, you can add these images to the Clip Gallery by clicking the Import Clips button. After you click that button, you're given the opportunity to navigate your hard drive and identify exactly the image you want to add to the Clip Gallery.

Give It a Scan, Man

If you have a TWAIN-compliant scanner attached to your computer, you can bring photographs or drawings right into word by selecting **Picture** from the **Insert** menu and then clicking **From Scanner**. Just don't spend a lot of time trying to figure out what TWAIN stands for, because it doesn't stand for anything. The folks at Hewlett-Packard invented TWAIN—a technology that allows software applications to communicate directly with desktop scanners without launching a separate scanning program—and gave it this name just because it sounds like it should stand for something.

When you use the From Scanner option, Word opens the resulting image in Photo Editor, a little mini-application that allows you to make some basic tweaks to your scanned image. (If From Scanner doesn't appear as an option, it means you didn't install Photo Editor when you installed Office. In that case, you have to go back and install the additional component.) After you finish making your adjustment in Photo Editor and close that application, your retouched photo appears in your Word document.

By the way, you don't have to use Photo Editor. Chances are if you have a scanner, it came with its own scanning software, and you probably installed that software when you set up your scanner. You can use this software to scan and save the image, and then you'll be able to add the image to your Word document using the Picture, From File procedure I talked about earlier in this section.

Automate with AutoShapes

If you need a simple graphic shape like an arrow or flowchart symbol, you probably don't want to hassle with hunting down the appropriate clip art. Word doesn't want you to, either. That's why the program includes a feature called AutoShapes.

Select **Picture** from the **Insert** menu and then click **AutoShapes to bring up** a floating AutoShapes toolbar. (Note that you can also access this feature by clicking the **AutoShapes** button AutoShapes ▾ on the Drawing toolbar.) This floating toolbar allows you to easily create shapes in six basic categories: Lines, Basic Shapes, Block Arrows, Flowchart, Stars and Banners, and Callouts.

Click one of these buttons to display the shapes available for that category. After you select a shape, click and drag the mouse pointer to define the dimensions of the shape. That's all there is to it.

Charting a Course for Graphical Marketing Materials

Charts and graphs can play an important role in your marketing materials. Rather than blather on in paragraph format about important statistics, it's much more effective to present the numbers in a colorful, eye-popping format. When you create your marketing materials in Word, you have two choices for adding charts and graphs.

If you already have the raw data you want to present stored in an Excel worksheet, you can create your chart using Excel's Chart Wizard. After the chart is complete, you can copy and paste it into your Word document.

If you need to create a chart on-the-fly—and you don't have the data stored in an Excel worksheet—you can do so by selecting **Picture** from the **Insert** menu and then clicking **Chart**. If Chart doesn't appear as an option, that means you didn't install the charting program when you installed Office. In this case, you have to go back and custom-install that component using the Office Setup program.

After you click **Chart**, an Excel-like datasheet appears on your screen with some sample data filled in. Just change the sample data to your own data and then close the charting application. The chart you defined appears in your Word document. From there, you can control the type of chart by clicking the **Chart Type** button that appears in the Standard toolbar when you select your new chart.

Understanding Your Printing Options

After you've finished the creative part of your desktop publishing project, you still need to turn your Word file into a printed document. Depending on the nature of your business and your own attention to detail, you may be perfectly happy printing these out on your own printer. However, in doing so, you do make sacrifices.

If you have a laser printer, you can achieve crisp output. On the other hand, if it's a black-and-white laser (and not many of us can afford color lasers) all your colorful graphics will come out as some shade of gray.

Likewise, a color inkjet printer reproduces all those vivid colors on paper, but the overall quality of the output is somewhat less than professional.

The next step up is to go to someplace like Kinko's and have your document output on a color laser printer. Then, at least in the case of Kinko's, you can have color copies of the original made at the same place. When color copiers first showed up on the scene, you could spend as much as $2 for a single copy. Now that the technology has been out for awhile, you should be able to have color copies made for somewhere in the general neighborhood of half a buck each.

Stripe-Tease

Many of the new inkjet printers boast (and some deliver) near-photographic quality color output. This might lead you to believe you can use your color inkjet to produce your color marketing materials. Nope! Unless you want to print out each one of them (all 200 flyers), you'll still have to take the color original you print out somewhere to be copied. So what's the problem? The inkjet printer's stripes of color (created by the back and forth path that the inkjet takes, applying color to your paper), while invisible to you, will stand out to the color copier at Kinko's, and they'll show in the copies.

The Least You Need to Know

- Microsoft Word offers many tools that help you bridge the gap between simple word processing and desktop publishing.
- The key to successful desktop publishing is subtlety. More often than not, you'll end up with a more professional look if you cut back on the number of visual elements. Don't fall in the trap of adding all sorts of extra garbage just because you can.
- Text is the most important part of your marketing materials—both the words you use and the manner in which you choose to present those words. Do whatever you can to ensure that both are top notch.

Chapter 14

Three Folds, No Waiting: Brochures, Flyers, and Print Ads

In This Chapter

- Create an attractive brochure to showcase your company
- Design a flyer guaranteed to attract attention
- Develop your own ads and ad campaigns

A few years ago, a friend of mine told me this story. He was at the grocery store and noticed a flyer from his gardener posted on the community bulletin board. Although the flyer included all the necessary information, it was hand-written—not a professional job by any means.

Well, my friend really liked his gardener, so he decided to do the gardener a favor. He took a copy of the flyer home and, using desktop publishing tools, turned the flyer into a work of art. The next time the gardener came by, my friend proudly presented him with the enhanced version of the flyer. However, my friend didn't get the response he expected.

The gardener politely informed my friend that he had created just such a flyer on his own personal computer, but after deploying it, his amount of new business went *down*. When he returned to the old, crude flyer, business went back up.

The moral of the story, clearly, is that the marketing materials that are appropriate for one type of business may not necessarily be appropriate for another type of business. Although I can't say for sure what was going through the minds of the people who saw the different versions of the gardener's flyer, I can venture a guess.

Most likely those who saw the hand-written flyer were left with the impression that here was a person who concentrated on being a good gardener instead of a flashy marketer. A gardener with a snazzy flyer might be one who spends too much time on his computer and not enough time pruning the hedge. In addition, people like to think of some services (like gardening) as non-technical, sort of homespun or old-fashioned. Good marketing relies on an understanding of the customers' perceptions of reality, which can often be much more important than the actual reality.

The bottom line is that your printed materials must present an image that's consistent with the nature of your business. If you own an auto repair shop, you don't want to produce printed materials with fancy script fonts and flowery graphics. Likewise, a brochure for an upscale caterer wouldn't go over too well if it gave a boring or unsophisticated impression.

Your materials should evoke the feelings that you want your customers to have about you—if you're a lawyer, doctor, or accountant, your materials should look solid, expert, and detail-oriented, making your customers feel safe and secure in your hands. If you're an interior designer, your materials should look sophisticated and creative, so your customers know you've got your finger on the pulse of design trends and that you have good taste, as well. That may seem like a lot to ask of a sheet of paper and some ink, but it's not. Subtle choices you make with regard to words, fonts, colors, and graphics can speak volumes.

Each piece of marketing material that you create should serve one of two primary goals: to convey information about your company as a whole, or to convey information about a particular product or service. I'll refer to the former as image marketing and the latter as product marketing.

Although some of each kind appears in any marketing piece you create, each piece should concentrate on either the image or the product. If you attempt to create a marketing piece that serves more than one purpose, the piece will lose focus and end up boring or confusing the reader. Remember too, that consumers can spot marketing materials that are all flash and no substance—don't underestimate them!

When you're on a tight marketing budget (and who isn't?), it can be tempting to cram a lot of information, ideas, and "message" into a single marketing piece. Don't give in to this temptation. First of all, people hate to read, especially when they didn't ask to read (as you did when you bought this book). If someone picks up your brochure or pries your flyer out from under their windshield wiper, they want to get the key information and a sense of what kind of company you are, with little or no effort. Give them what they want. Some do's and don'ts to keep in mind:

- **Keep text to a minimum** Don't waste your valuable space with lots of paragraphs. Use bulleted lists with short sentences and punchy phrases. Say "We use RepelEX, the most effective stain guard on the market" instead of "Our cleaning staff will apply RepelEX, the most effective stain guard on the market, to your carpets and all upholstered furniture." You don't need to tell them *where* you'll be applying the stuff, if you're a carpet cleaner, they don't think you're going to polish the silver.

- **Keep everybody happy** If you don't have a single "typical" customer, you can either make sure your information is distilled to the points that concern all your potential customers, or break the piece down into sections, one for each type of customer. If you choose the latter option, be brutally brief in your verbiage, and be sure to address the needs of the customers who are in the greatest numbers or who bring in the greatest revenue first (in case people don't read the whole piece).
- **Choose the right type of piece** Does your business need a brochure? If you can tell your story on a single sheet of letter-size paper, probably not. If you have several distinct services and many different types of customers with varied needs, you can't even scratch the surface with a flyer. Think about what you expect a company such as yours to use for marketing. Maybe you need more than one type of marketing piece—a brochure, a flyer, and a print ad, used together or at different times of the year, to complete your marketing picture.

After you've created all your cool materials, read Chapter 15, "Nail It Up or Send It Out? Distributing Information About Your Company" for some ideas on how to get them into your public's hands.

Designing a Snazzy Brochure

A brochure is an ideal tool for either image or product marketing. The question if you're just starting out is: Which one should you create first?

Start with the product brochure first. Of the two—product brochure and image brochure—the product brochure should deliver more of a hard sell. That is, if you only have time to create one or the other, the product brochure is likely to produce more direct results.

No matter what type of brochure you choose to create, or how many different ones you choose to create, it's important to keep a consistent look throughout all your marketing materials and other business documents.

Take a look at the business stationery you created in Chapter 12, "Keep Moving with Business Stationery." To whatever extent possible, you should try to give your brochures the same look and feel. You want to create some sort of visual identity for your business. The goal is that when someone sees one of your printed documents, they recognize it as yours even before they see the name. For example, if you saw the words "Pepsi Cola" printed in a bold, white, script font against a red background, you might think of Coca-Cola before you even had a chance to read the words. You want to create that same type of sight recognition with all your printed materials.

And Shoes to Match!

Chapter 12 discussed preprinted paper, but it's worth mentioning again here. If you purchased preprinted paper for your business cards and letterhead, chances are that the company who produced it also has matching paper designed specifically for various brochure formats. As mentioned in Chapter 12, Paper Direct (800-272-7377 or **www.paperdirect.com**) is a major supplier of such paper. But don't be afraid to shop around at a few larger office supply stores. You may find better deals (but fewer design options) there.

Trifold? Bifold? Building a Brochure

Trifold is the perfect size for a small business brochure. Because it is printed on letter-size paper, it's easy to reproduce. Because it folds down to the size of a letter, it's easy to fit in a business envelope. And because it's such a popular format, it's an easy size for which to find preprinted paper. As I said, it's perfect—almost.

What's a Trifold?

The term "trifold" can be a little misleading. At first glance, you'd think that a trifold brochure has three folds. Wrong! In fact, a trifold brochure has only two folds. The reason it's called a trifold brochure is that the two folds divide the paper into three panels. Take a regular sheet of printer paper, fold it over into three equal parts and you've created a trifold brochure.

For all the positive points of a trifold brochure, they can still be a little confusing to create. The problem is that it can be hard to identify the proper order of information. That's because you can't just flip from one page to the next like you can in a booklet.

Fold a sheet of paper into a trifold and you'll see what I mean. If you attempted to mentally assign a page number to each panel, it would be easy to identify the cover as page 1. But which panel would be page 2 or page 3? In what order is the reader likely to read the various panels?

You can take the guesswork out of this by filling each panel with information according to these simple rules:

- The cover of the trifold, which opens to the left, should contain some sort of simple headline.
- When you open the cover, you see a second panel that opens to the right. Use this panel for information that does not continue on into the inside of the brochure. For example, this panel could be used for a few customer testimonials.

- ➤ After you open that second panel, you see a three-panel spread. This is where you present the bulk of your information. Consider the left panel as page 1, the center as page 2, and the right as page 3. Then just add your information to those three pages.
- ➤ That leaves just one more panel. With the brochure laid out flat, it's the panel in the middle when you flip the brochure over. This is where I usually put the company name and logo, complete contact information (address, phone numbers, Internet addresses), and a copyright notice.

Stick to these guidelines and you're guaranteed not to confuse your readers with the flow of information. The next two figures show a basic trifold layout in Microsoft Word.

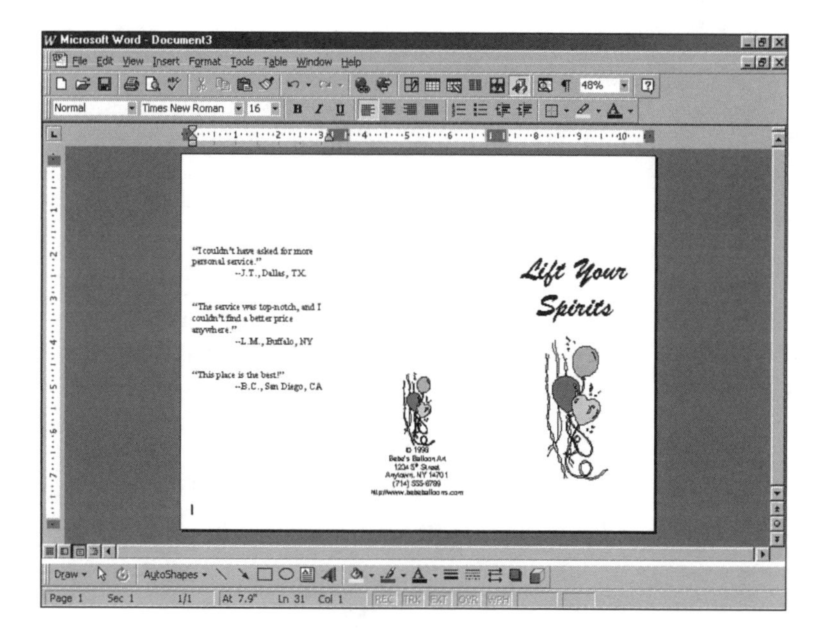

The three outside panels don't contain much information.

I know those figures aren't much in terms of graphical elements. My intent, however, was only to show the basic flow of the layout.

After you figure out how you want your trifold brochure laid out, the trick is to figure out how to pull it all together in Microsoft Word. In a general sense, working on a brochure is just like working on any other document. You type in words, you add graphics, and so on. However, you need to take four important steps to make your trifold brochure happen. Specifically, you need to:

- ➤ Set the correct margins for the document.
- ➤ Change the orientation of the document from portrait to landscape.
- ➤ Split the page up into three columns.
- ➤ Set the correct distance between the columns.

Most of the information goes on the inside.

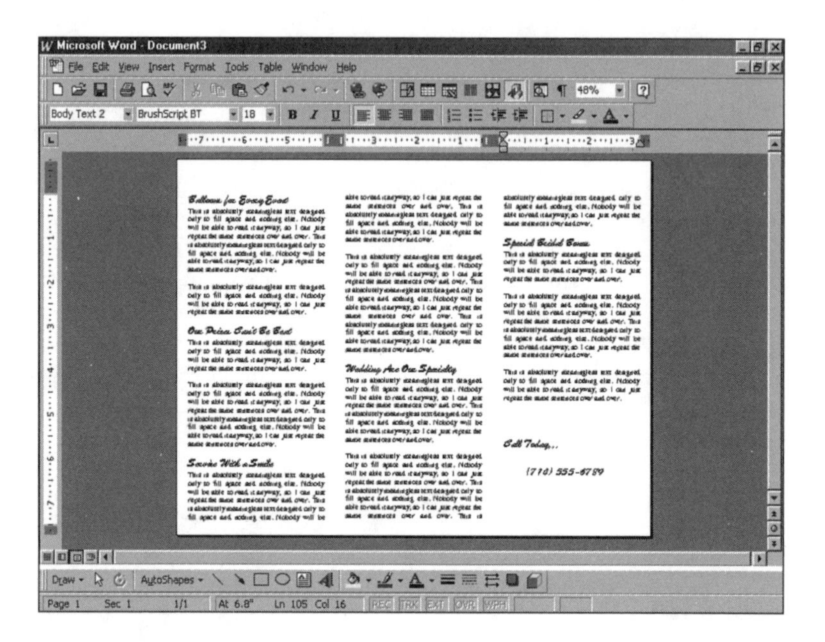

Even though four steps are involved, you only need to go two places to complete them. To set the margins and page orientation, select **Page Setup** from the **File** menu. The Page Setup dialog box appears as shown in the next figure. This dialog box defaults to the Margins tab; to change the page orientation, click the **Paper Size** tab.

After you're done with the margins, click the ***Paper Size*** *tab.*

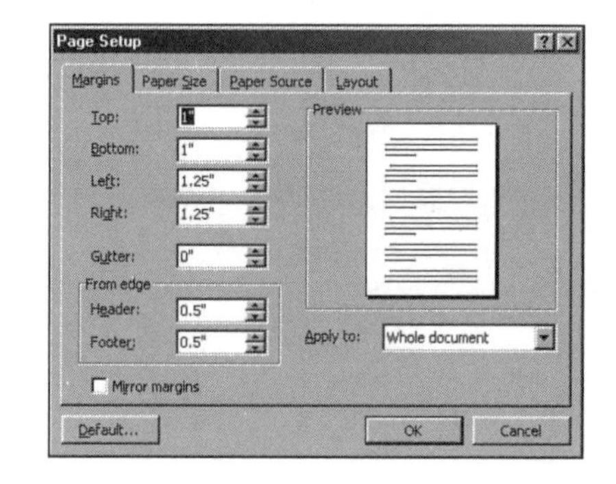

An important thing to remember when you're setting the margins is that you're dealing with tight quarters. You need to think of each panel in the brochure as an individual page—a page that is just a shade over 3 inches wide. That means that setting the margins to, say, 1 inch is way too much. For trifold brochures, I usually use a 1/4-inch or 1/2-inch margin, depending on how much whitespace I want to leave. Also, you should make the top margin about 1/2 inch larger than the others so the brochure looks like it has a little breathing room.

To change the number of columns, select **Columns** from the **Format** menu. The Columns dialog box appears as shown in the next figure. To switch to three columns, click the **Three** icon.

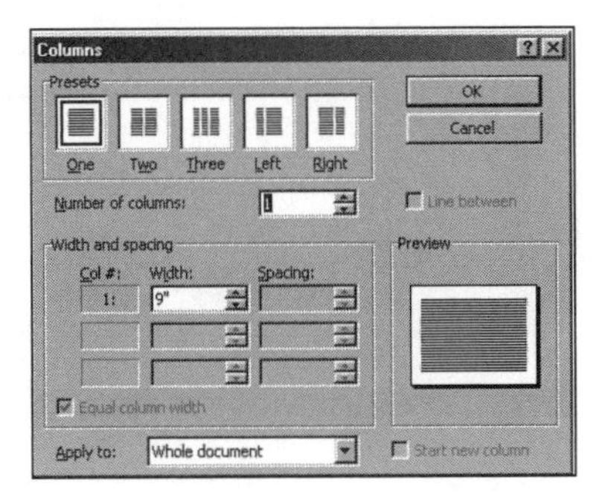

Word puts you in column control.

After you do that, you can accept the default value for column width, but you'll probably need to change the column spacing. To make sure each column is centered in its corresponding brochure panel after you make your folds, the space between columns needs to be twice whatever you set the right and left margins to. If you do that, each fold will run right down the middle between the columns of text on either side of the fold. In other words, each column of text will be centered in its corresponding panel.

The Ragged Right

In Chapter 13, "Printed Matter: Do-It-Yourself Marketing," you learned that whether you use left-aligned or fully justified text is largely a matter of personal choice. However, in the tight confines of a trifold brochure, left-aligned text just isn't as effective as justified text. Because the columns are so narrow, left-aligned text leaves the right side far too ragged. For your trifold brochure, make sure you use justified text.

Creating a Flyer That Soars

You know what happens to a lot of flyers? They get crumpled up and thrown away. Maybe they're turned into a paper airplane first, flown across the room, and then they're tossed. This isn't because flyers don't work as marketing materials, because they do. The reason this happens so often is because most flyers are terrible. Because a flyer is typically intended for a more casual audience than, say, a brochure, people think they can go wild with the design. I see so many bad flyers that I have to believe at least some of the businesses they represent are successful—it is mathematically impossible for every bad flyer I've seen to be the death-warrant for the business it advertises. If you can achieve success with an ugly flyer, all I can say is more power to you!

From a procedural standpoint, there aren't too many special concerns when it comes to creating your flyer in Microsoft Word. As long as you follow the various desktop publishing rules I presented in Chapter 13, you should be able to create a respectable document. However, that means following *all* the rules.

Start with an eye-grabbing, centered headline and maybe a subhead. Then move on to some important bullet points. After that, include any information that's better suited to short paragraph form. See the next figure for an example.

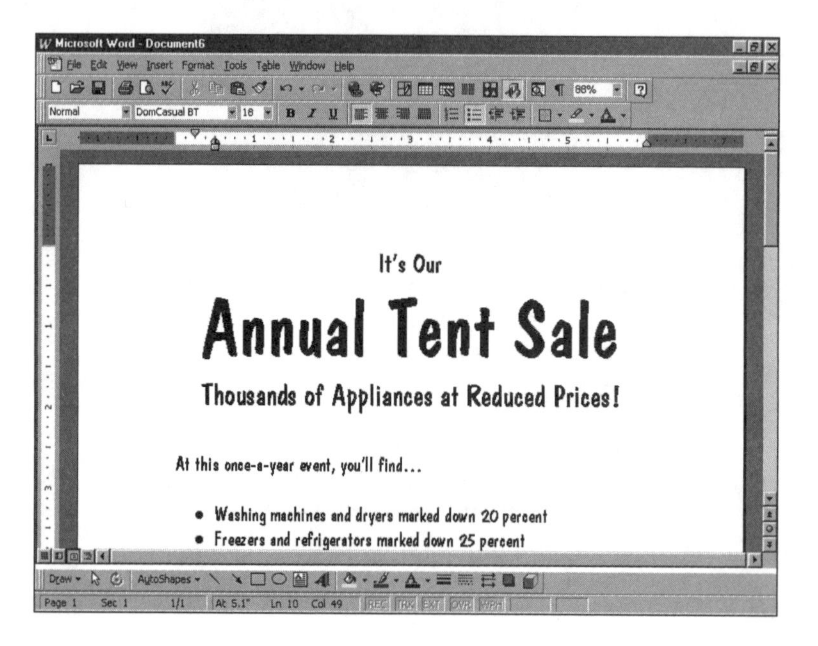

In a flyer, center your initial headlines.

When you're creating a flyer, the one area in which you can usually get away with a little craziness is the fonts. You want to stick with the two-font rule I mentioned in Chapter 13, but when it comes to a flyer, you can be a little more creative when it comes to which fonts you use.

That doesn't mean you don't have to consider readability. No matter what, you don't want to create the body of the flyer in a font that's difficult to read. The freedom of a flyer doesn't give you the go-ahead to advertise your tax accounting seminar with a font that looks like you're inviting people to a carnival. Choose fonts that match the tone people expect from a business such as yours. Because flyers are a bit more casual than brochures, you can choose more relaxed-looking fonts. A popular font to use for casual or "homey" flyers is Dom Casual (what an appropriate name!) or one of its variations. This is the font I used in the previous figure. I used it because it

Fonts, Fonts, and More Fonts

Font names aren't usually very illustrative. If I tell you that "Lucida Sans Unicode" is a great font, you probably won't have any idea what it looks like. To preview your fonts, choose the **Fonts** command from the **Format** menu, and scroll through the list. As you click different fonts, they appear in the Preview window. If you're just "window shopping", click **Cancel** to end the tour.

has a relaxed look and is also easy to read in larger point sizes. If "homey" isn't your style but you want a casual look, try Technical or AvantGarde.

One Microsoft Word feature that can come in particularly handy when you're creating a flyer is borders and shading. Select **Borders and Shading** from the **Format** menu and you're given the option to put a variety of borders around individual paragraphs or your entire document (but not both). You can also shade the background behind individual paragraphs. These tools are handy if you need to set off part of your text from the rest, or if you want to put a frame around your entire flyer.

Copies on the Cheap

People don't expect glossy, high-tech materials from most small businesses, even those in a high-tech industry. For most businesses, photocopied flyers are perfectly acceptable. Instead of wasting the time to print them off yourself or the money to have them printed at a commercial printing shop, print out a clean original and take it to the closest copy shop, such as Kinko's. Depending on what paper you choose, you'll only spend 5–10 cents per copy, and you'll end up with great looking flyers, too.

Your Ad: Speak Volumes in a Quarter Page

For the most part, creating a print advertisement isn't much different from creating a flyer. You have just so much space, and you need to fill it with information about your company. If you can create a decent looking flyer, you can just as easily create a decent looking print advertisement.

From a design standpoint, the big difference is that each publication you advertise in is likely to require slightly different physical dimensions for your ad. After you find out the exact size you need, just select **Page Setup** from the **File** menu and click the **Paper Size** tab. Click the **Margins** tab, and enter margins that leave a printable area equal to your ad's dimensions. For example, if your ad is 4.5 × 5 inches (a typical ad size in a lot of the newspapers and catalogs I have lying around), your top and bottom margins are 3.25, and your left and right margins are 1.75.

Doh! 500 Faded Flyers!

If you're making the copies yourself, do a few test copies first. Make sure the results are good enough before making hundreds of copies, and make sure the machine isn't low on toner—you don't want the last 200 of a 500-copy job to be so faded you can't read them. If you're having someone else (Kinko's, for example) make the copies, leaf through the stack for any losers before you pay for them.

Production can open up a whole new can of worms. Some publications accept what's called "camera-ready art." This means that you can print out your ad on your laser printer and give the hard copy to the publication. They'll handle it from there.

On the other hand, some publications only work with negatives (also called films in the printing biz). Chances are that you don't have the equipment in your home or office to produce your own negatives. That means you have to take your advertisement on disk to a service bureau. In the publishing world, a service bureau is a business that specializes in doing this sort of thing.

If you don't know of any service bureaus near you—and you probably don't if you've never needed such a thing before—check the yellow pages under Computer Graphics or Desktop Publishing. Make sure you call ahead, too. You need to know ahead of time whether they can handle your Microsoft Word file. Not every service bureau has every software package on the market, so you may have to make a couple of calls. In many cases, if they can't work with a standard Word document (.doc format), they can work with a Rich Text Format document (.rtf), and that format saves your formatting and graphics quite nicely.

How Did She Do That?

I figured out my margins by taking the height of the ad and subtracting it from the height of the paper: 11 minus 4.5 is 6.5. 6.5 divided by 2 (for the top and bottom margins) is 3.25. For the left and right margins, I subtracted the ad width from the paper width: 8.5 minus 5 is 3.5. That divided by 2 is 1.75. Got it?

Beyond all the design and production considerations lies one important issue that doesn't have anything to do with computers: In which publications will you run your advertising?

The biggest mistake that I've seen small businesses make is to assume that a lower advertising rate equals a better value for your advertising dollar. That's not the case. You need to remember that the whole purpose of advertising is to increase sales. If you run a cheap ad that doesn't produce more sales, you're just wasting your money.

Before you decide which publications to advertise in, take a look at all your options. See which publications your competitors advertise in. If an ad rep comes along with a deal that seems too good to be true and you observe that none of your competitors advertise in his publication, turn around and run the other way. Your competitors probably don't advertise there for a good reason.

Should Your Fingers Do the Walking?

Don't forget the Yellow Pages™ when you're looking into print ad space. You'll pay a monthly fee for your ad to appear in their book for an entire year (the fee varies around the country, by the size of your ad, and the number of phone books you put it in). You can provide the camera-ready copy for the ad, or use their in-house designers.

On the other hand, if you notice that similar businesses to yours routinely advertise in the same publication, that's probably where you want to be. Even if it means spending a little extra money, these other companies have already proven for you that this is the place to find just the type of customers you're looking for.

If your competitor's advertising choices aren't an option (do they do full-page glossy ads in national magazines?), look for publications that run ads for local businesses that you know are thriving. If the dry cleaner in town runs an ad in the local paper and you can never get a parking place in their lot, try an ad in that same local paper. Also, look for publications that have a good reputation and have been in business for a long time.

The Least You Need to Know

- The trifold brochure is the work horse of small business marketing materials, and it's easy to create in Microsoft Word.
- Flyers need to follow the same basic rules as any other desktop publishing project.
- Spend your advertising dollars wisely. A low price doesn't always equate to a better value.

Chapter 15

Nail It Up or Send It Out? Distributing Information About Your Company

In This Chapter

- Get your company noticed by the masses
- Discover new ways to distribute your marketing materials
- Build a powerful press kit

Marketing your business is more than creating flyers and brochures. If you don't distribute them, they won't do you any good at all. You have many options available to you for not only distributing your marketing materials, but for establishing your name in the minds of the public, and ultimately generating some business:

- **Seminars** Are you an expert at something? Can you demonstrate one of your services? Consider running a seminar at the local library (you normally can use their space for free as long as you don't charge for the seminar) or at a bookstore. If the bookstore sells books on the topic you're discussing, they'll be glad to have you. Call the store and ask to speak to the manager.
- **Community bulletin boards** Nail up a flyer on the bulletin board at your township or city hall's administration building. People coming in to complain about their trash pickup or apply for a passport have nothing to do but read your flyer while they stand in line. Try the bulletin board by the door on the way out

of or in to your grocery store. Remember to ask if it's okay to post something or it will just be taken down by the manager.

- **Piggy-back marketing** Is someone you know hosting an event? Can you slip one of your brochures into their handouts? If your service/product is a good match for theirs, you could get some good coverage. Their inclusion of your materials also works as an endorsement of you, which can't hurt. Some examples: Your friend does accounting, you do computer training. Put out a stack of your flyers at his tax accounting seminar at the local library.
- **Be a booster** Is your local high school about to publish their yearbook? Buy some ad space in the back. Same goes for football programs, handouts at the local craft fair, and church bulletins. Not every venue suits every business. If you have a lingerie store, it's probably not a good idea to run an ad on the back of the Little League schedule. If you mow lawns or paint houses, it's a great place for your ad.

If I Had a Hammer...

Sing with me now! No, nailing up flyers on telephone poles is not a good idea. Would you hire a roofer based on a rain-soaked, soot-stained fluorescent orange page tacked to a pole? Probably not. It looks cheap and it creates pollution (they eventually fall off). Signs on telephone poles, park benches, and pasted to sides of buildings are almost as unsightly as graffiti. Just say no.

More Than Marketing: Public Relations

So you're handing out your brochures at events, you're running an ad in the local paper, your flyers are on the bulletin boards all over town, and a stack of them are available in the vestibule at the library. That's great. I'm sure you also keep a supply of them in a box in your car in case any other opportunities for distribution present themselves. That's wonderful. But that's just scratching the surface. For many businesses, public relations is a real opportunity to spread the word about you and your business.

You might think public relations is only for big companies, but you're wrong. Everyone from disc jockeys to accountants can use some good PR.

Public relations (PR) is probably the least understood and most often overlooked aspect of marketing for small business owners. However, I can't blame the entrepreneurs for this. In a way, it makes sense that small business owners are confused by public relations—for two reasons.

First of all, public relations doesn't typically produce a direct result. Consider what is supposed to happen when you run a magazine ad: You run the ad. Somebody sees it and thinks, gee, I'd like one of those. Then they come to your shop and buy one.

An average PR campaign might result in a sale like this: Somebody is reading an article about your particular field and notices that you're quoted in the article. Then a couple of weeks later, that same person notices that your company is sponsoring a local charity event. A few weeks later, the same person notices your name on a banner and a Little League game. Finally, a few weeks after that, the person realizes a need for your product, remembers seeing your name around somewhere, and makes a visit to your shop or calls your 800 number.

Nearly any business can take advantage of these ideas. The following is a list of some inexpensive, creative, and effective public relations ideas:

- **Rah! Rah! Rah!** A small amount of money will purchase a banner at the local high school football field. Add a patch with your company's logo to the local Little League uniforms by becoming a team sponsor. You don't have to foot the whole bill, just chip in toward some of the costs of the team's operation.
- **Do something good for the soul** Buy a block of ad space in a program for the hospital fundraising dinner. Sponsoring a walker in an AIDS benefit doesn't cost much, and it's a great cause that benefits your company through exposure. Keep the higher motives for such good works foremost in your mind. The benefit to your company should never be your primary goal, nor should you boast about your charitable works. You'll look (and should feel) terrible.
- **Auction your services** You can auction your services at your church or through your local library or other benevolent association such as the Jay-Cees or the Lions Club. The fees go to the cause, but the exposure is yours.

It's a good idea to spread yourself around, give a little here, be seen there. It's not for everyone, but it can make a big difference in the long-term growth of your company.

Impressing with Your Press Kit

So you've found ways to make the public notice you and to market your company to them without spending a lot of money. Great! For some companies, however, this is only marketing to half the target audience. The other half is the press.

Why worry about the press? Because depending on the type of business you're in, you may be able to use their desire for news to your advantage. Local and city papers love to cover local business news. Your goal? Be that news.

The first step in developing relations with the press is to create a press kit. A press kit is a collection of informative materials that you present to members of the press. A basic press kit includes the following:

- A fact sheet of quick facts about your company in a bulleted list, such as contact information, nature of business, key clients, annual revenues, and so on
- A company history

- Brief biographies of the company's principals, which in this case may be just you
- A current press release (discussed in more detail later in this chapter)
- A brochure
- Your business card

Gather all these items together in a presentation folder. If you want to, you can have presentation folders custom-printed with your logos and colors. However, if you're on a tight budget like most small business owners, you can get perfectly respectable glossy presentation folders at your favorite office supply store—and they won't cost you an arm and a leg. Just make sure you look for a folder that has an inside cut to hold your business card.

You should put each of these documents on your company letterhead. Format-wise, all of these are similar—a simple heading and a few paragraphs—with the exception of the fact sheet. As I said, this is a simple list, something like the one shown in the next figure.

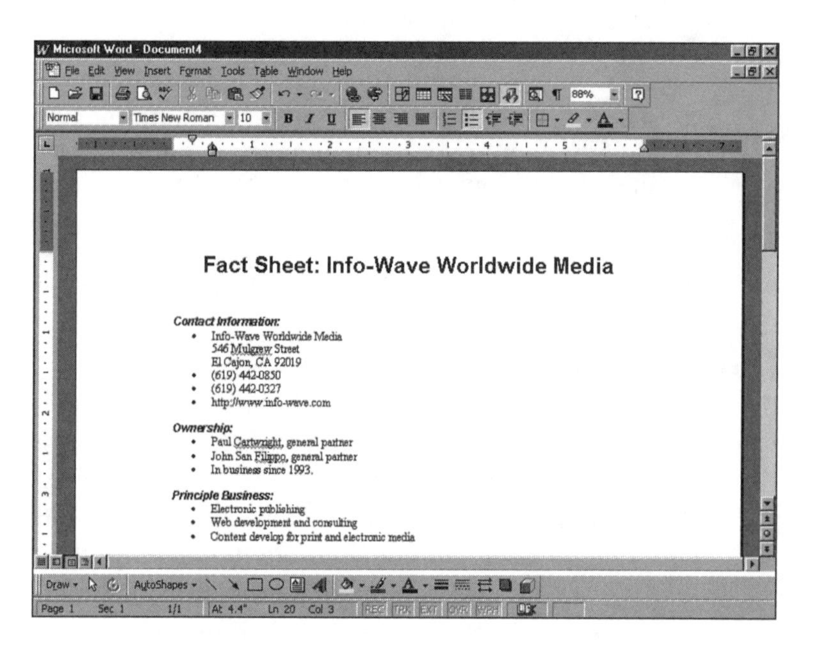

The fact sheet presents your company quickly.

When you send out your press kit you should include a cover letter that introduces you to the recipient. In this letter, you should volunteer your expertise as an interviewee in your particular field should the need arise. You'll be amazed at how many inquiries one little quote in a magazine article can bring to your business.

Braggarts, Boasters, and Name Droppers

Sure it's okay to exaggerate a little—"We cater to the needs of the Fortune 500 company" implies you're in with the A-crowd. In reality, you may have once done a small project for one Fortune 500 firm. As long as you're not technically lying, it's okay to puff yourself up a bit. Just don't pump your press release up with so much air that you risk looking silly if a reporter calls you for some background. You know that sound when a balloon deflates suddenly?

The reason you send out press releases is that you want some reporter who reads it to consider running it as a news item. The reporter doesn't care about how great your company is. He or she wants information that the publication's audience will find useful. That's how you need to approach your press releases. Think about what information will be useful to the people you ultimately want to reach with your press release, and then work backwards from there to write the thing. Your results should resemble the following figure.

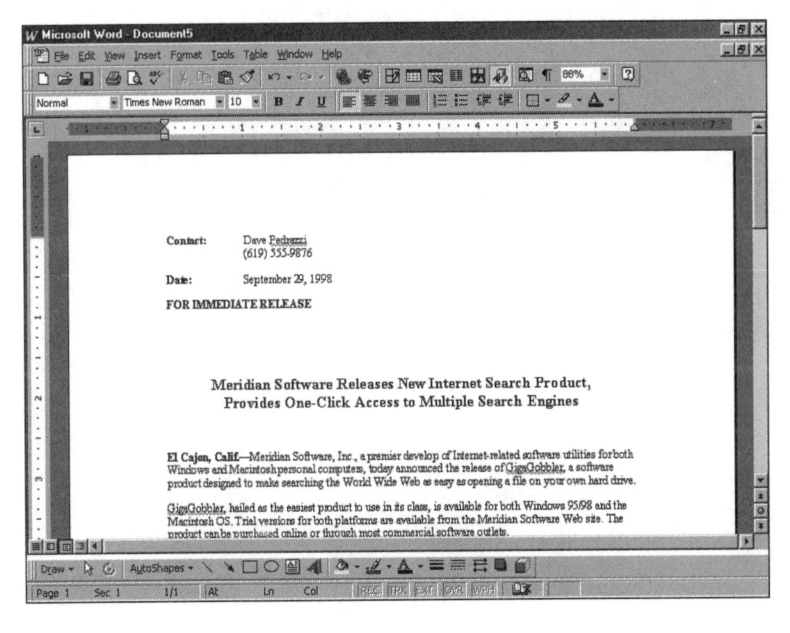

Contact: Dave Pedrazzi
(619) 555-9876

Date: September 29, 1998

FOR IMMEDIATE RELEASE

Meridian Software Releases New Internet Search Product,
Provides One-Click Access to Multiple Search Engines

El Cajon, Calif.—Meridian Software, Inc., a premier develop of Internet-related software utilities for both Windows and Macintosh personal computers, today announced the release of GigaGobbler, a software product designed to make searching the World Wide Web as easy as opening a file on your own hard drive.

GigaGobbler, hailed as the easiest product to use in its class, is available for both Windows 95/98 and the Macintosh OS. Trial versions for both platforms are available from the Meridian Software Web site. The product can be purchased online or through most commercial software outlets.

Be sure to order your information correctly.

Enough About Me. Let's Talk About YOU!

The description of your company requires talking about you, especially if you're the company. Remember to keep the paragraph short. Something like "In business since 1985, WingNut Auto Repair performs both major and minor car repairs for foreign and domestic models. Our mechanics are certified and continuously trained in the latest technology." If your company belongs to any trade or professional organizations, list those in your paragraph. Has anyone important ever said something nice about you? Include a quote. If you or one of your partners or employees have ever won any professional awards, mention that, too.

Storing Styles for Future Use

As you create your first press release, you should create different paragraph styles in Word for each type of paragraph. For example, create one for the heading, and so on. After you've created all your styles, save a copy as a Word template. The next time you need to write a press release, everything is set to go.

Making Sure Your Materials Meet the Press

Now you have a press kit, including your first press release. Now what do you do with them? Well, that depends on the exact nature of your business. It's up to you to decide which publications are likely to be interested in what you have to say.

Newspapers and general business publications are a sure bet. They're always looking for interesting stories on up and coming entrepreneurs. However, while you certainly don't want to ignore these publications, it's possible that the audience you're looking for doesn't read those publications. For example, if you run a carpet cleaning business, you can't be sure that anyone who needs your services is going to read the local business journal.

After you've identified any local, general readership publications, you need to stop and think what types of publications your prospective customers are likely to read. If you're selling directly to consumers, you want to look for consumer publications. Likewise, if you're selling to other businesses, you want to consider the trade publications these businesses are likely to read.

After you have a list of publications, it's time to gather additional information on each one. You need to get the address and phone number for each one, but that's not all. You also want the name of a particular person to whom you can send your press materials.

I can't overstate the importance of this particular point. If you blindly send your press releases to XYZ Magazine to nobody's attention, your materials probably won't even make it out of the mail room. On the other hand, if you put someone's name on the address label, you at least give somebody higher up on the totem pole the chance to throw out your stuff. If your materials are good enough, maybe they won't be thrown out, and they'll end up in an article.

Aw, Don't Be Shy!

Chances are you'll feel a little awkward calling around to these various publications, asking the name of this or that editor. Don't. It happens every day, hundreds of times a day. Publications are used to this sort of inquiry and are usually more than happy to give the requested information. Be sure you ask how to spell the name (is it Brown or Braun?) and note the name of the person who gave you the information, in case you have to call back.

Storing and Using Your Press Contact Information

After you have all the information together on each publication, you should record them all on your computer. The best place to do that is in Microsoft Outlook.

Because you're likely to keep more people than just press contacts stored in Outlook, I recommend you create a separate contacts folder called Press Contacts. This makes it easier to print mailing labels from Microsoft Word when you're ready to send out your press materials (more on that later).

To create a press contacts folder in Outlook, select **New** from the **File** menu, and then select **Folder**. This pops up a Create New Folder dialog box like the one shown in the next figure.

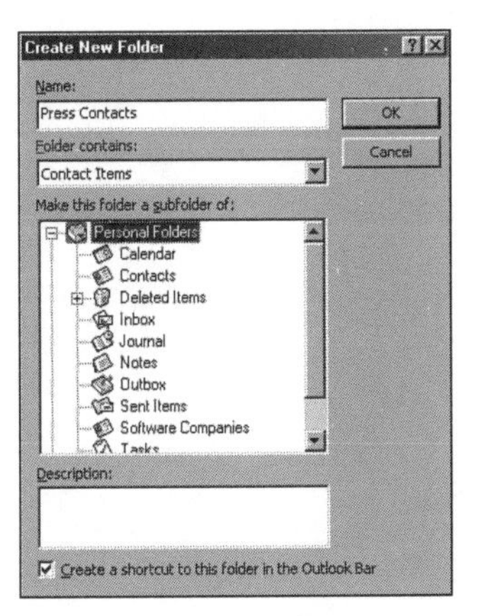

Create a new folder for your press contacts.

In the **Name** field, type **Press Contacts**. For the **Folder contains** field, select **Contact Items** from the pop-up. Then click **Personal Folders** in the folder list so your new folder doesn't appear as a subfolder under one of the others. Finally, click **OK** and Outlook creates your new folder.

Of course, just one more step remains. You need to add all your press contacts to the new folder.

If you're just starting your PR campaign, the first thing you want to do is send a complete press kit—including your first press release—to everyone on your press contacts list. From there on out, just send each one of them a press release as you write them. The key to making this easy is creating cover letters and mailing labels in Word from the names and addresses you have stored in Outlook. This process is called Mail Merge, and you can read all about it in Chapter 9, "Mass Hysteria? Marketing with Form Letters."

The Least You Need to Know

- Marketing doesn't stop with creating the materials. You have to be creative and assertive, finding new ways to get them in the hands of your prospective customers.
- Public relations is an important—but often misunderstood—component of your marketing plan.
- PR opportunities are all around you, and most of them don't cost much.
- Don't underestimate the power of the press to peddle your message.

Chapter 16

Ta Da! Creating a Sales Presentation

In This Chapter

- ➤ Create PowerPoint presentations that get results
- ➤ Add information from other Office documents
- ➤ Give your presentations some multimedia oomph
- ➤ Deliver your presentation in a variety of ways

If you're in the business of selling to consumers, you may never have to make a formal sales presentation. On the other hand, if you sell business-to-business, an effective sales presentation can make the difference between a closed deal and a missed opportunity. The good news is that Microsoft PowerPoint makes it easy to create a great looking sales presentation that you can give on your laptop computer, through 35mm slides, color (or black and white) transparencies, or on paper as handouts.

You'll choose your output method based on cost (35mm slides can be pricey, but look great), location of the presentation (a really large room requires projection through a computer or use of 35mm slides for a visually effective presentation), and personal preference. Some people prefer transparencies because they can transport and reproduce them easily, and they're cheaper to make. They also don't require a laptop or any special equipment to project your video display—you just need an overhead projector.

If you do use a computer and project your monitor's display for the audience, you can also take advantage of PowerPoint's multimedia tools for animation and sound, which may or may not appeal to you and your audience. The remainder of this chapter shows you the do's, don'ts, and things to consider in preparing a presentation and choosing your output method.

Creating a Sales Presentation

Creating the basic presentation in PowerPoint is a simple matter. When you start the PowerPoint program, you're presented with several options, as shown in the next figure.

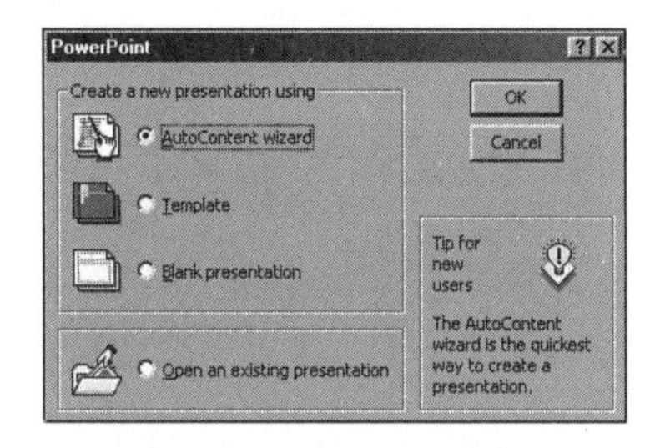

PowerPoint asks you what you want to do.

The program defaults to AutoContent Wizard, which may or may not be what you want. If you want to have PowerPoint ask you questions about the intended message and audience for your presentation and create a presentation for you, filled with instructional text (that you replace with your own text), then click **OK**. After a few seconds, PowerPoint launches the AutoContent Wizard.

When you get to the Presentation Type part of the wizard, the dialog box shown in the following figure appears.

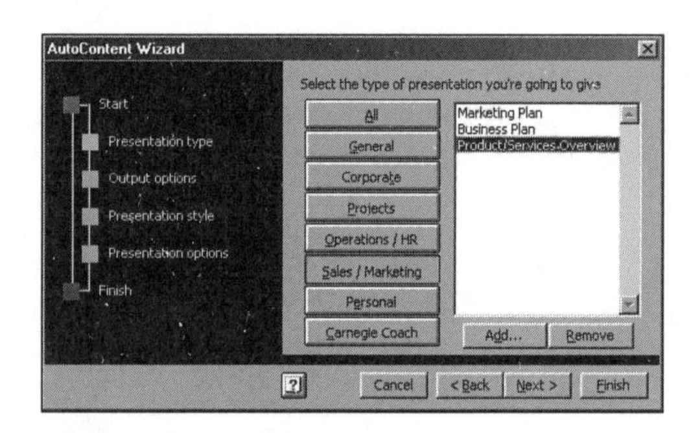

What kind of presentation do you want to create today?

Click the **Sales/Marketing** button and then click **Product/Service Overview** in the list on the right. After that, click the **Next** button until you get to Presentation Style. The following figure shows the dialog box that results.

Handouts: Should you or shouldn't you?

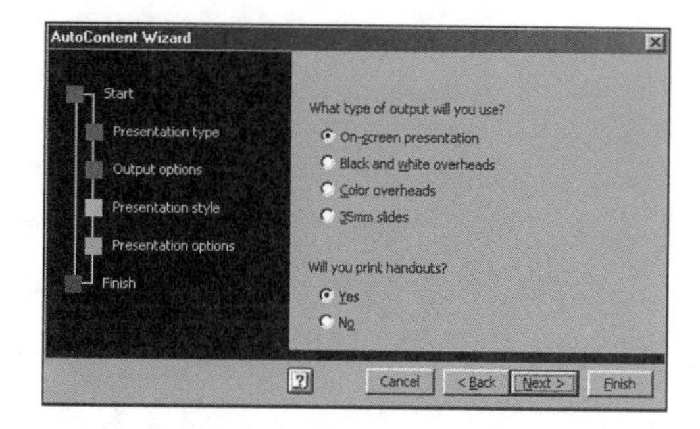

Here you can select the format of the presentation, as well as whether you intend to create handouts.

Give 'Em a Hand... Out!

Although it's up to you whether you create printed handouts, I strongly suggest that you always do. In the few cases where I didn't create handouts, people were invariably disappointed—if their seat didn't afford a great view of the screen, they needed them to follow the presentation. Handouts also extend your marketing opportunity, because the audience can take them back to work/home and potentially show them to others.

Click the **Next** button again and you're given the opportunity to add the name of the presentation, your name, your company name, and any other information you want on the first slide. After you've typed in that information, click the **Finish** button and PowerPoint automatically creates a fill-in-the-blanks sales presentation for you. The presentation looks similar to the one shown in the next figure.

The thumbnail image in the upper-right corner of the screen gives you an idea of what the slide looks like. If you want a different look, choose **Apply Design** from the **Format** menu and select a new design.

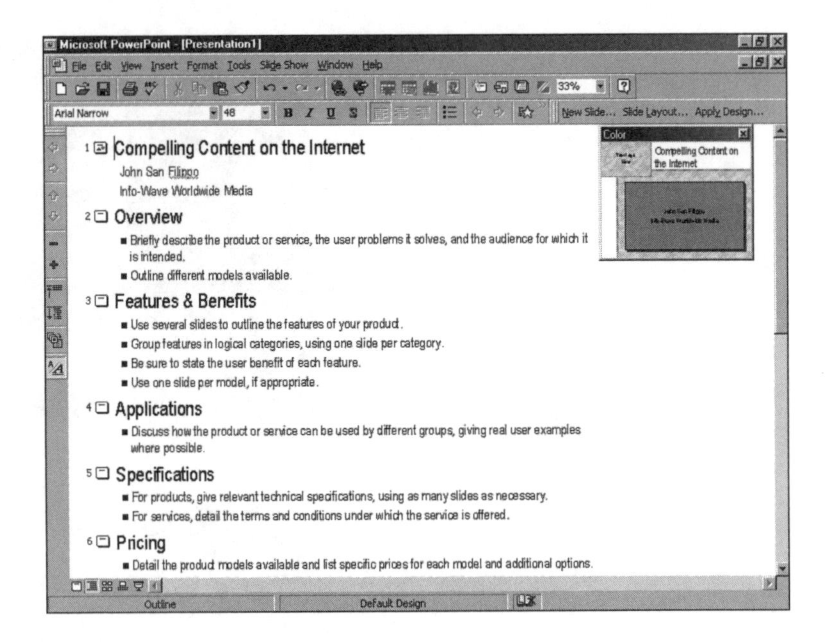

All you need to do is type in the information.

What Goes into a Presentation?

It's your presentation, right? I can share basic guidelines with you, but how you fill in the blanks is up to you. Is your presentation designed to sell? You can sell with an out-and-out sales pitch, with "Buy Now!" as your assertive message. You can also sell in more subtle ways—by doing a presentation that demonstrates a product or service, or trains someone to use your product or service. I once did a mini seminar (including a PowerPoint presentation) at a bookstore on how to build Web pages with Word. I sold 10 of my *Using Word 97* books, and got three new Web-design clients out of the evening. I didn't even tell people my company name, and although my books were on a table nearby, I didn't suggest anyone buy them.

Your goals for the presentation, your knowledge of the audience, the time, place, and duration of the show—all these things have an impact on how you build your presentation and what you put in it. The following list gives you some ideas for how to start your presentation (if you haven't used the AutoContent Wizard or find that the wizard's instructions don't really apply to you):

- Start with a Title slide. PowerPoint defaults to this layout for your first slide. The layout gives you a box for the name of your presentation and your company name. You can always add extra text boxes for your company slogan or the date.
- Follow that slide with a slide that informs the audience what topics will be covered in the presentation. A bullet list slide layout is best for this. Keep your bullet points simple. "Product Demonstration" is much better than "I will show you how the XJ5 works." Short, punchy phrases are much better than whole sentences when it comes to a presentation.

- Keep your topics in the order you listed them on the second what-we're-gonna-talk-about slide. If you shuffle the slides later, make sure to update the list to match.
- End with a Title Only slide, with a simple "Thank You."

Making Your Pitch Effectively

The slides and the content that comes between your first and last slides is up to you—depending on your topic and your message, you may need a lot of text slides or you may be up to your ears in charts and graphics. No matter what your slides contain, keep the following do's and don'ts in mind:

- Keep text to a minimum. I mean in the whole presentation and per slide. In bullet list slides, use no more than four bullet points. You can stretch it to five points if each one is very short.
- It's better to have a lot of slides than slides with a lot on them. People get bored easily, and their eyes will glaze over much faster if they see slides with two or three charts per slide, text boxes all over the place, or six or seven bullet points per slide. In a sales situation, boredom isn't the reaction you're going for, right?
- Let simplicity be your goal. Yes, you're a genius who can create a chart that shows six different types of information and how they all relate to the overall "big picture" of everything. But does your audience understand it at first glance? If you have to explain your chart, it doesn't belong in the presentation. Print it out with explanations on it and add it to your handout.
- Break up text-heavy slides with pictures. If you have two bullet slides in a row, don't follow them with a third slide that has text on it. Throw in a slide that has a photo or a clip-art montage on it. While that slide is onscreen, use the time to pace yourself, ask for questions, or make comments about upcoming slides. People like pictures better than words. Give them pictures whenever you can.
- When doing an organization chart, don't try to put the whole company on the chart if your whole company exceeds 15 people. Better to break the chart into two charts (on two slides) than to end up with tiny boxes with tiny text in them.
- Show the presentation on a large monitor or project it onto a wall or screen rather than showing it with transparencies or slides. The animation and sound you can add to an onscreen show will keep audience attention, unlike the sight of you flipping transparencies on and off the projector. If you use a large monitor, make sure it's large enough for everyone to see, and that glare is reduced or eliminated.
- Use color! Don't create a circus of color (stick with the templates and their prescribed color schemes to avoid clashing or too many colors per slide), but use it. Black and white is boring. If you must use transparencies, do them in color. If you don't have a color printer, take your presentation to Kinko's to have them printed.

- Rehearse thoroughly. You don't have to be perfect, but a lot of stammering and the appearance that you don't know which slide is coming next will make you look like you're either not confident in yourself or your product, or both.
- Move, but not too much. If you're in charge of moving from slide to slide (clicking the mouse or pressing keys), move around a bit by the table or podium, just to avoid looking like a talking mannequin. If you can, walk with the mouse in your hand, and click the button that way. You're on a leash (the length of the mouse cord), but you're more mobile.

With these ideas and suggestions in mind, you can avoid an amateurish presentation and feel more confident that you'll look like a professional. If you're not too crazy about public speaking, the knowledge that your presentation is well done will take that pressure off your shoulders!

Size Does Matter!

Remember how I said not to cram too much onto each slide? This means you have to be careful not to select too large a cell range in Excel or too large a table in Word for pasting onto a single slide. If you have a lot of Excel data or Word text to bring in, break it up over a few slides so you don't crowd any of the slides with too much data.

Adding Other Goodies

Office makes it easy to bring in pieces of text, numbers, and graphic content from other Office files and add them to your presentation. You can use Word text and tables and Excel worksheet cells and charts in your PowerPoint show, enhancing your presentation and reducing the amount of work that goes into putting it all together. If the content exists elsewhere, why not use it? Don't reinvent the wheel.

Suppose, for example, that you've stored your previous year's sales results in an Excel spreadsheet and want to make that information part of your presentation. The whole operation is as easy as copying from your Excel worksheet and pasting onto one of your PowerPoint slides.

If you want to use raw data, you can copy and paste a range of cells from your worksheet. When you paste onto your PowerPoint slide, the information shows up as a simple table that you can size and move at will. If you want to present the information in chart format, create the chart in Excel. Then copy and paste it into PowerPoint. Pretty easy, eh?

More Pie? Charting Your Numbers

A picture's worth a thousand words, right? Well, trust me, a chart is worth a million numbers. The word "numb" is right there in the word, and numbers can be mind-numbing, even to accountants and others who eat, sleep, and drink them.

When at all possible, show your numbers in the form of a chart. Don't list the sales of your product or the quantities sold in a table—turn the data into a chart! A nice colorful chart (a chart that's easy to interpret) is like that spoonful of sugar that Mary Poppins said makes the medicine go down. Show trends in sales or productivity, compare divisions, products, and people. Display the results of a survey. If you use a chart to show the numbers, people won't go to sleep, and they'll get the "picture"—the message your numbers are meant to convey—must faster.

The following figures show just what I mean. The first slide contains a lot of numbers. The second slide has turned those numbers into a chart. Which would you rather look at? More importantly, which would you rather stand up and talk about?

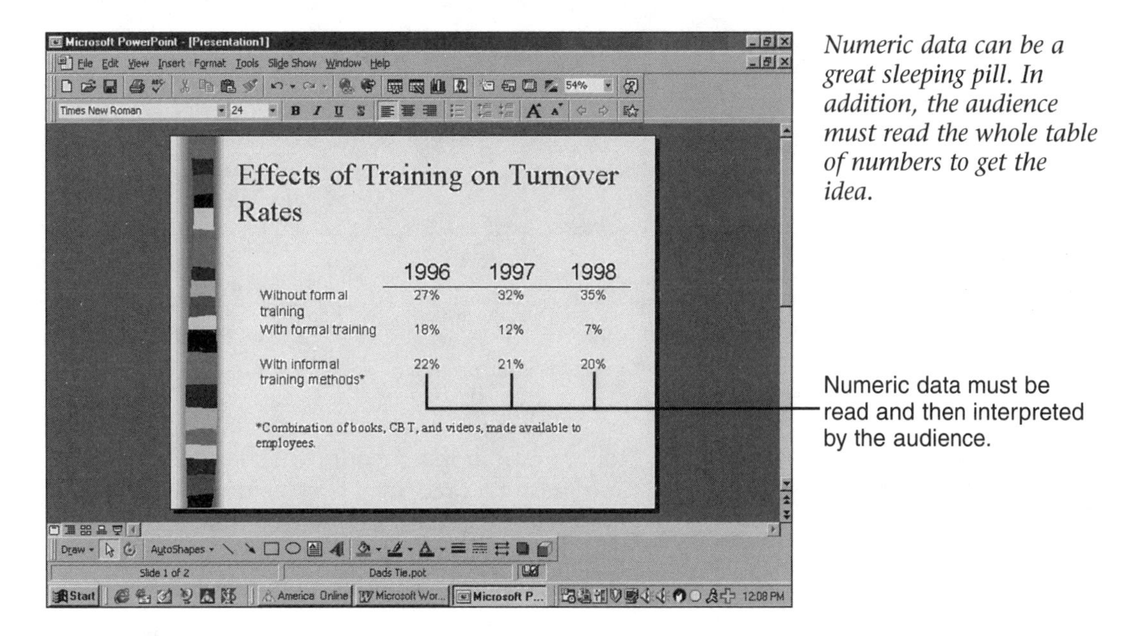

Numeric data can be a great sleeping pill. In addition, the audience must read the whole table of numbers to get the idea.

Numeric data must be read and then interpreted by the audience.

Lights! Camera! Action! Creating a Multimedia Event

Sound and animation can keep your audience riveted, and give a high-tech, creative feel to your presentation. The multimedia features of PowerPoint are the main reason that you should show your presentation onscreen rather than on 35mm slides or transparencies. You can, however, go overboard. For first-timers, the temptation is great to apply sound to every bullet point and graphic image that slides, pops, fades, or jumps onto your slide. Don't do it. Use one or two multimedia effects per slide—animate your title *or* your bullet points, not both. Use a sound when a graphic appears onscreen, but not as the slide moves off and transitions into the next slide. Be discreet, be subtle.

A chart shows the same data in a colorful way, and it's easy to see the overall idea, at a glance.

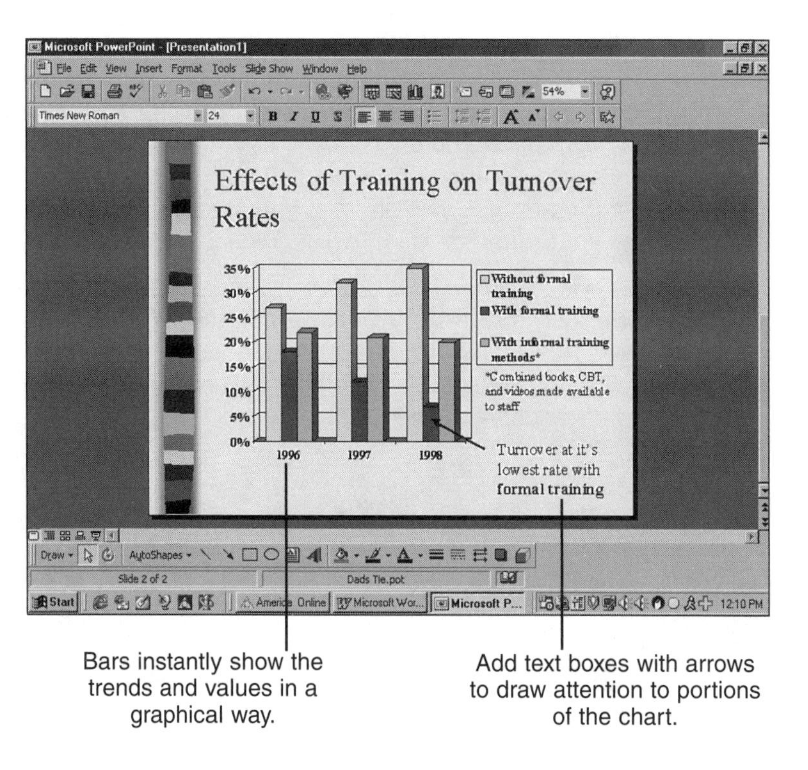

Bars instantly show the trends and values in a graphical way.

Add text boxes with arrows to draw attention to portions of the chart.

Data Sources

I already mentioned that if your data already exists in Excel, bring it over to PowerPoint rather than retype it. The same goes for a chart. If you already built one in Excel, copy and paste it into your PowerPoint slide. You can also use Excel data to fill the PowerPoint Datasheet and then build a chart with PowerPoint's charting tools.

In addition to PowerPoint's animation and sound tools, you can insert your own sound files (.wav and .midi files recorded by you, downloaded from the Web, or purchased on CD) and add videos to your presentation. Video is especially useful in training or demonstration presentations.

To add sound and video to your presentation, go to the slide where you want the event to occur, and choose **Movies and Sounds** from the **Insert** menu. The inserted sound or video appears as an icon on your slide, and you can position it anywhere (hopefully in a corner, out of plain sight) and resize it as needed. When that slide comes up in your presentation, double-click the icon to play the sound or video.

Squish! It's a QuickTime Movie

Movie files that end with the .mov extension were created with Apple's QuickTime technology. Although these movies can be created on both Windows and Macintosh computers, you need to be careful if you're using a QuickTime movie that was created on a Mac. Before the file is transferred to your Windows PC, it must be "flattened" on the Macintosh. This is a process that removes extra information from the file that can only be used by Macintosh computers. If you're getting a QuickTime movie from a Mac user, make sure you ask them to flatten it first.

Making Your Plea

You have the presentation done. You've printed the handouts and speaker notes. You have all the software you need loaded on to your laptop. Now all you have to do is give the thing. That's the hardest part of all. To make it a little easier, here's a list of important things to remember:

- Practice! Run through the presentation repeatedly until your familiar with the content and feel comfortable with the order of topics. Make some notes for questions you anticipate from the audience and allow time for them. Having some bright answers ready is a good idea, too.
- If you're presenting from your laptop, make sure you have both PowerPoint and a copy of your presentation loaded on your laptop.
- Arrive early so you can set up your equipment, make sure it all works, and still have time to take action if it doesn't.

Action!

You can also set timings for your presentation (the show itself and all the events that occur on your slides) so the presentation can run on its own. Choose **Custom Animation** from the **Slide Show** menu, and choose the **Timing and Play Settings** for the selected multimedia icon.

- If you still have time, run through the entire presentation with nobody in the room. You'll get a feel for the location, and it will make you more comfortable.
- If you're presenting to a small group—say 20 or fewer people—invite questions during the presentation. This can make the atmosphere more intimate. However, if you're presenting to a larger group, ask that questions be held until the end of the presentation. With a larger group, one question can lead to another and quickly steer you off course.
- When something goes wrong—and it will—don't get flustered. People understand that sometimes even the most well planned presentations hit a snag for one reason or another. However, you'll come off like a rank amateur if you let one little mishap blow the whole show.
- Be yourself. Some people tell you to always open a presentation with some humor. However, if you're not a natural joke teller, this could set the whole presentation off on the wrong foot.
- Keep an even pace. Listen to your own voice as you're talking. If you're talking like an auctioneer, slow down. Nervousness makes people talk faster, and at a higher pitch, because your throat tightens. Concentrate (if you're panicked about public speaking) on keeping a normal pace—the pace at which you talk in a meeting where you're comfortable holding the floor for a bit.
- Don't give in to rude people. Is someone chatting with the people around them? Try a little humor. As a woman, I can get away with "Do you have something to share with the class?" in a school-marmish tone, and people always laugh. If that's not you, try something good natured, but to the point. If you can't think of anything, ignore them.

Whatever You Do, Don't Start with a Joke

Unless you've done it a few times, presenting to even a small group can be more than a little frightening. If you're not comfortable with the idea of public speaking, you might consider checking the phone book for the local chapter of Toastmasters, International. This is an international group (as the name implies) that is devoted to self-enrichment through public speaking. Self-help organizations aren't for everyone, but if giving presentations paralyzes you and you *must* do them, it's worth finding a solution to your anxiety.

There Even When You Can't Be

Sometimes you may want your presentation to make the trip without you. For example, if you're in Baltimore and you have a prospective client in San Jose, it may not be feasible for you to fly cross-country to give a 20-minute presentation.

If this is the case, I suggest that you consider investing in a CD-ROM recorder. This is a device that can copy your information onto a CD-ROM that can then be used on any other CD-ROM-equipped personal computer. Hence, you can easily copy your sales presentation onto a CD and mail it off to San Jose.

Don't, however, make the mistake of sending that client your standard sales presentation—the one that normally includes you live and in person discussing the topics on each slide. Because you can't be there to give the presentation, you're going to have to create an alternate version that goes into a little more detail. Although it may not be practical to add every tidbit that you cover in your verbal presentation, you do need to add enough extra information to spark the customer's interest and answer most of the questions they're likely to have.

How can you be sure the people in San Jose have PowerPoint on their computers so they can see your presentation? Happily, they don't have to. This is where the PowerPoint Viewer comes in.

The PowerPoint Viewer is a standalone application that allows anyone running Windows 95/98 to view a PowerPoint presentation. (In fact, the Macintosh version lets Mac users view your presentation.) You're free to distribute this application on the same CD as your presentation so you never have to worry about who has the right software. A copy of the PowerPoint Viewer is in the ValuePack folder on your Office CD. However, you can find a more current version ready for download on the Microsoft Web site.

Another option for long-distance presenting is posting your entire presentation on the World Wide Web. This topic is covered in greater detail in Chapter 17, "Should You Weave a Web (Page)?"

The Least You Need to Know

- Creating a great looking sales presentation takes only a few mouse clicks in PowerPoint.
- Your PowerPoint presentation should serve as an outline—not the entire presentation.
- It's easy to add other elements to your PowerPoint presentation.
- Something will inevitably go wrong; don't sweat it.
- If you have a CD-ROM recorder, your presentation can go places where you can't.

Chapter 17

Should You Weave a Web (Page)?

In This Chapter

- ➤ Decide whether the Web is right for you
- ➤ Turn your office documents into Web pages
- ➤ Find additional tools to enhance your Web creation efforts
- ➤ Put your Web site online for the world to see

As someone who derives a large portion of income from the Internet and Web-related work, my short answer to the question posed in this chapter title is *yes*, you should have your own place in cyberspace. Maybe you're thinking that you run a relatively low-tech business, so why in the world should you be on the Web? A few years ago, you might have had a good point. Then, the only people on the Internet were... well, computer geeks. Today, however, the Web isn't just for geeks.

Stop and think about the demographics of the Web. According to survey after survey, the typical Web user has an above average education and an above average income, and statistics show that over 41 million users are surfing the Net on a regular basis. Who knew there were 41 million above average people in the world? Any business would do well to tap this resource.

What's more, these people are increasingly likely to turn to the Web, say instead of the yellow pages, when they're looking for a business. They may not always find what they're looking for on the Web, but they look there first. So if you happen to be the only dog grooming service in town with a Web page, you're likely to generate some business from cyberspace.

Perhaps you're wondering how you can justify the cost of a Web page. What cost? You have an Internet account, right? (If you don't, you should.) Today it's not uncommon for Internet service providers (ISPs) and online communities (such as AOL and CompuServe) to include with your account a few megabytes of space on their service to put your own Web page. If your ISP doesn't, maybe it's time to go shopping for a new ISP.

Now, I'm not trying to say that if you run a dog grooming service or a delicatessen that putting up a Web page should be your top priority. On the other hand, if you have a little spare time to fiddle around on your computer, creating a Web page can be fun, educational, and profitable.

The Ways of the Web

Just to make sure everybody's on the same page—no pun intended—I'm going to start this chapter with some basic Web facts that every person should know.

- The World Wide Web (most commonly called the Web these days) is *part* of the Internet, it is not the entire Internet. The Web uses the Internet (a global network of computers called servers) to store Web pages and transfer data from these servers (some of which are Web servers) to computers like yours.
- Two aspects of the Web make it different from most other Internet-based services such as email: First, the Web is based on hypertext. That means a simple mouse click on a hyperlink (a word, phrase, or graphic designated as hypertext) on one Web page can take you to an entirely different Web page on the other side of the world. Second, the Web is graphical. Before the Web, the entire Internet was text-based.
- A company's Web address is called its URL. (Pronounced either U-R-L or "earl.") This stands for Universal Resource Locator.
- A company's domain name is the part of the URL that normally comes after the www (World Wide Web) part. For example, Macmillan Computer Publishing's domain is mcp.com, and their full Web address (URL) is **www.mcp.com**.

When you're setting up shop in cyberspace, you have two choices for your URL. The cheapest option is to use your ISP's domain name. For example, suppose your company name is Acme Appliance and your ISP's domain name is sandiego.com. Your URL might end up looking something like this: **http://www.sandiego.com/~acmeappliance**.

This is all fine and dandy—unless you later decide to switch ISPs. Then your URL changes, too. Using the ISP's domain as part of your page's URL also makes for a really long address for Web surfers to type. Would you rather type **www.ispdomain.com/mydomain** or **www.mydomain.com**?

To avoid these problems, you can register your own domain name. Two sets of fees are generally required for registering. First, the company on whose Web server you're "renting" space charges a fee, anywhere from $50 to $250 per year. This range of fees is wide, as is the range of services these firms offer. If you just want the space and no help, no design assistance, no maintenance, no email addresses, the lowest rate will apply. The more help or extra services you want, the higher the yearly rate. Second, you must pay the InterNIC (the company that has the contract to manage domain names in this country) $70 every other year.

Mine, Mine, Mine

Some of the firms that rent Web server space (also known as Web hosting) offer to register your domain name for you, and include the costs payable to the InterNIC in your fees. Don't jump at this—it's better if you pay the InterNIC directly, because you'll own your domain name outright. If you switch hosting firms, you can easily take your own domain name with you.

All Web pages are made up of Hypertext Markup Language (HTML) code. This is a simple text coding system that allows for various formatting options. Web browsers, such as Microsoft Internet Explorer and Netscape Navigator, know how to interpret this code and can display your Web pages correctly.

In the early days, you had to know the various HTML codes and had to create your Web pages by typing all the code in a word processor or text editor. Today even the most rudimentary Web authoring programs create all the code for you. With the right software (such as Microsoft Word) you can make highly sophisticated Web pages without knowing any HTML at all.

Webifying Your Office Documents

Word, Excel, and PowerPoint all have built-in tools to help you create your Web pages. Each is a little different, so they are covered individually in this chapter.

[Yawn] Too Much Text!

Not all Word documents are good candidates for being converted to Web pages. Web pages should have mostly graphics, and very little paragraph text. Text should appear in lists and short bursts. If your document looks like a master's thesis, pare it down and add some graphics before converting it to HTML.

Word and the Web

Microsoft Word offers two ways to create Web pages. The first is to select **Save as HTML** from the **File** menu. Doing this converts your current document to the appropriate HTML code and saves it on your hard drive. This is pretty handy if you have existing documents (for example, marketing materials) that you created in Word and want to post on the Web.

You can also build a small Web site from scratch using the Web Page Wizard. To do this, select **New** from the **File** menu. This pops up the New dialog box as shown in the next figure.

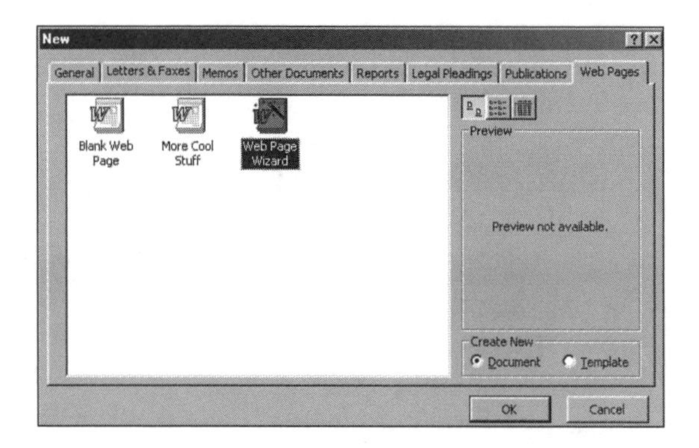

Word lets you create all sorts of documents.

In this dialog box, click the **Web Pages** tab, click the **Web Page Wizard** icon, and then click **OK**. The wizard takes you through a few options and when you're done, it leaves you with a simple but nice looking fill-in-the-blank Web page, complete with instructions. Check out the next figure for an example.

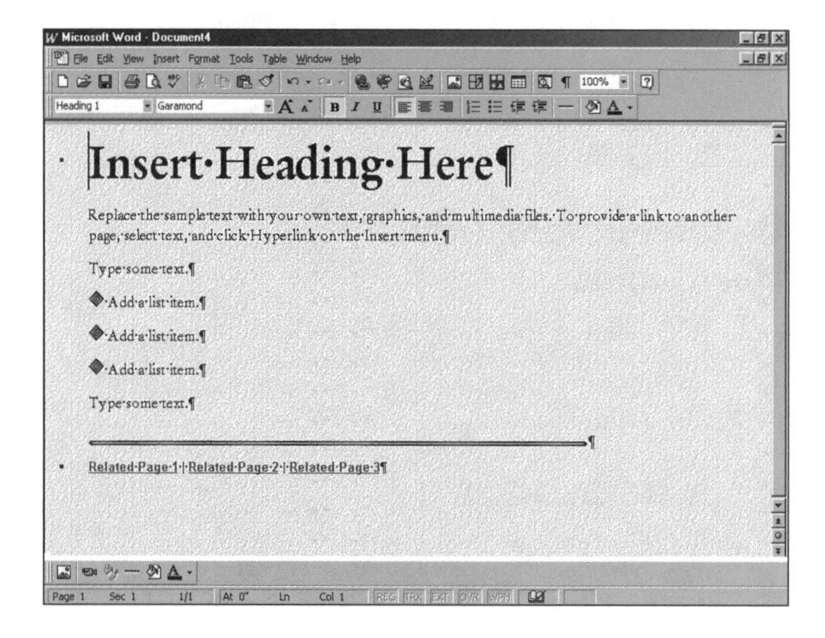

This page was created with the Web Creation Wizard.

After you've finished adding your own content, just save the document. Word automatically saves it as a Web page.

Excel and the Web

The File menu in Excel also has a Save as HTML option. However, due to the nature of spreadsheets in general, this option works differently than its Word counterpart.

The first step in converting your Excel data to HTML is selecting either a range of cells or a chart. If you select a range of cells, the data is converted to an HTML table that looks much like a Microsoft Word table. If you select a chart, the chart is converted to an HTML-compatible graphic.

Select **Save as HTML** from the **File** menu, and Excel launches its Internet Assistant Wizard. As long as you've already selected the cell range or chart that you want to convert to HTML, click the **Next** button on the first dialog box that pops up. However, you have to make a big decision when you get to the second dialog box as shown in the next figure.

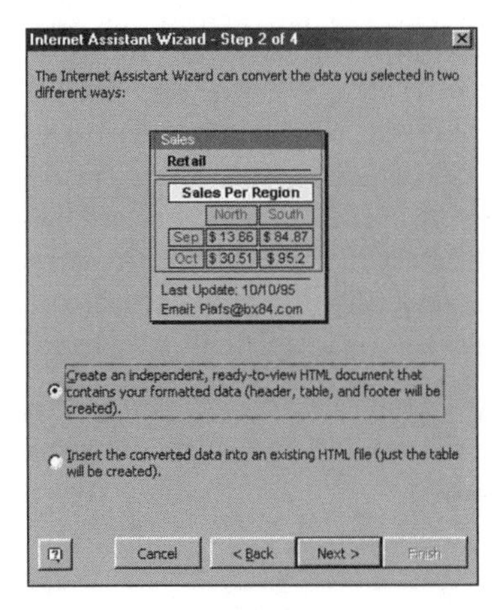

To create a new page or not to create a new page?

The decision you need to make here is whether you want Excel to create a brand spanking new Web page from your data or insert the data into an existing Web page. Now, chances are you don't want to devote an entire Web page to a single table or chart. That makes inserting the data into another page the logical choice.

The problem is that when you identify the Web page into which you want the data inserted, Excel has absolutely no idea where on that Web page you want the data. This is the tricky part.

For Excel to know where to put the data in the existing document, you need to edit that document's HTML code directly. I said earlier that you could create Web pages without knowing HTML, but I never said you could create *any* Web pages without knowing HTML. Unfortunately, this is one of those times when you need to know a little HTML. Even more unfortunate: That's a bit beyond the scope of this book.

On the other hand, suppose you do know the HTML ropes somewhat. Go into the HTML document and type **<!—Table—>** in the exact location where you want the

Excel data. Excel's Internet Assistant Wizard then looks for that code in the document you specify and replaces it with your chart or table.

PowerPoint and the Web

Like Word and Excel, PowerPoint's File menu offers a Save as HTML option. And like Excel, selecting this option launches a wizard, this one called (appropriately enough) the Save as HTML Wizard. However, out of all the Web-related Office wizards, PowerPoint's is by far the most powerful.

First things first, however. Why would you want to turn a PowerPoint presentation into a Web page (or more accurately, a series of Web pages)? In Chapter 16, "Ta Da! Creating a Sales Presentation," I discuss how easy it is to copy a presentation onto a CD and mail it off. The downside is that you have to repeat the process each time you want someone to see the presentation. Now just think how easy it would be to say to each prospective client, "Hey, just check out my Web site."

Now, back to the Save as HTML Wizard. The reason I said it's so powerful is that it doesn't just slap each slide on a Web page. Instead, the wizard starts by creating a main "table of contents" page that has links to each slide, as well as a "start here" button. Then each page includes a complete set of navigation buttons to help you move around the presentation. Finally, for anyone who doesn't want to wait for your lovely slide graphics to download, the wizard creates a text-only version that can be accessed from anywhere in the graphical presentation.

Take a look at the next couple of figures. The first one shows the main page as created by the Save as HTML Wizard and the second one shows one of the slide pages. As I said, this is powerful stuff.

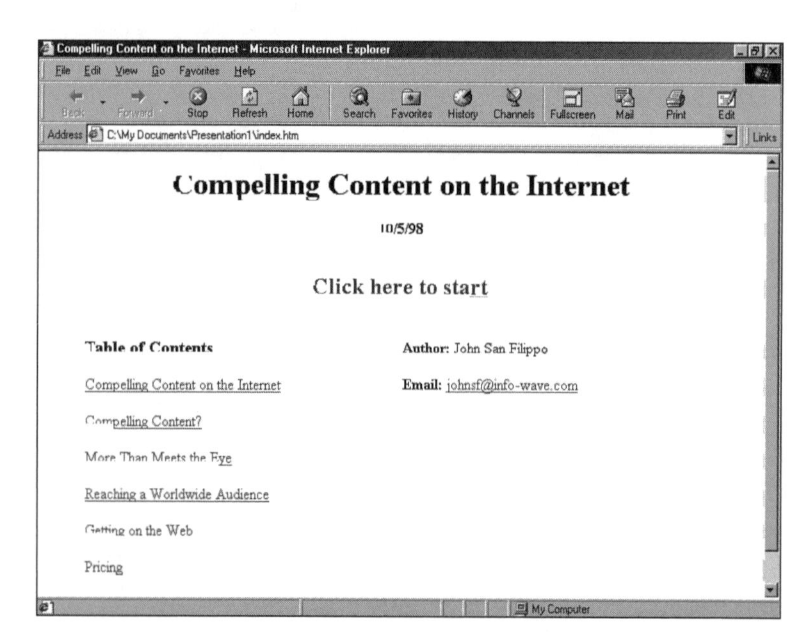

This is the main page according to PowerPoint.

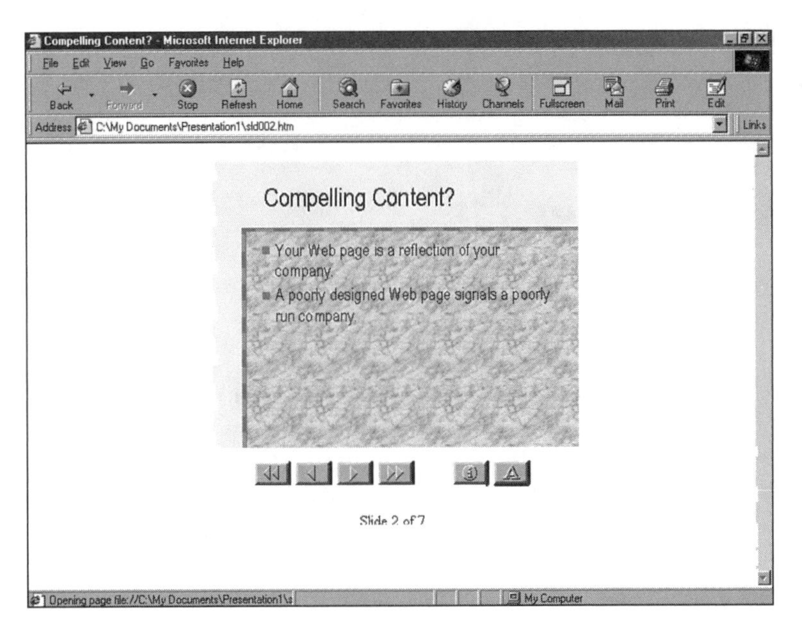

This is one of the slide pages.

Finding More Web Tools

Although the various Office applications—Word, Excel, and PowerPoint—do an adequate job of creating Web pages, you can only take them so far. After all, each of these programs was designed for something other than creating Web pages. The Web functions were added more or less as an afterthought.

If you get into working on your own Web site, a time will come when you're ready to move up to a program that was specifically designed for creating Web pages. After all, you can use a screwdriver to pound a nail once in awhile, but if you have to pound nails every day, sooner or later you're going to want a hammer.

Over the last couple of years, I've looked at dozens of Web authoring programs. Some were hot and some definitely were not. The following is my short list of favorites:

- The obvious choice (although maybe not the best choice) for a Web authoring package is Microsoft's FrontPage. Because it's a Microsoft product, integration with your Office applications is built-in. Plus, FrontPage is capable of some fairly sophisticated design. The downside is that it might seem a little too much for the beginning Web designer.
- NetObjects Fusion costs two or three times as much as FrontPage, but it's unmatched in its capability to create highly complex Web sites in record time. Like FrontPage, however, it suffers from feature overkill for some beginners.

- Adobe's PageMill is the program I recommend most often for Web newbies. The interface is simple enough that it shouldn't scare you off. Yet the program is powerful enough to create some top-notch Web pages.

Web Page Design Do's and Don'ts

Designing an effective Web page is much like designing an effective presentation (as we discussed in Chapter 16). The following is a list of things to keep in mind as you design your page, regardless of the software you use to do it:

- **Start with a plan** Like mapping out a brochure (which info goes on which panel?), mapping out a Web page and the links your visitors will follow is an important first step. Draw a flowchart that starts with your home page (the first page they see when they go to your site) and then the pages that can be followed from there. Make sure visitors can find their way through a logical series of links and pages that give them a complete picture of your company and services/products.
- **Use color** Even if your logo or letterhead is in black and white, use color for your text. This makes the page look more interesting. Don't go overboard—one or two colors per page is fine.
- **Use graphics instead of text** Instead of having all your links represented by text, throw in some graphic images (usually clip art) as the hyperlinks. A picture is worth a thousand words, and in the case of Web pages, this is certainly true.
- **Keep pokey modems in mind** Use small graphic files (not dimensions as much as file size) so it won't take forever to download your pages. Try to keep the largest graphic under 65K, other graphics under 25K, and the entire page, graphics and all, under 100K.
- **Make sure the tone of your page matches your business** If you're in a sober, serious line of work, don't have music playing and wild graphics on your page. Conversely, if yours is a fun business (birthday clown, disc jockey), make sure it's fun to visit your Web page.
- **When in doubt, check out the competition** Although you want your site to be better (more interesting, more informative), you don't want to miss that chance to steal some good ideas. While you're stealing these ideas (make that imitating them, the sincerest form of flattery), make sure you don't turn your page into a visual copy of theirs. If they have a dark background, make yours light. If they use music, make sure your music is different. Don't use any of the same graphic images, even if the pool of appropriate clip art is shallow. I often recognize graphics from one site on another, and I always shake my head.

Imagine 41 Million People Seeing Your Typos!

The exposure the Web gives you has a downside. If you mess up, millions of people may see the error. A friend of mine has a Web site, and he put it together rather hastily. It looked nice enough, and the overall layout was great. The problem? He transposed the numbers in his fax number (causing some poor woman to hear squealing and screeching in her ear every time she answered her phone) and he had several glaring typos in his text. If you're using any of the Office programs to generate your page, use the spell checker and proofread your page scrupulously. It also pays to have someone else check it out before you put it on the Web for all to see.

Getting Your Creation Online

All the Web authoring programs I mentioned in the previous section have built-in tools that help you transfer your Web files directly from your hard drive to your ISP's Web server. If you've created your Web page in one of the Office applications, however, you're going to have to do the job yourself.

Files are moved around the Internet using File Transfer Protocol (FTP). FTP is a standardized means of moving files from here to there in cyberspace, which is also how your files get from your hard drive to your ISP's Web server. If you're in the process of copying your files to your ISP's server, you're said to be FTPing them.

Obviously the key to this whole operation is a program that does FTP. If you don't have an FTP program, you'll need to find one somewhere on the Internet. Without this type of program, you have no way to copy your files to your ISP's server.

To connect to your ISP with your FTP program, you need three bits of information. The first two are your username and password, which you should already know. The third item is the name of your ISP's FTP server. For example, if your ISP is **ispname.com**, their server name is ftp.ispname.com. When you tell your FTP program to connect to **ftp.ispname.com** using your username and password, your FTP program is automatically logged onto the folder on your ISP's server where all your Web files reside.

From there, it's just a matter of following the directions for your FTP program to get the files from your computer to your ISP's computer.

Two Cows Walk into a Bar...

The best site that I know of for Internet-related software is TUCOWS (pronounced two-cows and located at **http://www.tucows.com**). TUCOWS stands for The Ultimate Collection Of Winsock Software. Originally a Windows-only archive, it has expanded to include Mac and even UNIX/Linux software. You're guaranteed to find plenty of FTP programs on this site.

Beware of FTP Encoding of Binary Files

Although your actual HTML files are simple text files, your graphics are called binary files. Instead of consisting of simple text characters, a lot of other information is stored in the file. The potential problem is that some FTP programs like to *encode* binary files when they're being transferred. Encoding kind of puts a wrapper around the file and is both necessary and appropriate in some situations. However, if the graphic files for your Web pages get encoded, no Web browser on the planet can read them. By whatever means your FTP program requires, make sure it doesn't encode your binary files.

The Least You Need to Know

- The World Wide Web has become an appropriate medium for just about every type of business.
- You can create Web pages from all your Word, Excel, and PowerPoint documents. You can also use Word to create brand new Web sites.
- Sooner or later, you may want to consider a more advanced Web authoring program.
- Your Web files are transferred from your hard drive to your ISP's service using a process known as FTP.

Part 4

You're Late! Scheduling Your Time and Resources

Even the most Type-A personalities among us can forget something from time to time. Whether it's a business meeting or to pick up your kid after soccer practice, running a small business can eat up your time and your mind, making it much easier to forget where you're supposed to be and what you're supposed to be doing. Chapters 18 through 21 show you how to budget your time, keep track of your comings and goings, and work effectively with coworkers or partners as you manage your efforts, your skills, and your time.

Chapter 18

Deciding on a Work Schedule

In This Chapter

- Determine a schedule that's right for you
- Schedule your time in the office
- Learn to delegate

If you're just getting your small business started, memories of your last job are probably still fresh in your mind. Some of them are likely fond memories; other may not be. Regardless, you're undoubtedly convinced that you're much better off now than before—and you are. I'm the first to agree that self-employment can make for a fantastic way of life.

After all, you get to make the decisions. You get to call the shots. You get to set your own schedule. Your get to do *whatever you want*. Well, not exactly. If you want to be successful out on your own, you have to put the needs of the business over your own personal needs.

The longer you're self-employed, the more you'll begin to appreciate the advantages of working for somebody else. Not that you'll regret having made the big jump. I never have. But you gain a real appreciation for the old saying, "The grass is always greener on the other side of the fence."

What's so great about working for somebody else? Well, for starters, a steady paycheck comes in awfully handy sometimes. So do health insurance benefits that are paid for right out of your paycheck before you ever see the money. Did your last employer have a 401(k) plan with matching contributions? Did your last employer ever cover the expense of a college course? Ever take a paid vacation?

Yes, being a working-class stiff does have some advantages. But the longer I'm self-employed, the one plus that I appreciate the most is this: When you're working for somebody else, you have to put almost no effort into time management. Think about it. Your employer tells you when you have to be in each morning, what time you should go to lunch, how long you should take, and when you should go home. Sure, you have to manage your time somewhat during the day just to make sure everything gets done. But by and large, your employer calls the shots.

I know what you're thinking. Yeah, my employer called the shots. My employer called too many shots. That's why I left in the first place. You're right, of course. But what you need to realize now is that responsibility for every minute of your day now rests in your hands—and that's a big responsibility. That's a responsibility that you must take seriously.

If you're running any sort of a retail operation, you have it kind of easy in this particular area. That's because your business exerts the same sort of time management control over you that your employer used to. If the sign on your door says you're open from 9 a.m. to 6 p.m. daily, you need to be there from 9 a.m. to 6 a.m. daily.

On the other hand, if you're involved in some type of service business—one that doesn't necessarily require you to be in a particular place at a particular time—time management represents a much greater challenge. Hopefully, this chapter will help you rise to it.

Planning Your Day

A few years ago, when I still found myself among the ranks of the gainfully employed, a coworker of mine quit his job to become some sort of an independent sales representative. I don't remember the name of the company nor the type of product he was selling, but I do remember thinking at the time that the field appeared to have some potential.

A few months later, we ran into each other, and I asked him how his new career was going. He confessed that he wasn't making much money. It wasn't his product that was the problem, nor was it his ability to sell the product. No, the problem was that each morning, he seemed to find himself inexplicably drawn to the beach, where he would bask for hours, planning all the work that he was going to get done the following day.

A couple of months after that, we ran into each other again. As I expected, this fellow had found another job with another company not much different from the job and company he had left behind. His own lack of discipline had doomed an otherwise promising business opportunity.

Lack of discipline, however, isn't the only thing that can foul up your workday. The flip side of no discipline is over-commitment. Instead of not doing anything all day long, you schedule too much. This can be a big problem as well.

The long and the short of it is this: If you expect any measure of success in the world of the self-employed, you must manage your time effectively. Effective time management requires two things:

- The discipline to do what you're supposed to be doing, when you're supposed to do it
- A realistic expectation of how much time you need to allocate for each of those things

Scheduling Your Time in the Office

As I mentioned earlier in this chapter, if you're involved in some sort of retail operation, your time is pretty much scheduled for you. You have to be at work from open to close, and probably then some. On the other hand, you have much more flexibility (and room to foul things up) if you're running a service-oriented business from your small office or home office.

It's only natural that you want to take advantage of this newfound flexibility to enhance your life. For example, if like me, you're working from home, it's reasonable for you to want to do things like pick the kids up from school. If a daily task like that is a priority, all you need to do is schedule your office time around that.

As with most other areas of your business operations, Microsoft Office can be an invaluable tool as you set out on your quest for optimum time management. Specifically, Microsoft Outlook is likely to become your best digital friend as you begin to juggle your daily priorities.

Over the years, I've tried plenty of PIMs (personal information managers—software that helps you organize your time and resources). I've tried the big-name PIMs like ACT! and Goldmine, and I was never impressed. They all seemed too complicated and bloated with features I wouldn't use in a million years. I had just about given up PIMs altogether when I started fiddling around with Outlook.

Much to my amazement, Outlook made sense to me from the moment I launched it. It provided powerful tools, but didn't seem to be overkill. The interface worked the same way I thought. In short, I was hooked.

Scheduling your time in the office is often more a matter of scheduling your time out of the office and then seeing what's left over. After all, when you're setting a meeting or scheduling a phone call, you check your calendar to see what time is filled, then assume that the rest of the time is empty.

A problem can arise, however, when you check your calendar and overlook those daily tasks like picking up the kids from school. It doesn't matter that you may be sitting in your home office wearing Bugs Bunny pajamas; you need to maintain a professional attitude for your customers. The last thing you want is to have to call a client and tell them you need to reschedule a meeting because you forgot you had to pick Junior up from preschool.

This is one spot that Outlook can get you out of. When you set up an appointment in Outlook, a feature called Recurrence saves the day. Using this feature, you can set up an appointment once and then have it repeated either daily, weekly, or monthly on your calendar for as long as you want. You can even set up yearly recurrences, although I haven't found too much use for that.

For example, suppose you need to take Junior to his karate lessons from 3–4 p.m. every Wednesday. Using the Recurrence feature, you can set up Junior's karate lesson as a single appointment and then have it repeated every Wednesday until the end of time. That way, you'll never accidentally schedule another appointment when you're supposed to be hanging out down at the dojo.

I'll take a moment to walk you through the whole process. Keep in mind, however, that Outlook is flexible enough that there are several ways to set up an appointment. I'm presenting the method I use most.

You can display your calendar in Daily, Weekly, or Monthly view (your choice). If you're in Monthly view, double-click the day on which you want to enter an appointment. If you're in Weekly or Daily view, click once to display the hours of the day, and then double-click the time slot you want to fill. In any case, the double-click opens an Untitled Appointment dialog box, as shown in this figure.

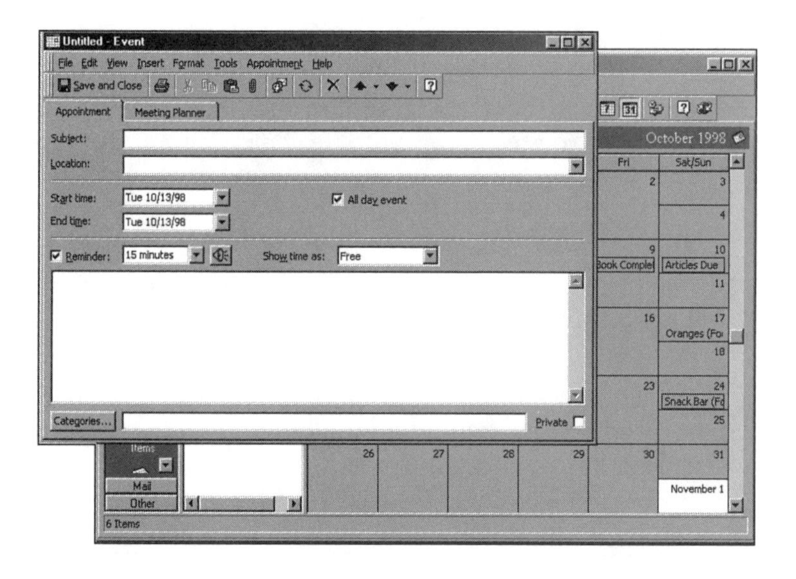

Enter all your appointment information here.

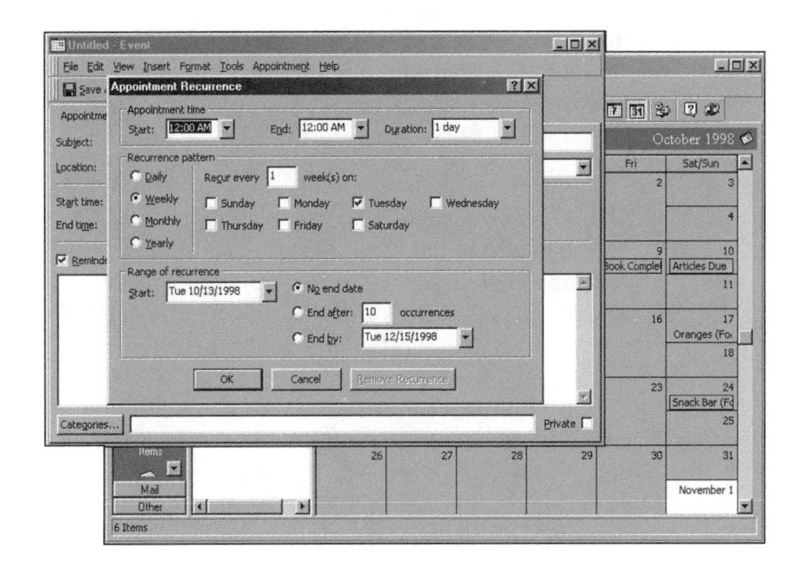

You can repeat an appointment as often as you want.

After you've typed in the various details of this event, click the **Appointment** menu and select **Recurrence**. This brings up an Appointment Recurrence window like the one shown in the following figure.

Outlook gives you different options, depending on which recurrence pattern you choose, as follows:

- If you choose Daily, you have the option to repeat the appointment every day, every so many days, or every weekday.
- If you choose Weekly, you can have the appointment repeat every week or every so many weeks. You can also choose which day or days of the week on which the appointment should occur.
- If you choose Monthly, you can have the appointment repeat on a particular date or day (for example, the second Tuesday) every month or every so many months.
- Finally, if you choose Yearly, you can have the appointment repeat on a particular date or a particular day of the month (for example, the second Tuesday of October).

If the situation is only temporary, the bottom portion of the Appointment Recurrence window gives you various options for discontinuing the appointment after a period of time.

Scheduling around your recurring appointments is only one piece of the time-management puzzle. Another common mistake for new entrepreneurs is to think that

Pssst! Remember Me?

After you've gone to all the trouble of setting an appointment (recurring or not), don't miss it because you forget to check your calendar in Outlook or you lose track of time while working at your desk. Set a Reminder—an alarm that will sound or display a message 15 minutes prior to the appointment. If you need more or less lead-time, reset the time.

Get Back to Work!

Be careful of any lunch or break-time activity that is hard to break away from. Don't plunk yourself down in front of the TV if you tend to be a couch potato—you'll find yourself there hours after your favorite show ended. If the weather's wonderful, be firm with yourself about coming back in the house and getting back to work. Spring fever can hit at any time of the year.

they can pop out of bed fresh at 6 a.m. and work straight through until 6 p.m. Even if you're young and inspired enough to pull that off now, I can guarantee it won't last for long. You need to work hard, but you shouldn't be a slave to your business.

I highly recommend that you schedule—and that means adding it to Outlook as a Recurring Appointment if you have to—at least 30 minutes for lunch each day. A full hour is even better if you have the time. This allows you to clear out your head of the morning's clutter and get a fresh start on the afternoon's tasks. If you can, take the time to get out of your office, away from your desk. A change of scenery (and a chance to stretch your legs) can contribute to your ability to work through the afternoon.

Likewise, you should schedule 10–15-minute breaks for the morning and afternoon. Again, getting up to stretch and maybe take a little walk is good for both the mind and body.

Of course, you're the boss now. That means you don't have to schedule your lunch right at noon if you don't want to. For example, I like watching reruns of *Law & Order* on A&E every morning at 10 a.m. I count this as my lunchtime. So instead of going break-lunch-break, I go lunch-break-break. This works out just fine for me.

Flexibility is what makes self-employment so alluring, and staying flexible is what keeps your business moving forward. Typing an appointment into Outlook isn't the same as carving it in stone. If you need to juggle a few things now and then, go ahead and juggle. Just make sure that when you juggle, you record everything in Outlook. If you don't, you may end up dropping a bowling pin on your head—so to speak.

Just Say NO

A certain entrepreneur I know had trouble saying "No" to friends who called her during the day to talk or invite her to lunch. Her friends knew she worked at home, and figured that meant two-hour phone calls and long lunches would be just fine—after all, there's no boss hovering around, right? Wrong. Her lack of spine when it came to possibly hurting her friends' feelings cost her hours of productive time. A potential solution? Get Caller ID from your local phone company, and screen your calls. If that doesn't work, be firm. Say "Gotta go!" after the pleasantries are exchanged. Offer to call back when you're less busy. After a few "Gotta go's", friends will catch on and begin to respect the demands on your time.

Can't Do It All? Then Delegate!

"If you want something done right, you have to do it yourself." Sometimes, for the sake of small business owners everywhere, I wish these words had never been spoken. If you're just starting out in business, these words are probably ringing in your ears at this very instant. It's almost a universal affliction. Every new entrepreneur feels that he or she has to do absolutely *everything*.

Although the old saying certainly has some truth to it, it's equally true that sometimes there just aren't enough hours in a day to do it all. That leaves you with two choices: You either don't get everything done that you need to, or you delegate to someone else. This should be a no-brainer.

Of course, if I tell you to delegate some of your daily tasks, I'm making a rather large assumption that you have someone to delegate to. But if you're just starting out, you don't have anyone to delegate to, do you? Well, unless you live and work in a cave, you probably do.

If you ask someone to run an errand for you or undertake some other task, add it to your Outlook to-do list, and also include it as an appointment item. For the appointment date and time, use the date and time by which the task should be completed. That way, you can follow up with the person to make sure they came through.

Okay, so you're single and don't have anyone to help you out with the business. Does that mean you can't delegate? Not necessarily.

When you have a 9-to-5 job, your life is segmented into two distinct components: work and everything else. However, when you're self-employed, work and play tend to become one, big, intertwined... well, mess. Not necessarily a bad mess, but a mess none-the-less. If you can't find anyone to delegate work-related tasks to, perhaps you can delegate some non-work tasks.

Many years ago, a friend of mine told me of an acquaintance of his who was accomplished in his particular field—so much so that he decided to strike out on his own. I'll call this fellow Bob for the sake of discussion.

Like most new entrepreneurs, Bob felt the need to tighten the old belt and cut out as many unnecessary expenses as possible. In fact, Bob became somewhat of a penny-pincher, refusing to spend a cent unless absolutely essential.

As such, Bob fired his gardener and also began working on his own car—all in a valiant effort to save money. Well, as time went by, Bob couldn't figure out why he wasn't making as much money as he expected. The truth was, he was spending too much time in the garden, under the hood and elsewhere, and not enough time bringing home the bacon. Eventually, Bob had to crawl back to his former employer and ask for his old job back. "He had to ask for his old job back" are nine little words you never want to hear spoken about you.

Anyhow, my whole point here is this: Don't be another Bob. You expect people to pay you for your expertise in a particular field. Don't be afraid to pay for someone else's expertise in some other field. I know it's cliché, but time really is money. If you spend too much time trying to save money instead of delegating some tasks to someone else, you're going to end up losing money.

When you finally do have employees, one more aspect enters into the delegation equation: trust. Although you may not want to delegate tasks to your husband or wife, it's probably not for lack of trust. But when you're dealing with what ultimately amounts to a total stranger, trust is probably your top concern.

A fine line lies between reasonable trust and stupidity. On one side of the line, you don't want to be so paranoid that you end up spending more time monitoring them than you would have doing the job yourself. On the other side of the line, it's unwise to put full and blind trust in someone you don't know.

The key is to build trust gradually. You do this by delegating a little at a time, increasing the employee's responsibilities as you become satisfied with his or her current performance. Along the way, you may want to deliberately give her or him the opportunity to screw up just to see what happens. Just make sure it's in a controlled environment.

The Least You Need to Know

- Effective time management is essential to any successful business.
- Microsoft Outlook helps make short order of the time management challenge.
- It's important to make realistic expectations of your own time.
- No matter what your situation, sometimes you have to delegate tasks to someone else.

Chapter 19

Appointments: Be There or Be Square

In This Chapter

- Plan a successful business meeting
- Prepare all your meeting resources
- Run a business meeting like a pro
- Follow up after the meeting

Whether you call it a business meeting or business appointment, the idea seems pretty simple. You schedule a time and place to meet someone else. Then you show up. A snap, right? Well, if the best thing you can say about your performance at a business meeting is that you showed up on time, you may not be in business long.

Throughout the course of your business, you communicate in many ways—letters, email, telephone calls, advertising, and so on. Out of all the ways you're likely to communicate, however, a face-to-face meeting is by far your most powerful medium. You've probably heard it said before, maybe you've even said it. You've talked to somebody on the phone several times and then finally meet them in person. So you say, "It's nice to match a face to the voice," or something similar. No matter how far telecommunications advance, personal meetings will always be more personal, more legitimate, more appealing, and more effective—that's just the nature of human beings.

Beyond that, a personal meeting gives you the best opportunity to reach a meeting of the minds with your client or prospective client. If you send a letter, you're just guessing at the information you think the other person wants to know. Even on the telephone, you're not able to read the other person's body language. However, after a well-run business meeting, everyone that leaves the room should be on the exact same page, so to speak.

A business meeting can be a valuable tool. Don't take it lightly.

Sounds Like a Plan

Although business meetings represent a powerful means of communication, they do have drawbacks. Depending on how many people need to attend and how busy each person is, they can be hard to schedule. In fact, don't be surprised if rescheduling meetings is the norm in your business life.

Meetings also take a lot of time. You have to prepare for the meeting, you have to travel to the meeting, and after it's over, you have to travel back. You don't want to become a meeting junkie and start scheduling meetings for every little thing that comes up. A meeting is a tool that must be used judiciously. That being the case, the last thing you want to do is fail to prepare properly for a meeting.

The first step in preparing for a meeting is determining the reason for the meeting (and in the process, determining if you really need a meeting). To determine the purpose of a meeting, you have to focus on the expected outcome. What are you trying to achieve? When the meeting is over and everyone is shaking hands, what will each person be thinking? What will they be expected to do? The purpose of your meeting should not be, for example, to discuss such-and-such. Instead, it should be to reach a decision about such-and-such.

Next, you need to decide who should be present at the meeting. Remember, people are busy. You don't want to invite someone who doesn't really need to be there. If you do, you risk their resenting a waste of their time; or if they jump in and get involved in something that doesn't concern them, you risk extending the meeting with unwanted discussion that annoys everyone else at the meeting. If this happens too often (more than once), people may become mysteriously busy whenever you call a meeting.

At a typical business meeting, two parties are represented: you and your prospective client. Hence, you need to decide if anyone from your company (or perhaps an independent consultant that you plan to use for this particular job) should attend. Don't bring someone else from your organization just to make it look like you have "people." Bring only those who are likely to make a substantial contribution to the discussion.

Determining who from your client's organization should attend can be a little trickier. Depending on the nature of your business and your familiarity with the client, you may have no idea at all. The key to making sure the right people are there is making sure your client knows the exact purpose of the meeting and asking the client to invite whatever other employees he or she wants to attend.

Outsmarting the Fox

Wondering who has the most clout at your client's company? A salesman I know talks about identifying the "fox." The fox is the person who makes decisions. Don't assume that the fox has to be the president or a high-level manager. In many firms, the president's secretary is the fox. The fox influences the people in power; he or she has the "real" decision maker's ear, and makes effective use of it. It takes time to identify the fox—and you may not be able to do it on your first few meetings or on a warehouse tour—but it's worth the time. If the fox doesn't like you, it doesn't matter if you're *dating* the president of the company—your days with that firm are numbered.

After you have both your purpose and your list of attendees in mind, it's time to schedule the meeting. If you have everyone's email address, Microsoft Outlook provides a convenient means for calling a meeting. However, unless you're the really big cheese and everyone else bows at your command, I recommend avoiding email to schedule a business meeting. The Meeting Maker can be a great tool, however, for finding out who's free at the time you want to have the meeting. You may not be high enough on the food chain to demand everyone's presence, but at least you'll know if anyone's lying about being busy!

Because everyone's on a different schedule, the meeting time you want is not likely to be the meeting time you get. If you attempt to use email to schedule a meeting between more than two people, you're likely to find yourself in the nuthouse before you get a meeting time nailed down. When it comes time to schedule your business meeting, just pick up the phone and dial. And after you have the meeting scheduled, don't forget to add it to your Outlook calendar.

The last step in the planning process is to decide exactly how the meeting will flow. If you're the one calling the meeting, you're going to be expected to run the show. That means you better know where the show is headed next. If you go in blind with just a topic in mind, the meeting is likely to meander all over the place and you may find you've reached the end of the road without getting what you came for.

You're best bet is to create an outline in Word. Maybe you thought all those outlines you wrote in junior high and high school were a little pointless, but that format is ideal for a business meeting. An outline provides a nice framework for mapping out exactly what points you want to cover in the meeting.

The most important part of your outline is making sure you bring it with you. People won't think less of you because you're following an outline, in fact, they're likely to be impressed with your organizational skills. If you've created a particularly nice looking outline, you may even want to consider bringing copies for the others at the meeting so it's easier for them to follow along and stay focused.

On Your Mark, Get Set...

On the day of the meeting, first make sure you have all your materials and equipment together. If part of your meeting is going to include an electronic presentation (see Chapter 16), make sure you have the following:

- Your laptop computer.
- A copy of your presentation loaded on your laptop.
- A copy of PowerPoint loaded on your laptop.
- Your projection equipment. (If you're relying on your client's equipment, a quick call to double-check might be in order.) Bring extra bulbs for your projection equipment.
- Enough copies of your handout for everyone at your meeting, plus a few extras just in case someone else shows up.

If you're taking other people with you, call them at least an hour before your departure time to remind them of the meeting.

One thing that some people tend to forget until the last minute (myself among them on occasion) is to know exactly where it is they're going. If you've never been to a client's site, it may not be as easy to get there as you think. Even if you know the general area, getting to a particular suite in a crowded business park can often be a challenge. The last thing you want to do is open your business meeting with, "Sorry I'm late, but I got a little lost." For all intents and purposes, you're saying, "Sorry I'm late. I didn't take the time to prepare."

You have a couple of options to help you get where you're going:

- Call the client's office and ask the receptionist for directions. However, if it's a smaller organization and you want to appear more self-sufficient, you may want to consider one of the other options listed here.
- Click the MAP button to connect to Microsoft's Expedia Street Finder and get a map and directions that you can print out and take with you.
- Assuming they have one, check the client's Web site to see if it includes directions to the office.

- Use the mapping feature on a portal site like Yahoo! (**www.yahoo.com/py/maps.py**)to generate a detailed map from your office to your client's office. These give you turn-by-turn instructions and also include expected times for each leg of the trip.
- Buy a good map and become familiar with it. Remember to keep it in your car, and keep it within reach while driving.

Help from Above

If you own a laptop, consider purchasing a Door-to-Door Co-Pilot from TravRoute Software. This package includes mapping software and a GPS (Global Positioning Satellite) unit that plugs into your laptop. The end result is that you type in where you want to go. The GPS unit figures out where you are now, and the software tells you how to get where you want to go through the laptop's speakers, monitoring your progress along the way via the GPS. (I have one and it's incredible.)

It's Show Time!

As the person who called the meeting, you're expected to run it. I can't stress this point enough. The biggest mistake you can make at your meeting is to think you can say, "Okay, let's start," and the meeting will then run itself. You're the one in charge.

Use your outline to control the flow of the meeting. If someone begins to stray off topic, don't be afraid to tactfully redirect the conversation back to where it should be. Nobody is going to be offended—or I suppose I should say nobody *should* be offended—if you say something like, "Maybe we should come back to that after we finish discussing this."

This brings up a couple of important points. First, no matter how well you plan your outline, somebody at your meeting is going to bring up something that you didn't think of. You have to allow for this. Don't be so rigid in following your outline that you exclude an important point. Even if you think it's not important, the fact that somebody else does means that it is.

This all points to the need to take notes. If you say you're going to come back to a topic someone raised, you need to come back to it at some appropriate point. The problem is that if you're following your outline, you may forget—unless you take the simple step of writing it down.

If it fits somewhere else in your outline, write it in there. Otherwise, just make a note to yourself somewhere else. What you don't want to do is force the other person to bring up his or her topic a second time. By mentioning it yourself at the appropriate time, you show that you're genuinely concerned with the other person's needs.

When I'm at a business meeting, I take two types of notes. The first ones are similar to what I just described—little notes to myself for later in the meeting. For example, if someone says something that raises a question in my mind, but it's not quite the right time to interject, I'll write the question down so I don't forget. I learned this the hard way when during a couple of meetings early in my career, I interjected to ask a question, only to realize that I had forgotten the question. Boy, did I feel dumb.

The second type of notes is for recording the actual events of the meeting. To be perfectly honest, I don't take extremely detailed notes. I find that if I spend too much time writing, I often miss something important. Instead, I jot down the major points and rely on my memory for the details later.

That doesn't mean this is the best approach for you. Other people I know are able to take very detailed notes and still keep up with the conversation. Whichever type of note-taker you are, the important thing is that you do take notes.

As the person running the meeting, it's your responsibility to know when the meeting is over—and then to say so. That's not to say you should cut someone else off in the middle of a sentence. However, after your meeting goal has been achieved and the conversation begins to drift elsewhere, it's time to wrap things up. Some good physical cues (to accompany your tactful "Well I think that wraps things up!") are stacking your notes and papers in front of you, putting your pen away, and thanking everyone for coming to the meeting. Putting your coat on and looking impatiently at your watch is *not* a good idea.

Get It on Tape

Depending on the exact nature of your meeting, you may want to consider using a portable tape recorder to take your notes for you. For example, when I'm interviewing someone for a magazine article, a microcassette recorder often comes in handy. Rather than just spring a tape recorder on someone and make them feel uncomfortable if they don't care to be recorded, your best bet is to check with them ahead of time.

The Follow Up

Any time the terms of an agreement are questioned in a court of law, one of the goals of the judge or jury is to determine if there was a meeting of the minds between the involved parties. In other words, did both parties agree to the same thing.

Amazing as it may seem, two people sitting in on the same meeting listening to the same exact words can walk away with entirely different interpretations. With your meeting, you set out to achieve a specific goal and perhaps you believe that you did. But that doesn't guarantee that everyone else got the same idea. That's why it's important to follow up after a meeting. Good meeting notes make the follow up process easy.

The best way to do this is in writing—either by letter or email. Although the main purpose of your follow-up letter is to confirm the outcome of the meeting, it also gives you an opportunity to show some good business manners.

Don't Use that Tone with Me!

The tone of the letter should match the tone of your relationship—don't be overly stiff and conservative if this is a client you've had drinks with or known for a long time. Don't be too familiar or flippant if the client is relatively unknown to you (even if the client has been familiar and flippant with you). Strive for a professional tone that contributes to your growing relationship with the client.

Open your letter with a few words of thanks. Let the person know that you appreciate the time and effort they took to meet with you. Then, almost as an afterthought, write a few sentences that explain your understanding of the outcome of the meeting. Close by inviting the person to contact you if he or she has any questions.

The Least You Need to Know

- The key to a successful business meeting is planning.
- If you call the meeting, you're the one in charge.
- You should make every effort to be punctual.
- Different people interpret things in different ways. Make sure you write a follow-up letter after the fact to confirm your understanding of the meeting's outcome.

Chapter 20

Mastering Your Calendar 101

In This Chapter

- ➤ Create a paper version of your electronic calendar
- ➤ Take your electronic calendar on the road
- ➤ Access your electronic calendar from anywhere in the world

From a technical standpoint, creating an electronic calendar in Outlook is simple. You click the **Calendar** icon in the Outlook bar, double-click a date, and type in your appointment information. No fuss, no muss. As long as you're sitting in front of your computer, your calendar is at your fingertips.

The only problem is, you probably don't conduct your business in front of your computer (unless you have some weird line of work like writing computer books). The challenge is to have your appointment information with you when you need it, which is likely all the time.

Fortunately, three general ways exist to package your appointments to go:

- ➤ Commit your electronic calendar to paper and take it with you.
- ➤ Store your electronic calendar on a device that you can take with you.
- ➤ Store your electronic calendar somewhere where you can get to it no matter where you are.

All three of these options are covered in this chapter. Chances are that each person who reads this book will find one method more appropriate than the others, but you can certainly employ all of them if you want.

The Paper Chase

Long before laptops, palmtops, and personal digital assistants appeared on store shelves, businesspeople around the world relied on good, old-fashioned, paper-based organizers. I bought my first Day Runner years ago and it's still an important part of my everyday business life.

What's changed over the years is that a good portion of the pages in my Day Runner were printed from my computer. Rather than scribble notes, addresses, and appointments in the Day Runner, I can keep them neatly organized in Outlook, and then create a neatly organized printout to carry around in the Day Runner.

The key to creating these handy-dandy printouts is making effective use of Outlook's print styles. These styles allow you, among other things, to print your calendar in a format that will fit right into whatever type of paper organizer you happen to use.

When you're viewing your Outlook calendar, select **Page Setup** from the **File** menu, and you're presented with five style options:

- Daily Style
- Weekly Style
- Monthly Style
- Tri-Fold Style
- Memo Style

Printing your calendar in a tri-fold format can be handy if you just need something to stick in your pocket, but I don't use it much. I've never found much use for the Memo style, either. The real workhorses here are the Daily, Weekly, and Monthly styles.

Select **Weekly Style**, for example, and you're presented with a Page Setup dialog box that includes three tabs: Format, Paper, and Header/Footer. Each tab presents a variety of options, but the most important tab for our purposes is the Paper tab. Click the **Paper** tab, and the Page Setup dialog box looks something like the one in the next figure.

Pay particular attention to the Page Size area on the right side of the screen. If you scroll down through this list, you'll discover that Outlook can produce a printout to fit just about every popular paper organizer out there.

In my case, I use a Day Runner Classic organizer. By selecting Day Runner Classic as my page size, I can print two pages of my Outlook calendar on a single sheet of letter-sized paper. Then all I do is fold it in half, hole-punch it, and pop it into my Day Runner.

When you prepare to print your calendar, Outlook lets you choose which print style to use. Select the one you want and in no time at all, a hard-copy version of your calendar is ready to go.

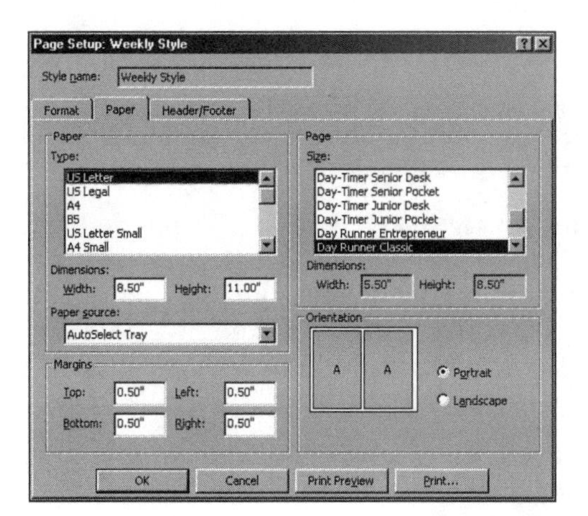

Choose your paper and a whole lot more.

Skip the Origami

Depending on the size of the paper in your printer and the size of the pages in your organizer, a simple fold may not be enough to fit your printout into your organizer. You may have to do some cutting. If so, just don't waste your time with scissors. Instead, by a small paper trimmer. It's faster, more accurate, and I can guarantee that you'll find other uses for it. Don't forget to buy a hole punch, preferably set to the ring configuration of your book or one that adjusts.

But This Calendar Says I'm Free on Wednesday!

If all you have with you is a paper version of your calendar, it stands to reason that you'll make changes and additions to that paper version. The important thing is to remember to record those changes and additions in Outlook when you get back to your computer. Otherwise, you're asking for obvious trouble.

Hit the Road, Jack

If you're lucky enough to have both a desktop and laptop computer, you have the luxury of taking your electronic calendar with you when you go. The problem in a two-computer environment is making sure the calendars on both computers match up.

Windows 95 introduced a great feature called the Briefcase. Using the Briefcase, you can easily copy a file from your desktop system to your laptop, revise it on the laptop, and then put the updated version back on the desktop system. Unfortunately, your Outlook calendar isn't stored as a separate file that you can move here and there at will. This means that for purposes of making your calendar mobile, the Briefcase isn't of much use.

To copy your electronic calendar from one copy of Outlook to another (that is, from your desktop to your laptop), first export the calendar as a free-standing file. Then import the information in that file to the second copy of Outlook. For this, the easiest way to go is with a dear, old floppy disk. So before you get started, make sure you have a blank, formatted floppy disk in your floppy disk drive. Here's how it works.

First, select **Import and Export** from the **File** menu to launch the Import and Export Wizard. The first screen of this wizard looks like the one shown in the next figure.

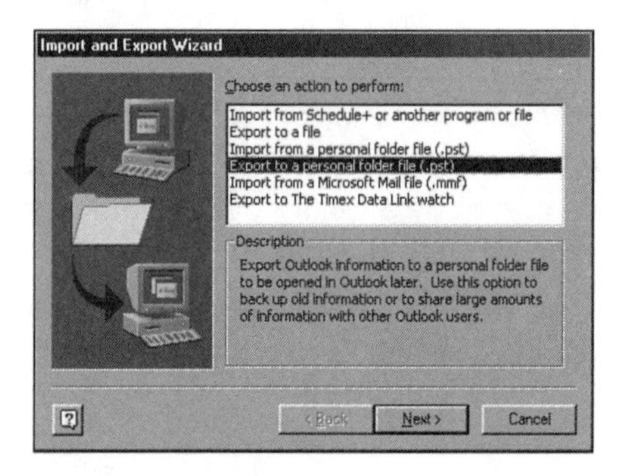

It's time to export your calendar.

From this list, select **Export to a Personal Folder File**, and then click the **Next** button. On the next screen, you're presented with a list of all your Outlook folders. If the **Calendar** folder isn't already selected, click it, and then click the **Next** button again.

On the next screen, you identify the name and location of the exported file by clicking the **Browse** button. Just make sure you tell the wizard to put the file on the floppy disk. One final click on the **Finish** button puts the new file on the floppy disk.

You're half way there. Now you just need to import the file into Outlook on your desktop. Before you begin, make sure the floppy disk is now in the drive on your laptop.

Start off the same way by selecting **Import and Export** from the **File** menu to launch the Import and Export Wizard. But instead of exporting, you want to select **Import from a Personal Folder File**.

On the next screen, use the **Browse** button to locate your calendar file on the floppy disk drive. Then on the next screen, tell Outlook where to put the imported information, as shown in the following figure.

Export It!

If you've upgraded to Outlook 98, the wizard works a little differently. First you select **Export to a File**. Then you select **Personal Folder File** from the next list.

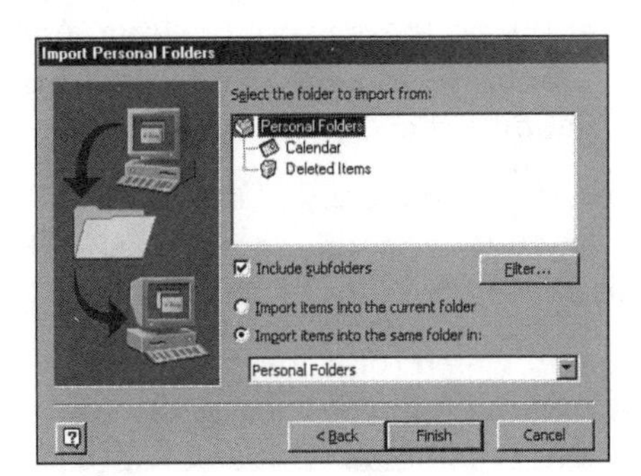

You can tell Outlook where to stick the file.

At the top of this screen, click the **Calendar** folder if it isn't already selected. (In case you're wondering why a Deleted Items folder appears too, that gets added any time you export a folder.) However, the absolute most important thing to remember about this screen is to select the **Import Files into the Same Folder in Personal Folders** option. If you select the other option, Outlook creates a whole new Calendar folder instead of adding the information to the existing calendar folder.

One click on the **Finish** button updates the calendar on your laptop. If you make changes or additions on your laptop, just reverse the process to get the new information back over to your desktop system.

And Now for 007 Fans...

The problem with using your laptop computer as a carrying case for your electronic calendar is that it's not convenient. Just to check an appointment, you need to pull out the laptop, start it up and run Outlook. If you're in a hurry or in the cramped confines of an economy-class seat on a plane, this is clearly not the ideal solution.

Option two is to print out your calendar (as described earlier in this chapter) so you can just pop open your organizer when you need to check an appointment. Of course, your organizer is buried at the bottom of your briefcase. And it's so stuffed with... well, stuff, that you have to flip more than a few pages to get where you want. No, this isn't the ideal solution either.

As a near-perfect solution for those who need a copy of their calendar with them, but don't need to actually change anything, I heartily recommend a Timex DataLink® watch. This is one of the coolest "toys" I've ever owned.

By flashing bar codes on your computer screen (or through an optional "electronic eye," if you're using a laptop), the DataLink software can transfer all sorts of personal information into your wristwatch. Even better, Outlook has DataLink connectivity already built-in. All you do is run the Import and Export Wizard, and select the DataLink option. Outlook blasts whatever information you specify right onto your watch.

Going Global with Your Calendar

One alternative to taking your calendar with you (whether in paper or electronic format) is to keep your calendar somewhere that's accessible no matter where in the world you happen to find yourself. For that, you need an international computer network that can be accessed from your desktop or laptop, from your wireless communication device, from special terminals in airports, and so on. In short, you need the Internet.

Sure, the Internet is everywhere these days. The $64,000 question is: How do you use the Internet to get to your personal calendar information in Boise when you're on a sales trip in Baton Rouge?

Lucky for you, this is much less of a problem than you might think. That's because a number of free (if you don't count the "cost" of having to look at banner advertising) Web-based calendar services have sprung up over the last few months. Using one of these services, you can maintain your appointment calendar (and other personal information, depending on the service) on that company's Web server. When you need to see your calendar, you connect to the Web site, type in your username and password, and you're there.

You're probably wondering a couple of things right now. First, what does this have to do with Outlook? Second, what happens if I happen to be one of the few places on the planet that doesn't have Web access? Fortunately for me, both of these questions have the same answer.

Any Web-based calendar service worth its salt allows you to download an Outlook-compatible file that you can use to update your Outlook calendar. Two such services that come to mind are WebCal (**http://www.webcal.com**) and PlanetAll (**http://www.planetall.com**). The only drawback, at least as of this writing, is that you can't move calendar data in the other direction. In other words, if you schedule an appointment in Outlook, you have to manually type it in on your Web-based calendar. You may want to check one of these services to see whether this has changed by the time you read this.

The Least You Need to Know

- ➤ If you use a paper-based organizer, you can create printed versions of your Outlook calendar.
- ➤ It's easy to take your Outlook calendar on the road (and then back again).
- ➤ Using a free service, you can access your calendar via the Web from anywhere in the world.

Chapter 21

Getting It Done with To-Do Lists

In This Chapter

- Create and manage a basic to-do list
- Use to-do lists to manage a project
- Keep your project moving

Way back when I got my first paper-based organizer, I was amazed with how many different types of information I could jam into a single little binder. At the time, I suspected I would never use all the features in my Day Runner, and wondered which ones I would come to rely upon the most.

Of the numerous features offered in a Day Runner, the one I found myself getting the most mileage from was the to-do list pages. I didn't need a lot of complicated planning pages; I just needed a place to write down the things I needed to accomplish on any given day. Over the years, this has proved valuable.

If you're running a small business, chances are that you wear several different hats. During the course of the day, you're likely to have a number of otherwise unrelated tasks to perform. That's where a to-do list comes in handy.

Maintaining your to-do list in your mind is a hit-or-miss proposition. Just picture it. You finish one task and it's time to move on to the next one. Your mind locks in on one of the unfinished tasks on your list, but unfortunately it doesn't lock in on the most important one. You end up forgetting about that more important task until it's too late.

This can't happen if you have all your tasks written down and prioritized. You complete one task, check it off on your list, and move on to the next one. The end result is that you use your time much more efficiently. Eventually, that should convert to a dollars-and-cents advantage for your business.

TaskPad Basics

Let me open this section by saying that in the world of Microsoft Outlook, the function that most people call a to-do list is called the TaskPad. From here on out, I'm going to use the term TaskPad when referring to your electronic to-do list just to stay consistent with the software. When you read TaskPad, just think "to-do list."

In Outlook, the TaskPad is visible as an integrated part of the Day view, or by clicking the Tasks folder. Working in the Task folder affords you the most flexibility in building and editing tasks, but many users like to see to-do items onscreen at all times. The next figure shows the TaskPad conveniently displayed in Day view.

Try manipulating your default view to include your Personal Folders list, making access to the Tasks folder much easier.

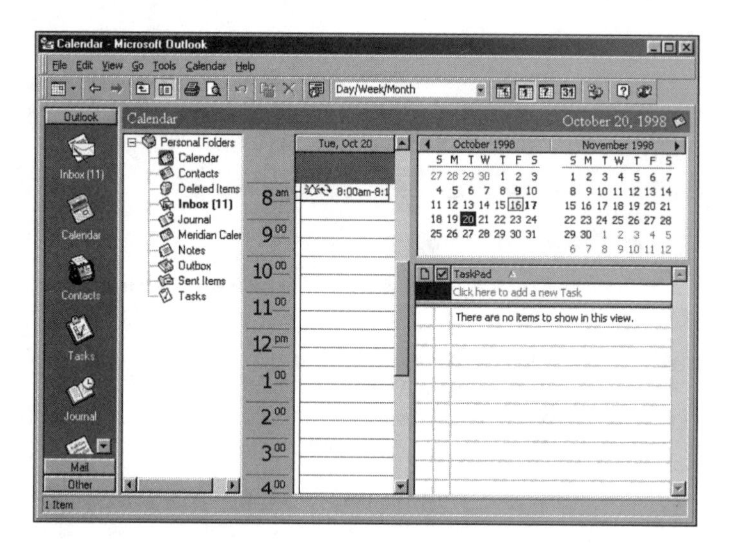

Adding a new task is simple stuff. First click the mouse in the TaskPad where it says **Click Here to Add a New Task**. Then type in the task and press the **Enter** key. Your new task automatically pops down into your task list.

After you've completed a task and want to remove it from the list, click the checkbox immediately to the left of the task's name. After you check off a task, the task appears as strike-through text and eventually drops off the list.

Simple enough, right? But if that's all the TaskPad can do, it's not much better than a paper to-do list. If you think an electronic to-do list should be able to do more for you, you're right.

When you double-click an existing task in the TaskPad, you're greeted with a Task window like the one shown in the next figure. I'll cover some of the key features of this window now; others I'll save for the discussion of project management later in this chapter.

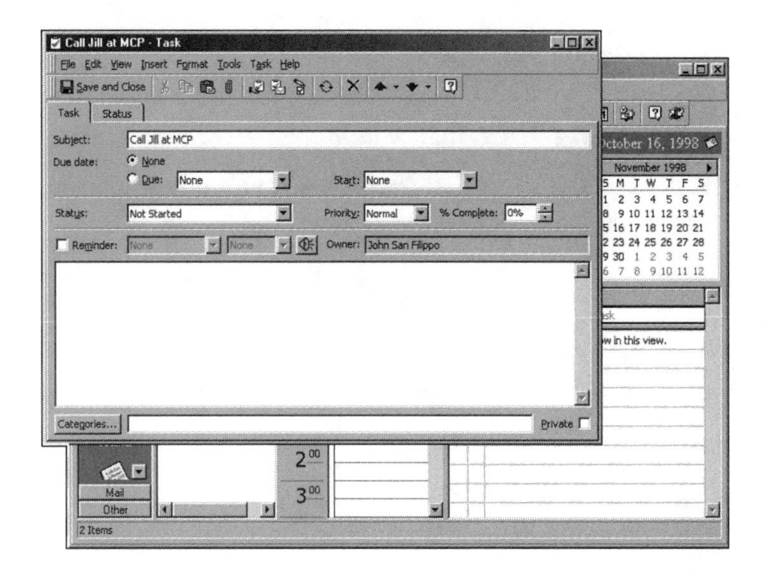

You can customize any task.

Note the Due Date option buttons. When you first create a new task, the None button is selected by default. However, if you click the Due button, you can select a due date from a pop-up calendar. Doing this means that the task will not appear on the TaskPad until the date you specify. This helps keep the TaskPad from becoming unnecessarily cluttered with tasks that aren't due yet.

If you have a task that, for example, can be done anytime between next Tuesday and next Friday, choose a start date in the **Start** field. This causes the task to appear on the TaskPad for the entire date range specified by the start date and due date.

The next important feature is the Priority field. Here you have three choices: low, normal, and high. Giving each task a priority helps you identify on-the-fly which tasks are more important than others so you know which one to direct your attention to next. I don't find myself using low priority much—I guess all my tasks are of at least normal importance. But I do like being able to distinguish between normal- and high-importance items.

The final TaskPad feature I want to point out now is the Reminder area on the Task window. Maybe you want to be reminded the day before an important event or meeting. Or maybe you want to be reminded that morning. Whatever the case, Outlook lets you specify a reminder date and time for any task. The reminder will pop up on your computer screen just like one of Outlook's appointment reminders. To set the default time for task reminders, choose the **Tools** menu and select **Options**. Then choose **Tasks/Notes** from the Options dialog box.

Tweaking Your Task View

While viewing your Outlook calendar, select **TaskPad View** from the **View** menu to see a number of options. Typically, the default selection is Today's Tasks. However, with that view selected, the TaskPad only displays tasks for the current date, even when you click another date on the calendar. I find that the Active Tasks for Selected Days view is much more useful. With this view selected, when you click a date on the calendar, the tasks for that day appear in the TaskPad.

Sort by Priority

The problem with assigning a priority to a task is that you have to double-click the task to check its priority. You can get around this in Outlook in two ways. The first is to select **TaskPad Settings** from the **View** menu, and then select **Show Fields**. Here you can tell Outlook to include the priority information in the TaskPad.

Rather than clutter the TaskPad with another field, I prefer to have Outlook sort and display my tasks by priority. To do this, select **TaskPad Settings** from the **View** menu, and then select **Sort**. This pops up a window that enables you to tell Outlook to sort by, among other things, priority. This way, you always know that whatever item is at the top of the list has the highest priority.

Project Management à la Outlook

For the most part, the tasks on your TaskPad are just that—individual tasks such as calling this person or reordering that item. However, on occasion, you may encounter a task that involves several steps. In short, the task might constitute a full-blown project (or maybe a mini-project). In those cases, you'll probably want to employ some of the TaskPad's project management features.

Double-click an existing task and you'll see a Task window like the one shown in the next figure. This window may look familiar from earlier in the chapter.

Of particular relevance to the aspiring project manager are the Status and % Complete fields. The Status field provides the following options:

- Not Started
- In Progress
- Completed
- Waiting on Someone Else
- Deferred

Need More Power?

If you find your projects becoming larger, more complicated, and more resource-consuming, you may want to consider a true project management software package like Microsoft Project. Project is basically the TaskPad on steroids and can help you make short order of even the most complicated projects.

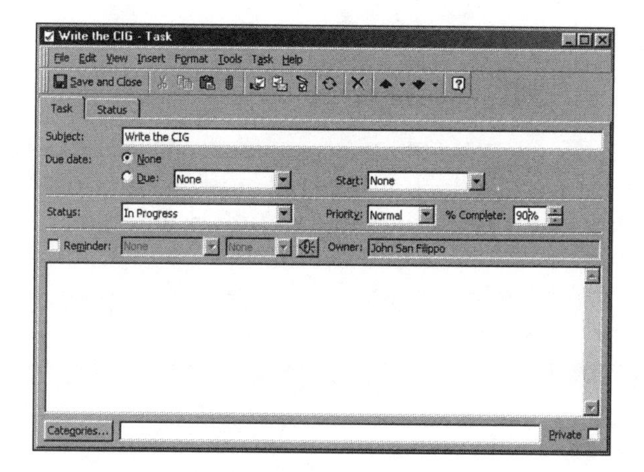

The TaskPad offers some project management tools.

You select whichever option is appropriate for the current state of the project.

The % Complete field gives you two options. You can change the number of 25% increments by clicking the little arrows to the right. Or you can click in the field itself and type any number you want.

Now click the **Status** tab near the top of the window (not to be confused with the Status field). This tab, as shown in the next figure, allows you to track all sorts of information associated with your project. Just enter the information as it becomes available and you'll always have it to refer to if necessary.

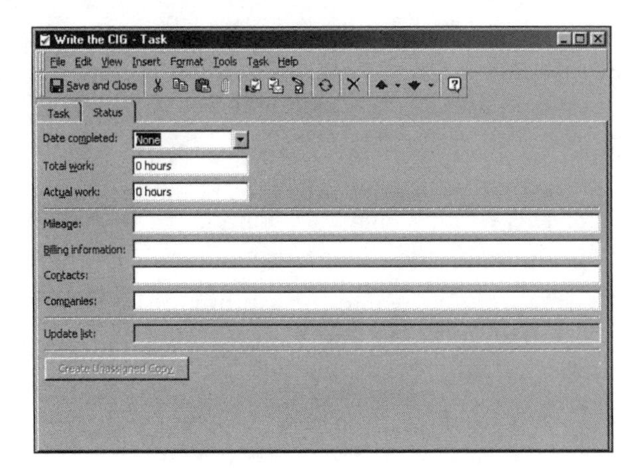

Outlook lets you track all the details.

Oh, Just Do It!

Outlook allows you to delegate your tasks to other people, assuming your delegates are on your network, by using Outlook as their task management tool. In the Untitled Task dialog box, choose **Assign Task** from the **Actions** menu, and choose the delegates from your list of users. A message is sent to them, notifying them of the assignment, which they can refuse or accept. If they accept it, you can track their progress within your own Task folder.

Project Management 101

Managing a successful project is more than learning how to schedule tasks in Outlook. The key to project management is making the most efficient use of both your time and your resources, especially your human resources. Projects often require input from several people, and as project manager, it's your job to make sure these people are pulling their weight.

Depending on the nature of the job at hand, project management may involve scheduling multiple tasks and multiple appointments. The more individual components in a project, the more chances that something can go wrong.

As I mentioned earlier, you need to keep an especially watchful eye when you're relying on other people to perform certain tasks in support of your project. The reason is that they may or may not be as concerned as you are about the timely completion of your project.

I'm good at scheduling my time and then sticking to my schedule. Like Dirty Harry said, "A man's got to know his limitations." I know mine and I take them into consideration when I'm planning a project.

However, the big mistake that I seem to make over and over again—no matter how old I get—is relying on other people to do what they say they're going to do when they say they're going to do it. I don't mean to sound overly pessimistic, and I also don't mean to imply that anyone ever tries to intentionally sabotage my projects. But the simple truth is that everyone has a million things to do, and you can't expect all your business associates to share identical priorities with you.

Don't Forget to Call

If the pressure of juggling the efforts of several people seems overwhelming, let Outlook give you a little support. Remind yourself to call your associates (a good idea if your "team" isn't all on Outlook) by dragging the associate's contact record (drag with your right mouse button depressed) to your TaskPad. Edit the task to include a reminder, minutes before the call is to be made.

If you're managing a larger project that involves several people, do yourself a favor and add reminders for the other people to your TaskPad. They agreed to do the work and most likely have a sincere desire to do what they say. If they're busy, chances are a friendly reminder from you will be most welcome.

Another Book for Your Night Table

Are you overwhelmed by the subject of project management? If you're new to the field and have some big projects to tackle, that's understandable. Unfortunately, it's impossible for me to include everything you need to know in one short chapter. If you really need to master this subject, I recommend investing a few dollars in a copy of *The Complete Idiot's Guide to Project Management*.

The Least You Need to Know

- An electronic to-do list offers many advantages over a paper-based list.
- You can manage all your tasks and even small projects within Outlook.
- Managing the people involved with a project is often the most important part of project management.
- If you have some large project to manage, you may want to consider a copy of Microsoft Project or a copy of *The Complete Idiot's Guide to Project Management.*

Appendix

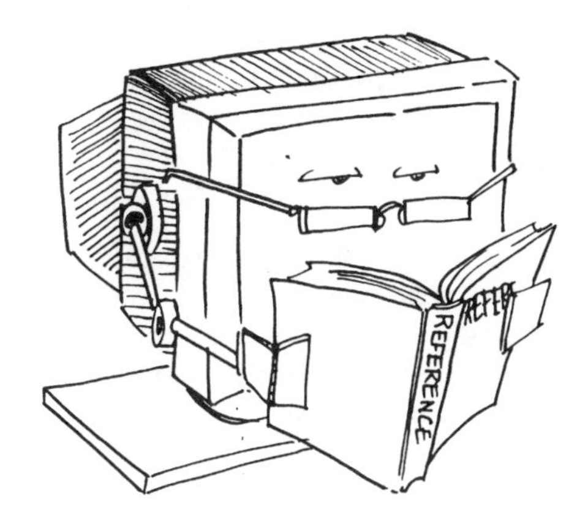

Small Business Resources

As a reader of this book, you're likely to be interested in two things: running your business and using Microsoft Office. With that thought in mind, I've divided this appendix into two sections. The first section covers online resources that help you in your use of the Microsoft Office suite of programs. The second section guides you to online resources for your small business, and provides great information even if you're not an avid Microsoft Office user.

Online Resources for Office Users

Check out the following online sites that help you to make more effective use of the Microsoft Office suite of programs:

Microsoft Office Update

Located at **http://officeupdate.microsoft.com** and part of the Microsoft corporate Web site, this is the logical starting point for advice and assistance using Microsoft Office. Probably the most important part of this site is the Office updates. Anytime Microsoft issues some sort of fix, patch, or other update to an Office product, you'll find it here first. I suggest that you check here regularly to make sure you have all the latest versions.

You can also download free add-ons for Office. For example, at this writing, the site offers a collection of free clip art. This is where you can find, for example, a Word template that sucks in calendar information from Outlook and formats it as a table in Word. Once the template does its thing, you're free to format the calendar in any manner you want. This is just an example of the type of tools you can find on this site.

If you're still using Outlook 97, you can download Outlook 98 from this site. However, if you're connecting over a standard analog modem, you may want to go run some errands while you're waiting. The file is about 30 megabytes. On a 28.8Kbps modem, that translates to about three hours of download time. If you'd rather spend money than time to get Outlook 98, you also have the option to order it on CD for $10, which covers the shipping and handling.

To use the Office Update site, you do have to complete a brief online registration. This includes selecting a user name and password. The good news is that Microsoft puts a "cookie" in your browser so that you don't have to retype your sign-on information each time you connect. Make sure you write your password down and keep it handy, though. The first time you try to access the Office Update site from other than you're usual computer, you'll remember this reminder when you're prompted for your password and you don't have it. You can't say I didn't warn you!

One final thought: If you're interested in more general information about Microsoft Office—for example, when Office 2000 is supposed to ship—you may want to check the official Office home page at **http://www.microsoft.com/office**.

Yi-hah! It's Tip World!

You'll find this interesting site at **http://www.tipworld.com**. Here you can subscribe to numerous Internet mailing lists, each of which provides you with a "tip of the day" on the specified topic. For example, you find daily tips under these headings: Windows 98, Small Office/Home Office, Mobile Computing, Microsoft Office, Microsoft Word, Microsoft Excel, and Internet Explorer—this is just a portion of the list of products for which you find tips.

Did I tell you everything at Tip World is free? The whole thing is advertiser supported, so don't worry about having to provide a credit card number.

Shhhh! You're Inside Microsoft Office 97

Located at **http://www.zdjournals.com/o97**, this site is the online arm of the magazine of the same name. As with Tip World, this site is a valuable source of Office tips, tricks, and advice. The difference here is that you can find the information you need right on the Web site; there's no need to wait for a daily tip of the day.

Of course, some people like getting all sorts of relevant information in their email inboxes. For that crowd, this site offers its own Office tip of the week, delivered right to your email door.

Just when you thought the excitement was over, get this! This site also includes back issues of the magazine—very useful if you need to check an article and you've thrown out the issue in which it was published.

The Insider's Guide to Office 97

This ClNet site, located at **http://www.cnet.com/Content/Features/Howto/Ofc97tips**, is yet another Microsoft Office tip fest. One interesting note: In addition to topics organized by individual software packages (for example, Word or Excel), this site offers a special tip section that covers working with Office over a LAN or the Internet.

Baarns Office Resource Center

Baarns Consulting Group, located at **http://www.baarns.com**, pays the bills by providing Office-oriented consulting services. To promote the business, Baarns has developed a very impressive site.

Like just about any other Office site, you can find plenty of tips and tricks here. However, what makes this site a real find for the Office user is its free software. That's right, free software. For example, you'll find a cost estimating form, an inventory tracker, and a time and billing log, just to name a few.

An important point to consider here is that these templates are free—not freeware. There's a difference. Freeware is software that you're allowed to give to anyone you want in just about any medium you want. Although some programs on this site are free for your use, you're not supposed to pass them around to your friends. If someone you know wants one, you should direct him or her to this site. After all, these people created this site and all its freebies to promote their business. It's only fair to let them do so.

Of course, there's a truckload of Office templates and programs that you can buy, too—both from Baarns and from other sites to which this one is linked. I suggest setting aside a little time to explore this site and see what it has to offer.

The Spreadsheet Page

This site, coutesy of JWalk and Associates and located at **http://www.j-walk.com/ss**, provides useful information for users of all major spreadsheet programs (and even minor ones for that matter). Given that Excel is the world's most popular spreadsheet package, it's no wonder that Excel is given ample coverage on this site.

Aside from all the serious stuff you find here, this site boasts the world's only online collection of spreadsheet jokes. For example, here are the Top 10 Signs That You Purchased a Bad Spreadsheet:

10. A sticker on the box reads, *Now Supports DOS 1.2.*
9. It is part of a software suite called "Office Schmoffice."
8. User testimonials on the box are written in Arabic.
7. The help file consists of three words: "Don't ask me."

6. The Setup disk reads, "Disk 1 of 1".
5. The Setup routine displays "Another Sucker" as the default username.
4. The user manual is scribbled on the back of an old envelope.
3. The technical support phone number is 555-1212.
2. The only way to get a hard copy of your work is to photograph the screen.
1. When you press F9, a message box tells you to dig out your calculator.

Usenet Newsgroups

Although you're likely to find more information than you can use on the World Wide Web, don't forget that there's more to the Internet than the Web. One place to look for loads of information is on the Usenet. Microsoft hosts dozens of newsgroups, all starting with *microsoft.public*. Many of these relate to Office in general or to specific Office programs.

The added benefit of a newsgroup is that in addition to picking some good information, you can exchange ideas and problems directly from other users. Instead of reading what Microsoft has to say about Office, or what some consulting firm has to say about Office, you can get it straight from the horse's... er, user's mouth. How to find an Office newsgroup? Follow the newsgroup links on AOL, use your browser's search tools, or try Yahoo.com (or any other major search site). Type **Usenet** in the search text box, and you come to another search window that searches only newsgroups. Enter **Microsoft Office** in that search text box, and you find groups devoted to this topic.

Stephen Bullen's Excel Page

You have to travel all the way to the United Kingdom for this one—or at least your browser does. Located at **http://www.bmsltd.co.uk/Excel**, this site offers another nice collection of free Excel downloads. Fortunately, most of the files are relatively small, so you can download a lot of great software in just a little time.

WOW! It's Woody's Office Watch

Subscribe to this weekly newsletter from esteemed Office guru Woody Leonhard. It's full of Microsoft Office tips, suggestions, and the inside dope about Microsoft's doings —software releases, bugs, political stuff. To subscribe, go to **www.wopr.com**, and check out the Office Watch site.

Online Resources for Small Businesses

You may find the following online resources useful even when your computer is turned off:

/smallbiz

This site, located at **http://www.microsoft.com/smallbiz**, is Microsoft's small business resource center. Sure, there's plenty of hype about Microsoft products on this site, but there's also plenty of genuinely useful stuff, too.

One area you might enjoy is called Reader Success Stories. These are articles written by small business owners about how they've used Office to further their business efforts. Reading these is a great way to pick up new ideas for streamlining and automating your own business.

Quicken Small Business

Between its Quicken and QuickBooks products, Intuit has a pretty good lock on the PC-based do-it-yourself financial management market. With that kind of success, the company can afford to put together a top-notch small business site—and it has. Located at **http://www.quicken.com/small_business**, this site is short on hype and long on valuable information.

Departments include Starting a Business, Managing Your Business, Marketing, Legal Issues, Office Technology, Benefits and Retirement, Employees and Payroll, and Taxes and Accounting. You also can find a collection of online business tools, as well as late-breaking small business news.

One thing I especially like is the inclusion of the Small Business Message Boards. Covering a variety of topics, these Web-based discussion areas give you the opportunity to exchange ideas with other entrepreneurs who may have already overcome the issues you now face.

Small Business Administration

No small business Web-surfing expedition is complete without a trip to the SBA Web site, which you find at **http://www.sba.gov**. Here you find information about a variety of topics, including business expansion, financing, disaster assistance, and local SBA resources, among others. There's even an area to help you with Y2K planning.

Perhaps the most valuable asset on this site is the online library. This collection of digital documents includes various forms, SBA publications, FAQs, reports, and much more. There is even a shareware download page.

Better Business Bureau

Although the resources on this site, located at **http://www.bbbonline.org**, aren't nearly as comprehensive as those on the SBA, I still suggest you check this one out. I suppose I just like the goal of the BBB: to promote ethical business practices.

If you're doing business online, you'll want to check out the results of a BBB Online survey about increasing consumer confidence in online shopping. The survey results boil down to two main points. To increase consumer confidence, all you need do is address the issues of data security and business reliability.

Don't worry. I didn't tell you what happens at the end of the movie. The survey results bring up some very good points, and the recap provided on this site is well worth reading.

Homebased Business Channel

Even if you don't work from your home, you're likely to find some useful information on this site, located at **http://www.entrepreneurmag.com/homebiz**. In addition to scads of general information, you can also search various databases to find the home-based business that's just right for you. An online chat room rounds out this nice collection of small business resources.

Business Owner's Toolkit

Found at **http://www.toolkit.cch.com/**, this site includes the usual assortment of free information. However, what really sets this site apart is its for-pay online services. For a nominal fee, you can check business credit reports, perform trademark and patent searches, and engage in a little competitive intelligence.

How nominal is nominal? I guess that all depends on your point of view. If you only need to use these services a couple of times a year, you probably won't squawk over the $4–$5 hit your credit card takes each time you use one of these services. However, if for some reason you need to rely on them heavily, you could really get nickel-and-dimed to death.

SBFocus.com

No doubt you already have your own favorite Internet search engine. For general searches, try DogPile, which is actually a search engine that searches other search engines. However, when you're looking for information on a very specific topic, sometimes only a specialized search engine will do. That's where SBFocus.com, located at—you guessed it—**http//www.sbfocus.com**, comes in.

This unique search engine is dedicated exclusively to helping you find small business articles on the Internet, wherever they happen to be. Just type in a keyword or two and you're likely to get back a list of links from around the world. These articles could be located anywhere, from the Web site for *Business Week* magazine to that of the Social Security Administration.

The Mining Company Guide to Small Business Information

The Mining Company takes an interesting approach to finding what you need on the Internet. The premise is that you're better off with a personal guide than some automated search engine. To this end, The Mining Company contracts with experts from various fields to create online resource centers in their particular area of expertise. These guides share in any revenues from the advertising on their particular area.

At this writing, the Guide to Small Business Information, located at **http://sbinformation.miningco.com**, is moderated by a fellow named Ed Martin. You can read his biography, which seems impressive, online. What's more impressive is the collection of online resources Martin has accumulated at this site. In addition to its own content, the site includes hypertext links to other Internet resources in categories such as Accounting, Associations, Business Plans, Buying & Selling a Biz, Direct Marketing, Financing Your Biz, Franchising, Government Help, Health and Safety, Home Businesses, International Business, Just for Fun, Legal, Management, Marketing, Network Marketing, Retail, Sales, Small Biz Books, SOHO, Software & Shareware, Starting a Small Biz, Venture Capital, Web Marketing, and Woman-Owned Biz. That enough for ya?

Usenet Newsgroups

There are more Usenet newsgroups relating to business than you can shake a compact disc at. There's no shortage of discussion of general business topics here. And with more than 30,000 newsgroups and new ones being added daily, you're likely to find some discussion specific to your particular industry.

Glossary

The following is a list of terms and definitions that will help you interpret some of the high-tech or esoteric business terms you may find in the book. Many of these terms have been defined in context, through my "Whaddya Mean by That?" elements (Excuse the repetition, but I wanted you to have one place to go to look up terms.) Here you go!

absolute reference In a spreadsheet formula, the cell that will remain constant in all pasted or copied repetitions of the formula.

alignment A word processing term that describes text placement relative to the margin. Your choices are left (aligned along left margin), center (equal distance from both the left and right margins), right (aligned along the right margin), and full (left-aligned with no ragged right edge).

browser Software program used to search the Internet and Web for information based on search criteria entered by the user.

byte 8 bits. So what's a bit? A 1 or a 0, the two characters in the binary number system. Data is stored and transmitted through and between computers in binary.

camera ready Printed original documents suitable for clean reproduction, usually the original given to a printing firm for generating flyers, brochures, and other marketing pieces.

CD-ROM Stands for Compact Disk, Read Only Memory. A compact disk bearing data that can only be read and copied to another storage device—a CD-ROM disk cannot be altered by the user.

cell In a spreadsheet, the individual boxes on the spreadsheet are called cells.

client Your computer is the client when you're attached to a *server*, meaning that the server is accommodating the needs of your computer, supplying requested programs, data, and access to devices.

clip art Drawings that have been created on a computer (or by hand and then scanned) and saved as a graphic file. These images are typically added to documents and presentations to add visual impact. Microsoft Office comes with its own selection of clip art, and there are many sources for additional images, such as computer stores and the Internet.

Clipboard A term for your computer's memory when it is used to hold a selection that you want to move (cut) or copy from one document to another or within a single document. Cut or copied content is pasted to its new location.

compressed file Also referred to as a *zipped file*, a compressed file is one that has been reduced in size through a file compression program such as PKZIP or WinZip. This is normally done to speed transmission over the Internet or to make the file fit on a floppy disk. Compressed files must be expanded to their original size before you can open or view them.

computer virus See *virus*.

CPU Stands for Central Processing Unit. The brains of your computer, normally referred to by its product number/name, such as 486 or Pentium (really a 586). This chip is about the size of a large postage stamp and is attached to the *motherboard* inside your computer.

crash When a program stops working, it is said to have crashed. If the problem is significant, your whole computer can crash, requiring you to reboot (restart).

database A collection of information, such as a name and address list. A database can also be a collection of lists (also known as tables) that share some sort of logical connection—such as tables containing customer and product information—used to generate reports on customer activity and who bought what.

default What your computer will do if you don't tell it to do otherwise. Default settings are created to make your computer programs easier to use without any required intervention. For example, when you start a new document in Word, default fonts, margins, and line spacing are all set for you.

domain name Part of one's Web or email address. In the email address **laurie@limehat.com**, "limehat" is the domain. In the Web address **www.microsoft.com**, "microsoft" is the domain. Domain names are controlled and administered by the *InterNIC*.

dots per inch Also referred to as "dpi," this term refers to the resolution of a printer—the greater the dpi, the more detailed and crisp that printer's output will be. Most printers (inkjet and laser) range from 600 to 1,200dpi.

download To copy a file from a Web page or other Internet site to your computer.

driver A file that tells your computer how to communicate and work with a device attached to it, such as a printer, monitor, or a sound card.

email The slang term for electronic mail.

field Each *record* in a database is broken down into fields, such as First Name, Last Name, or Address.

filter When referring to a database, a filter is a set of criteria presented to the database by the user, requesting that only the records meeting the criteria be displayed. An example might be State=PA to show only records for customers in Pennsylvania.

flame An angry response to an email or comment in a chat room. People sending flame messages are called flamers.

font Another word for "typeface," meaning the style of type applied to text. Microsoft Word's *default* font is Times New Roman.

FTP (File Transfer Protocol) The Internet relies on strict standards for handling the flow of data. This term refers to the rules for the transmission of files to and from FTP sites, Internet locations created for the storage and retrieval of files.

gigabyte (GB) 1,000,000,000 (billion) *bytes*.

highlight To drag through text in a document or cells in a table or spreadsheet with your mouse, selecting the content for formatting, editing, or deletion.

HTML (HyperText Markup Language) The programming language used to create Web pages. Microsoft Office enables you to build your Web page content and then save the file in HTML format, eliminating your need to know how to write HTML programming code.

HTTP (HyperText Transfer Protocol) The set of rules governing the transfer of Web text. The http:// at the beginning of a Web address is used to invoke this method of data transfer, setting the stage for the successful display of the Web page in question.

hyperlink Text or graphics within a Web page that when clicked, take you to another page. Hyperlinks can also be added to Word, Excel, and PowerPoint documents to allow access to other files from within that document.

Internet A global network of computers that store information. These computers can be accessed by anyone with an *ISP* (*Internet Service Provider*) or who belongs to an online community such as AOL or Prodigy.

InterNIC The administrative governing body of the Internet. Although no one owns or controls the content or use of the Internet, this organization must exist to make sure each user has a distinct domain name and protocols are maintained.

ISP (Internet Service Provider) This type of firm sells you (for a monthly or annual fee) access to the Internet and normally provides one or more email accounts. To access the Internet, you dial into the ISP's local *server* and from there you can jump to any other server via *hyperlinks*.

lurk To view newsgroup postings without joining the newsgroup.

mail merge A word processing term for combining a form letter or labels and a database for the purpose of a mailing. When you receive a letter that tells you "You may have already won!" and it starts with Dear Bill (or whatever your name is), you've received the results of a mail merge.

megabyte (MB) 1,000,000 (million) *bytes*.

megahertz (MHz) Your computer's megahertz rating tells you how fast it processes data.

memory The amount of memory your computer has determines how many simultaneous tasks it can handle. Your computer's transient tasks (opening a program, printing a document, using the Clipboard) use its memory. Memory is also called *RAM*, and Windows 98 requires at least 32 *megabytes* of memory to run properly.

merge fields When performing a *mail merge*, merge fields are inserted in the form letter or label to indicate where data from the database should be inserted.

modem The device inside or attached to your computer that allows it to use phone lines to transmit data.

motherboard A large circuit board inside your computer to which your *CPU* and other devices are attached. By placing these devices on one board, they can all communicate with each other, via the circuits in the board itself.

network A group of computers connected for the purpose of sharing data, software, and peripheral devices such as printers.

newsgroup On the Internet, newsgroups form to enable people with common interests to share ideas and information. Articles and messages are posted to the newsgroup and emailed to the group's members. You need not be a member to read these postings.

OCR software Optical Character Recognition software converts a scanned document into editable text.

operators In a spreadsheet formula (or any mathematical process), the symbols (+, -, *, /) that indicate which mathematical function should be performed, such as 5+6. When doing math on a computer, the * represents multiplication and the / represents division.

Parallel port A female port on the back of your computer to which printers, external drives, and some scanners connect.

points Text is measured in points, a measurement system in which there are 72 points to an inch. On this basis, you can assume that each character in 12-point text will be roughly one sixth of an inch square.

query In database terminology, a query is similar to a filter—a set of criteria is presented, and only the database records matching it are displayed. In Microsoft Access, a query can draw data from one or more *tables*.

RAM Random Access Memory is the method by which data is stored in your computer's memory. Open space is randomly chosen and used to house tasks until they are completed, at which time another task takes its place in the same or another randomly selected spot.

range A block of cells in a spreadsheet, selected by dragging through them with the mouse. After a range is selected, its content can be formatted, edited, named, or deleted.

record If you think of the phone book as a database, each listing is a record. When you store a database in Excel or Access, each row is a record, and each record is made up of *fields*.

sanserif Sanserif fonts have no flourishes or wings on the tips of the letters. Common sanserif fonts are Arial, AvantGarde, and Helvetica.

scanner A device used to transfer a document, drawing, or photograph from paper to the computer. Using technology similar to a photocopier, a laser "reads" the paper document/image and converts it to a graphic image (or text file, through *OCR software*) on your computer.

search engine A program that "surfs" the Web for information based on a user's requests. Common search engines include Yahoo! and Lycos.com.

serif Fonts with flourishes or wings on the ends of the individual characters. Times New Roman, Courier, and Bookman are common serif fonts.

server A computer that serves other computers by storing communal data and programs to assist the *client* computers in retrieving it. A Web server is a computer that stores Web pages and allows other computers to access and display these pages.

shareware Software that can be freely copied and used without registration or formal purchase. Although generally at no cost, many shareware programs request that money be sent to the programmer after you've "tested" the software; and the programmer may have crippled the software in some way to prevent your using it without buying the full-running version.

sort A database term that refers to the order in which records are displayed or printed. You can sort by any field in your database (by Last Name, for example), and choose ascending or descending order. Most databases allow you to sort by more than one field.

spam To send unsolicited emails to many email addresses, a sort of mass mailing. Spamming often causes angry recipients to *flame* the sender of the unsolicited email.

table In word processing, a set of columns and rows created to give structure to text. In database software, a table is a group of records, such as a name and address list.

template A cookie cutter for documents, spreadsheets, or presentations. Templates contain the formatting and setup required to start a file, including any common text or numeric content.

unzip To expand a *compressed* or *zipped file* to its original size so that the file can be opened and used.

upload To copy data from your computer to another computer via the Internet.

URL (Uniform Resource Locator) Pronounced by saying the letters "U-R-L" (although some geeks say "Earl"), this is another term for a Web address. For example, Macmillan Computer Publishing's URL is **www.mcp.com**.

VBA (Visual Basic for Applications) Similar to Visual Basic (a programming language), Microsoft has built VBA into the Office suite to allow users to create their own applications and tweak the way Word, Excel, PowerPoint, and Access work.

virus A program written for the expressed purpose of causing your computer to malfunction. Their damaging results range from annoying to devastating, depending on the goal of the virus-maker and when/if you realize you have it. Antivirus software such as Norton Antivirus or McAfee VirusScan are popular tools to prevent and cure computer viruses.

World Wide Web A global network of Web *servers,* containing Web pages and the data linked to them.

WYSIWIG What You See Is What You Get. A term created to describe how Windows-based software displays text and graphics onscreen just as they will look when printed.

zipped file Slang term for a *compressed file*. Programs such as PKZIP and WinZip compress a file to a smaller size for faster transmission over the Internet and to enable larger files to fit on floppy disks. To use or view a zipped file, it must be *unzipped,* or expanded to its original size.

Index

B

C

D

E

F

G

H

I

J-K

L

M

N

O

P

Q-R

S

T